FIDEL

AND

GABO

FIDEL
AND
GABO

A PORTRAIT OF THE LEGENDARY FRIENDSHIP BETWEEN
FIDEL CASTRO AND
GABRIEL GARCÍA MÁRQUEZ

───────────── ★ ─────────────

ÁNGEL ESTEBAN AND STÉPHANIE PANICHELLI

ENGLISH TRANSLATION BY DIANE STOCKWELL

PEGASUS BOOKS
NEW YORK

To Yani

★ ★ ★

FIDEL AND GABO

Pegasus Books LLC
80 Broad Street, 5th Floor
New York, NY 10004

Translation copyright © 2009 by Diane Stockwell

First Pegasus Books edition 2009

Interior design by Maria Fernandez

Library of Congress Cataloging-in-Publication Data is available.

ISBN: 978-1-60598-058-4

10 9 8 7 6 5 4 3 2 1

Printed in the United States of America
Distributed by W. W. Norton & Company

CONTENTS

INTRODUCTION

★

ART AND FLIES

W E ARE LOVERS. LOVERS OF CUBA, AND OF GREAT LITERATURE. Cuba was a vast empire's sparkling crown jewel in the sixteenth century, and it has been fiercely coveted from the nineteenth century on. At first, there were the tobacco and sugar crops that were appealing; later, Cuba's spectacular coastline and climate became the draw. Spain did not want to lose it. The United States' relentless efforts to take it never ceased. This is, simply, the history of Cuba. And in the midst of it, a revolution. Not yours, nor mine. But was it really the Cubans' revolution? The years of Soviet-made Lada cars and vodka cast some doubt. And what about now?

This book was born out of more than just love. It also sprang from idleness and admiration, two magic words to the Greeks. Idleness is the opposite of industry. Those who work hard don't catch flies. Contemplation is needed to create art, and idleness and admiration facilitate it. This is also true with science. Only people who are willing to waste a lot of time are capable of truly appreciating, or creating, a work of art. So, this book grew out of a fascination for two things: Cuba and literature; a place, and the literary works of a Nobel laureate; a charismatic man who has been in power for almost half a century, and his best friend. A commander who now has his own writer. Macondo in Havana. Strolling through Old Havana, down the Malecón or Fifth Avenue, with its nocturnal flowers, is an experience, nothing more. Whoever tries to completely capture it in a single description will fail. In the same way, reading *One Hundred Years of Solitude or Love in the Time of Cholera* is an experience. Summarizing it or trying to explain how one feels when reading it is a hopeless task. When we read great literature, or walk idly along a Caribbean beach, attracting flies, we're wasting time, and this enriches us, making us happier, more human.

But fascination has a limit, imposed by circumstance. Fascination without limit is called God. Nothing human is perfect. But nothing is completely imperfect either. Everything in nature possesses admirable qualities, as well as weaknesses, pluses and minuses, heads or tails. In this book you will find, idle reader and fly catcher, the secrets of a friendship as solid as a rock, with all its lights and shadows. We are talking about flesh-and-blood people, not icons or superheroes. We will tell the story of Fidel Castro and Gabriel García Márquez ("Gabo" to his friends), with its highs and lows, like any other *zoon politikon*, as Aristotle would say. A personal, political, and literary friendship. Castro, who for years would not let the Colombian Nobel Prize winner into his inner circle, later would openly accept his conspiring overtures. Gabo, obsessed with power, political bosses, and the highest levels of diplomacy, saw in the Cuban patriarch a model that all of Latin America could follow to one day build its own socialist state, a contented society without class differences, more Rousseau than Marx. Castro, who did not have an intellectual on his island who could serve as a mouthpiece to communicate his revolutionary achievements, found in García Márquez the best candidate for the task to come out of the entire Caribbean region since the time of cholera. Gabo, who had always turned down the requests of political parties and leaders in Colombia to serve as minister, ambassador, or presidential candidate, put on his campaign hat to become a politician in his own way: moving within the circles of political power, controlling and directing it, making decisions without pounding his fist on the table, issuing mandates without a scepter in hand, using his fame in his rounds of glittering social obligations, ferrying proposals from one country to another, as the bearded Commander's exclusive ambassador-at-large to the world.

Idle contemplator, in these pages you will read about how Fidel was on the brink of his own destruction as he ventured into the political turmoil of Bogotá in 1948, passing close by his future friend in the city streets before they had ever met, and, who knows, maybe even helping him in perhaps the first serious crisis he would face in his life. You will read about a young Colombian journalist's first trips to Cuba to witness the dawn of an equally young Revolution, his work for the press agency launched by Che Guevara, and his run-ins with communists and Cuban exiles. You will see him attempt to slip through the olive-green bars of paradise, efforts that were futile in the sixties and early seventies but very successful after 1975. You will also listen in on Fidel and Gabo's first conversations, when love-at-first-sight quickly blossomed into a strong—and by necessity symbiotic—relationship. You will walk through the Caribbean region's halls of highest political power and watch as control of the Panama Canal changed hands; you'll witness the birth of the San-dinista movement and observe its military development and tri-umph; and you'll learn about the various components driving socialism internationally in the struggle against capitalism. You'll fly with García Márquez from Spain to France, from Cuba to Colombia, from Panama to Venezuela, from Nicaragua to Europe, and you'll notice that his new friends are almost all powerful heads of state, while intellectuals and writers are increasingly of less interest to him. You'll understand why he won the Nobel Prize, wholly deserved, at a very young age, and you'll find that in the criteria for receiving the Swedish prize, political character is no less important than literary or aesthetic considerations. You will question those who were behind the maneuverings on his behalf for the prize, and you will figure out why they had such an interest in his winning. Later on, you will visit the mansion that Gabo was given in the best neighborhood in Havana as another prize for his commitment to the Revolution and as a token of his friendship with Castro; and you will chat with people who frequently spent time there. You will look on as the Nobel laureate, along with various artists and Cuban political figures, founded the best film school in all of Latin America; you will stroll its grounds, talk to its directors, and even peek into a classroom as García Márquez conducts a seminar or Steven Spielberg delivers a lecture. Finally, you will discover the statements that García Márquez has made in the press about Cuba and its leader, and the articles in which Castro has publicly acknowledged his relationship with Gabo. You will see them photographed together with their arms around each other, attending the Mass given by the Pope in the Plaza of the Revolution, at Martí's feet. Much of this information comes directly from them: García Márquez has made many statements in interviews and articles about Fidel and his world, Cuban politics and Latin America, and so forth, and Fidel has penned articles on García Márquez and on literature. And we have personally interviewed many of their friends, writers from developing countries, journalists, and European and American politicians. Some of them have given us uncensored anecdotes, lengthy stories, details of demonstrated friendship or reproach, and pointed observations on their personalities. In certain cases, for understandable reasons, some sources have asked to remain anonymous. We have protected their identities, and we have been consistent in all of the notes that accompany the text. We would like to thank all of the people who were interviewed, and all of the people and institutions that have supported us, for their selfless collaboration in our research and for their invaluable assistance.

In his book *Y Dios Entró en la Habana*, Manuel Vázquez Montalbán says that the relationship between Castro and Gabo is so "human" that "a theory of friendship must be considered." In the following pages, you will see this theory and its history developed. Gabo, who feels "like a foreigner everywhere else except in the Caribbean," is the happiest man in the world in Cuba, and he describes the island and its leader as "the land of friendship." And the only times that he really feels completely like himself are when he is with his friends. He confesses that what makes him happiest is getting an unexpected call from a friend, who's just calling to ask how he's doing, and he asserts that he writes to be loved. He has occasionally declared that he needs this feeling so much that he has gotten on a plane and traveled to the other side of the globe just to spend a few hours with a friend. Cuba, his house in Havana, and spending time alone with close friends, all relieve him of his fame, a condition which makes it impossible for him to go unrecognized anywhere on earth. He thinks, perhaps as a way to better understand his friend, that "there's nothing more similar to the solitude of power than the solitude of fame." A well-deserved fame that he seems to sometimes tire of, especially when he says things like "I am so goddamn sick of 'García Márquez'."

There have always been writers who have tested the durability and sincerity of friendships. One talented Spanish poet, a colleague of ours at the university, dedicated a book to us, emphasizing ironically that we were "colleagues, and, in spite of that, friends." The most extreme version of this outlook may have been summed up many years ago by another no less ironic Spanish poet, Enrique Jardiel Poncela, who stated: "The day you dine in absolute solitude, you can say: *I had dinner with a friend.*" The deep mistrust throughout the history of human relationships is bluntly portrayed in the Castilian saying "Don't have faith in anyone, not even in your father." Gabo, however, believes that friends are forever. And Fidel has shown that, even if in the past his friendships have not lasted, his relationship with his friend from Colombia has taken giant leaps forward as the years have passed. For his part, García Márquez has said that he will not ever return to Cuba if Fidel dies before him. This relationship brings to mind José Martí, who valued friendship even more than love, and believed that friendship was the truest manifestation of love. Here is his verse:

Si dicen que del joyero	*If they say from the jewelry chest*
Tome la joya mejor,	*to choose the most precious stone,*
Tomo a un amigo sincero	*I would choose a true friend*
Y pongo a un lado el amor.	*And leave love alone.*

This idea didn't originate with the Cuban poet. Medieval philosophers who studied Aristotle defined the love of friendship as the most pure and most valuable form, since it is characterized by giving without expecting anything in return, doing a favor without needing an expression of gratitude, but with the unspoken understanding that makes it an even exchange—friends don't need to ask, or to be asked: they just give. Serrat said it better: "What's mine is yours, what's yours is ours, and what's mine is ours." Fidel, bereft of close friends after the death in 1980 of Celia Sánchez, who was his comrade-in-arms, his secretary, and his lover, found in García Márquez an alter ego, someone he would like to be in another life. Gabo, fascinated by power, with a natural talent for conspiracy, as he freely admits, saw in the Cuban leader an opportunity to develop his political instincts and indulge his obsession. The unbearable lightness of being becomes bearable when friends support each other, like a house of cards. Now let's catch some flies, idle reader, and turn the page.

PART ONE

———— ★ ————

LOVE IN SPRINGTIME

CHAPTER ONE

★

GODS AT PLAY

"Gabo and I were both in Bogotá on that sad April 9, 1948, when Gaitán was killed. We were the same age, twenty-one years old; we witnessed the same events, we were university students studying the same subject: Law. That's what we thought anyway. Neither of us knew anything about the other. No one knew who we were, we didn't even know ourselves.

"Almost a half century later, on the eve of a trip to Birán in the Far East, Gabo and I were talking in Cuba, where I was born on the morning of August 13, 1926. Our meeting had the feel of an intimate family get-together, where old memories are shared and colorful stories told, in a gathering with some of Gabo's friends and some other comrades of the Revolution."[1]

And so begins the most literary piece that Fidel Castro has ever written, two months into his seventy-sixth year. It is a short article about his best, and perhaps only, friend, Gabriel García Márquez. Two of the most important personalities in twentieth-century

Latin American history were in the same city on one of the worst days that that city, the Colombian capital, had ever experienced since its founding in 1538. Their paths probably crossed, running through the streets in the midst of the chaos, not knowing where they were going or even why they were running. Maybe their eyes met for an instant on a street corner, or maybe they tripped over the same woman struggling to pull herself up off the ground after being knocked down by a boy careening past on a bicycle. The son of the telegraph operator from Aracataca tried to get back to his rented room to at least save manuscripts of the stories he had written the week before. The student from Cuba surmised that it was too late now to meet with the leader Jorge Gaitán again, Colombia's shining hope, the political figure-of-the-moment who had taken a real interest in the problems of Latin American college students; who had met with student representatives to adopt a unified position in the face of the always conflict-ridden relations between the United States of "North"America and the Disunited States of South America.

★ ★ ★

Gabo was born in Aracataca, a small town in the north of Colombia, on March 6, 1927, with the umbilical cord wrapped around his neck, while his mother bled profusely. Doña Luisa Márquez not only survived the birth, but she would go on to bring ten more children into the world. When the next son was born, Gabito was sent to live with his grandparents, and this proved to be a formative experience that would shape his character, as the future Nobel Prize winner developed an avid interest in the stories of political bosses and strongmen, spending hours with his grandfather, hearing about the amazing feats of the men who fought in the civil wars at the dawn of the century. His grandmother, who spent the days singing to herself in a sort of delirium, was a constant target for her grandson's questions, always wanting to hear stories of the wars:

"Grandma, who is Mambru, and what war was he in?"

And, not having the slightest idea, but with an overactive imagination, she replied calmly: "He was a man who fought with your grandfather in the 1,000 Days' War."

As we now know, the Mambru of the old, popular song (the one that Gabo's grandfather was so fond of singing) is none other than the Duke of Marlborough, and when García Márquez went on to include him as a vibrant character in his novels and stories, he preferred his grandmother's version to the actual truth. That's why Marlborough appears disguised as a tiger, losing all of the Colombian civil wars, alongside Colonel Aureliano Buendia.[2]

When Gabo was seven years old, Nicolas Márquez took his grandson to number 5 San Pedro Alejandrino, in Santa Marta, where Simón Bolívar, the great liberator of America, had died. The grandfather had already told his grandson about this illustrious figure many times. When he was six, Gabito had gazed upon the image of a dead Bolívar on a calendar his grandfather owned. So, while still young enough to play with toy soldiers, the boy's interest in this and other American leaders grew, characters who would later figure into his novels, stoking his particular fascination with power. He learned to read and write at the Montessori school when he was eight years old, and his teacher, Rosa Elena Fergusson, would be Gabo's first muse, since he thought that the verses she recited in class, "forever embedded in my brain," were a direct manifestation of her striking beauty. At nine years of age, while digging through one of his grandparents' trunks in what would be one of the most pivotal moments of his life, he found an old, tattered book with yellowed pages. At the time, he didn't know that the book's title was *A Thousand and One Nights*, but he began to read, and he felt positively transformed. He said to himself:

> I opened it, and I read that there was a guy who opened up a bottle and out flew a genie in a puff of smoke, and I said, "Wow, this is amazing!" This was more fascinating to me than anything else that had happened in my life up to that point: more than playing, more than painting, more than eating, more than everything, and I didn't lift my nose from the book again.[3]

Over the next several years, having to support a large number of growing children, the García Márquez family moved often: from Aracataca, to Barranquilla, to Sucre. In 1940, García Márquez returned to Barranquilla to attend the Jesuit school of San Jose, where he wrote his first verses and stories for the magazine *Juventud* ("youth")[4]. Three years later, just before his sixteenth birthday, he had to leave home and find a job to finance his education, since his parents, who by then had eight children, could not afford to feed everyone and also pay for their schooling. He went to Bogotá and felt completely disconsolate in such a faraway, huge, cold city, where no one knew each other and the local customs were so different. He received a scholarship and began studying at the National Boys' School of Zipaquira, where the bug he had first caught when he opened up *A Thousand and One Nights* quickly replicated inside of him, until it was a chronic, unstoppable virus. He read and wrote diligently, studying all the classics of Spanish literature. He delighted in his teachers' sage knowledge and lived an almost monastic existence, spending many hours poring over his books . . . or staring down at a blank sheet of paper, trying to compose a poem. He fully participated in the school's literary activities, and in 1944 he wrote his first story. Three years later, Gabo entered law school in Bogotá, a city of 700,000 inhabitants, over 6,500 feet above sea level, similar in many ways to the plains of Spain, with a vibrant cultural life that centered around the downtown cafés. The future Nobel laureate would spend more time at the cafés than attending classes, and he met the most important writers of the day there. He would also discover a few literary jewels: Kafka's *The Metamorphosis*, which aggravated the bug for literature even more, prompting him to write stories of his own in a frenzy; classics like Garcilaso, Quevedo, Góngora, Lope de Vega, San Juan de la Cruz; and his own contemporaries like the Generation of 1927 and Neruda. Soon after, his interest would focus almost exclusively on the novel, until he came to believe that his vocation for literature was so strong that he should drop out of law school altogether. . . .

★ ★ ★

Fidel Castro grew up in a rural working-class family. In the small town of Birán, near Santiago de Cuba in the far southeast of the island, his childhood playmates were field workers on the sugarcane plantation in Mañacas. Surrounded by nature and animals, Castro explored the forests on horseback, swam in the river, and when he was five years old was enrolled in the small local country school. At six and a half, he was brought to the province's capital, Santiago de Cuba, to continue his studies in a parochial boarding school. His revolutionary outlook can be traced back to those early childhood years; for when he returned to the plantation, he organized a workers' strike against his own father, whom he accused of exploitation! For his final years of high school, because of his high grades, his parents enrolled him in the Jesuit school of Belen in Havana, the best school in the country, where Cuba's aristocracy sent their children. Future conservative political affiliations were often cemented there.

In October 1945, Castro entered the University of Havana to

7

study Law. It would change his life. He had come from an uneventful, tranquil environment, where the only things that mattered were getting a good education and being a good Christian, and now he found himself in a place where the struggle for survival was what counted. The campus was roughly divided into two rival political groups, which exerted effects on the city as a whole through acts of violence and financial influence: the Revolutionary Socialist Movement (Movimiento Socialista Revolucionario, or MSR), headed by the ex-communist Rolando Masferrer, and the Insurrectionist Revolutionary Union (Unión Insurreccional Revolucionaria, or UIR), led by the ex-anarchist Emilio Tro. Fidel was immediately gripped by political ambition, and his goal was to lead the Federation of University Students (Federación Estudiantíl Universitaria, or FEU)—that is, the entity that represented the entire student body—a very coveted position for members of either of the two rival factions. He tried to attract the attention of the leaders of MSR and UIR, aware of the fact that he could not accomplish his objective without the support of some influential group; but by the time he was in his third year, he hadn't moved beyond the position of vice president for the law school's own student council. For the next election, he decided to run for president of the FEU, regardless of his affiliation with either of the two parties. He carefully laid the groundwork. He read many of the works of the great Cuban revolutionary and writer José Martí and took from them a very seductive, powerful philosophy, and also a lengthy compilation of facts to bolster his carefully composed speeches. He also began to act outside of the university, organizing demonstrations against Ramón Grau San Martin's government. "The papers were talking about him," notes his biographer, Volker Skierka, "sometimes in grandiose terms. A charming, talented speaker, young, tall and athletic, dressed handsomely in double-breasted suits and ties, his black hair slicked back, with his classic Greek profile, at twenty-one years old he cut an impressive figure, the type that mothers of marriageable daughters dream about."[5]

But he wasn't just talk. After a meeting with the president, Castro proposed to his fellow activists the possibility of grabbing the president and throwing him from his balcony in an effort to kill him, which would set off the student revolution in a highly dramatic fashion. Around that time, Castro is alleged to have been involved in three actual assassination attempts: the first in December 1946, when a member of UIR was shot in the lung; the second in February 1948, when Manolo Castro, the national Director of Sports, was shot and killed outside a movie theater; and the third shortly thereafter: a police officer, Oscar Fernandez, was fatally shot outside his home; before taking his last breath, he identified the student leader as the trigger man.[6]

Castro's interest in Latin American politics gradually intensified. He aligned himself with a movement for the liberation of Puerto Rico; he traveled to the Dominican Republic in a failed attempt to oust the dictator Rafael Trujillo; and he expressed solidarity with student movements in Argentina, Venezuela, Colombia, and Panama, which were fighting to end colonialism within their countries and stop the infiltration of imperialism from the United States. To that end, he organized a congress of the student assemblies of Latin America in early 1948, to be held in April of that year in the Colombian capital, coinciding with the Ninth Inter-American Summit of Foreign Affairs Ministers, where the creation of the Organization of American States (OAS) would be decided, and where Washington aimed to thwart the "communist threat" under General Marshall's watchful gaze.

★ ★ ★

Playtime was over. The destinies of our two little gods collided in Bogotá on that bloody April 9, 1948. What became known as the

"Bogotazo" riots would claim 3,500 lives over the coming days and over 300,000 more in the subsequent fighting in years to come.[7] On April 7, Castro met with Jorge Eliécer Gaitán, the popular liberal leader of the opposition in Colombia. In spite of his youth, Gaitán had managed to consolidate the party at a time when the country desperately needed someone to put an end to the climate of violence and oligarchy, and no one doubted that he would win the presidency in the next elections. At his meeting with the student representative from Cuba in his office on Seventh Street, the two had liked one another. Gaitán promised to help Castro and his colleagues secure a location to hold their anti-imperialism conference, and to close the proceedings with a massive public demonstration. They planned to meet again two days later, at two o'clock in the afternoon, to finalize the details. Shortly before that, as Fidel and his friends wandered around the neighborhood, waiting for the appointed time, a lone, deranged gunman, Juan Roa Sierra, shot the presidential candidate at point-blank range. As Gaitán stepped out of his office at 14-55 Seventh Street, between Jimenez de Quesada Avenue and Fourteenth Avenue, he was shot three times: in the brain, the lungs, and the liver. Three bullets ended the life of the great hope of Colombia, marked the beginning of one of the darkest eras of the country's history, and sparked a civil war that would drag on for decades.

At that very moment, in a rooming house for low-income students on Eighth Street, very close to the scene of the assassination, second-year law student Gabriel García Márquez was about to have lunch. His watch read five minutes after one. He knew what had happened immediately. Gabo and his friends ran to where Gaitán had collapsed bleeding on the sidewalk. By the time they got there, Gaitán had already been taken to the Central Clinic, where he would die within a few minutes. Confused by the growing chaos, the students lingered in the area for a little while, trying to make sense of the street disturbances erupting around them and the shouts and screaming, growing louder. The city was burning. They decided to go back to their rooming house. As they rounded the corner and crossed their street, they discovered the worst: their house was on fire, too. They couldn't go in and rescue their personal belongings. Clothes, furniture, books, everything would be reduced to ashes. Gabo tried to run into the inferno, but his friends held him back. His desperation stemmed from the imminent loss of his most treasured possessions: the manuscripts of the stories he was writing, especially "The Story of the Faun on the Streetcar," and the pieces that had already been published in *El Espectador*.[8] Luis Villar Borda, a friend from the literary scene, ran into Gabo at around four o'clock that afternoon at the intersection of Jimenez de Quesada Avenue and Eighth Street. Dasso Saldívar describes the encounter:

> Coming upon his friend in such a disoriented state, on the verge of tears, made quite an impression on Villar Borda, since over the past year, seeing him at university functions and lecture halls, Gabriel had never displayed any passion at all for anything political, much less for bipartisan national politics in particular. . . . So, finding him so out of sorts, he said, puzzled,
> "Gabriel, I didn't know you were such a Gaitánist!"
> Then Gabriel replied, his voice breaking, "No, what are you talking about, it's that *my stories burned!*"[9]

Gabo made one last desperate attempt: to save the typewriter that must have still been at the pawn shop. He had recently left it there as a guarantee, to get some cash to pay off some debts and bills. Seeing how Seventh Street and its cross streets were engulfed in flames, his brother Luis Enrique and he had the same premonition. Gabo recalls in his memoirs:

Enraged crowds, armed with machetes and all kinds of sharp tools looted from hardware stores, destroyed the shops on Seventh Street and its cross-streets and set them on fire, with the help of mounted police. One look was enough to convince us that the situation was out of control. My brother read my mind when he shouted:

"Shit, the typewriter!"

We ran to the pawn shop, which was still intact, with the iron gates locked up tight, but the typewriter wasn't where it always had been. We weren't worried, assuming that we could get it back after all this was over, not having realized yet that that terrible disaster would never be over.[10]

Fidel Castro, Alfredo Guevara, and the rest of the student delegates who had left their hotel to meet with the liberal leader watched people running by, shouting "They killed Gaitán!" Thirty-three years later, Fidel recounted in an interview with Arturo Alape the things that struck him most about those days: crowds of furious, indignant people running around, committing acts of violence with total abandon. They smashed windows, looted stores, destroyed public and private property. The mob reached the plaza in front of Parliament; hundreds of people crowded in front of the door, while a man futilely tried to address the throng from a balcony. The police could not contain the mob, which broke into the government building and proceeded to destroy everything in its path, heaving desks and chairs out of the windows. Fidel instinctively joined up with the group of insurrectionists running through the streets, one more revolutionary; he dashed into the third division police headquarters, making off with a shotgun, fourteen bullets, boots, and a police captain's hat before heading out to war.[11] Eventually, Castro came to the conclusion that this was not a revolution, but a riot. When he joined his friends again, he learned that the police were looking for him because it was the Cuban *communists* who had provoked Gaitán's death and the insurrection.[12] In light of the situation, they decided to go to the Cuban embassy and stay there, to avoid any further trouble in the midst of the increasingly chaotic uprising.

A few years ago, together with his close friend Gabriel García Márquez, the Cuban leader recounted the dramatic twists and turns of those unforgettable, hair-raising days. Both have stated on numerous occasions that their friendship began for literary reasons. Fate coincided with history on April 9, 1948; a typewriter, a simple machine made of metal and plastic that can transport you to heaven through transcendent writings inspired by the muses, was the catalyst of their union—if not in actual terms, at least in an imagined, fantastic, magical way, as *real* things often are in the Caribbean. Fidel recalls this conversation with Gabo:

> While I stood there watching, perplexed, the people dragged the assassin through the streets, mobs set fire to shops, offices, movie theaters, and apartment buildings. Some people were hauling around pianos and armoires on wheels. Someone shattered glass. Others defaced signs and marquees. The most vocal unleashed their frustration by shouting from the street corners, garden terraces, and smoky buildings. One man vented his fury by attacking a typewriter, beating it, and then to save himself the laborious effort, he threw it up into the air, and it smashed to bits when it hit the pavement.
>
> As I spoke, Gabo listened, probably confirming to himself the certainty that in Latin America and the Caribbean, writers don't have to make very much up, because reality is more interesting than anything you could imagine, and maybe the challenge is to make that incredible reality

believable. As I was finishing telling my story, I knew that Gabo had been there too, and the coincidence was very telling, maybe we had run through the same streets and witnessed the same harrowing events, which had made me just one more character in that suddenly roiling mob. I asked the question with my usual dispassionate curiosity:

"And what were you doing during the Bogotazo?"

And he, calmly, entrenched within his vibrant, provocative, exceptional imagination, answered simply, smiling, ingenious with his natural use of metaphor:

"Fidel, I was that man with the typewriter."[13]

★

CHAPTER TWO

IF THE RIGHT TO KNOW IS NOT A RIGHT, THEN IT MUST BE A LEFT

T HE WIZARD OF MACONDO HAS BEEN KNOWN TO SAY ON OCCASION that while his political convictions are firm and unchanging, his literary convictions fluctuate somewhat. There are no formulas or absolute truths in literature, but in politics, there are principles, and those took root at the deepest levels of Gabo's consciousness from a very young age. García Márquez freely acknowledges that the stories his grandfather, a liberal colonel, told him about the Colombian civil war; about the vicious massacre of the banana workers on strike in 1928; and about other political, sometimes cruel, events in Colombia's history, could have influenced him from earliest childhood.[1] Still, the first inklings of his interest in politics can be more directly traced to his elementary school days in Zipaquirá, where some of his teachers had received a Marxist education at the Escuela Normal during the years the Leftist president Alfonso Lopez had been in power: "At that school, the algebra teacher taught us about the history of materialism; the chemistry teacher gave us books on Lenin; and the history teacher lectured us on class struggles. By the time I got out of that cold dungeon, I didn't know north from south, but I had two very strong convictions: that good novels should be a poetic translation of reality, and that humanity's destiny in the near future was socialism."[2] He further stated, in his conversation with Plinio Apuleyo Mendoza: "I want the world to be socialist, and I believe that sooner or later it will be."[3]

His contacts with communism have always been tangential. He attended a few meetings of a communist cell when he was twenty-two years old, but he never became a sympathizer of the party. He had a highly variable, sometimes conflictive relationship with the communists, but he never openly criticized or denounced them. During an interview in 1983, after making some comments about the United States, Gabo challenged his interviewer:

> I notice you haven't asked me the one question all interviewers start with.
>
> What question is that?
>
> You haven't asked me if I'm a communist.
>
> Okay. Are you a communist?
>
> Of course not. I am not, and have never been. Nor have I belonged to *any* political party.[4]

In another, earlier conversation, his position on communism is clear, especially with respect to the situation in Cuba and Latin America: "The old communist parties are made up of honorable, chaste men, sterilized by dogma and coddled by a revered Soviet mother, who is now more interested in making shrewd business deals than in sponsoring the revolution. This is clear in Latin America. Aside from the economic aid that it has given to Cuba, which has been very substantial, the Soviet Union has had no qualms about negotiating with the most reactionary regimes on the continent, with no regard for politics."[5]

After his trip touring the communist countries in the late 1950s (Poland and Czechoslovakia in 1955, and later East Germany, the USSR, and Hungary), he wrote a series of articles titled "The Iron Curtain" where he expressed his "disapproval of what has happened there."[6] He traveled with Apuleyo Mendoza and his sister Soledad. The three returned completely disillusioned. The socialism they had seen there had nothing to do with the socialism that they followed. It was almost an antithesis of Marxist ideas. They could only conclude that the "real socialism" exported by the Soviets did not work. In fact, it strangled the countries where it had been installed by force. Referring to his writings, García Márquez remarked, "The central premise of these articles is that within the so-called popular democracies, there wasn't authentic socialism, and there never will be, following that path, because the dominant system had not been based on the particular conditions of each country. It was a system imposed from the outside by the Soviet Union, through local communist parties, dogmatic and unimaginative, which couldn't conceive of doing anything except forcing the Soviet system onto a reality that it didn't fit."[7]

Gabo understands socialism to mean a system of "progress, liberty, and relative equality"[8] where *to know* is not only a right, it is a left, as the popular Cuban singer-songwriter Silvio Rodriguez suggests in his song "Escaramujo."[9] "I spend my life questioning, knowing the answers can't be a luxury," the song says. And the writer from Colombia seemed to be very sure that this open character of informed socialism, far from the rigid dogma typical of the Soviet Union, would be a valid, workable system for Latin America in the future. In 1971, he affirmed his aversion for Soviet-style socialism, and also his faith in the success of a form of socialism suitable for his continent: "These unscrupulous transactions are only symptoms of a system that resembles socialism less and less. But in spite of this, I continue to believe that socialism is a real possibility, that it is the right solution for Latin America, and that there needs to be a more active level of militancy."[10] One of his first experiences of open engagement with the Leftist world would be his trip to Cuba in 1959, which was preceded by a few articles in which he praised the young lawyer Fidel Castro's efforts to overthrow the Batista regime, the springtime of a love that would not be consummated until autumn.

THE TRUTH BEHIND "OPERATION TRUTH"

In the earliest stirrings of the Revolution, the name of one Cuban rebel in particular began to circulate around the world. García Márquez had also heard of Fidel Castro. In 1955, in Paris, the Cuban poet Nicolás Guillén met with Gabo and Mendoza and told them that "a guy half out of his mind"[11] was trying to overthrow the Batista government, and that he was the only hope his native country had for a better way of life.

Mendoza and García Márquez were always interested in hearing about what was happening on the Caribbean island. They listened to Radio Rebelde, the voice of the Cuban opposition, every day, and read everything they could about "The Queen of the Caribbean." In 1957, in his piece "Cuando era feliz e indocumentado," García Márquez refers to that lawyer and his group of rebel fighters, and in February 1958 he wrote an article titled "Pedro Infante's Out. Batista Stays," where he alludes to the guerrilla struggle of the *barbudos* (bearded ones) as "problems in maintaining public order in the Western province,"[12] which were beginning to pull the rug out from under Batista. Soon after, Plinio Apuleyo Mendoza interviewed Manuel Urrutia, who had been appointed provisional president of the future revolutionary government, and García Márquez published an article on Emma Castro, the Cuban leader's sister. In that interview, Emma exalted her brother as Cuban to the core, regardless of bloodlines, and García Márquez implied solidarity and sympathy for the guerrillas and for Cuba in general, presenting a human image of their leader, untainted by the publicity coverage. He pointed out Castro's culinary talents, especially the spaghetti that he cooked for his fellow inmates in prison, and highlighted his charming, animated conversation; his willingness to listen; his leadership skills as demonstrated at the university; and his dedication to his studies, especially at exam time: "After learning everything on every page of a book, he would rip out the pages and destroy them, burning the pages. He knew that he absolutely could not forget what he had learned, since he had eliminated the possibility of going back."[13] Then Emma gave a brief family history, revealing that Fidel was very athletic; he was also absent-minded and would lose his books all the time, except the ones written by Martí. She pointed out her brother's skill in handling firearms, his love of hunting, his rebellious streak, and how his parents had suspected that their son was already involved in the student revolution against Batista before he had told them. After summarizing what he knew about Fidel's experience in the "Bogotazo" of 1948, Gabo expressed solidarity with the Cuban's mission, before describing what had become of each of the revolutionary's family members since he had picked up arms:

> One of Fidel's great accomplishments is that he was able to bring together the 150,000 Cubans who supported the revolution from the United States. He inspired them with his announcement to the people of Cuba: "Before the end of the year, I will land on the island." In less than one month, he raised $160,000, traveled to Cayo Hueso and then to Mexico, where his brother Raúl put him in contact with the Cuban leaders of the movement in exile.[14]

This article, while very positive in tone, was nevertheless, according to Fidel, strictly informative. Over time, he would remark to Gabo that his first writings about Cuba and the revolution were not completely committed to the cause, and that he had essentially been watching the bulls from the grandstands. Within a few months, Batista had to flee the country, and the trials for the captured members of his government began. To demonstrate that these were war criminals, and not simply followers of the ousted dictator, as they were portrayed in the United States press, Fidel Castro organized "Operation Truth" and invited journalists from around the world to attend the public trials, which took place in the sports stadium in Havana.

On January 19, 1959, García Márquez and Plinio Apuleyo Mendoza traveled to Cuba. They had their first contacts with Castro during that trip. Plinio told us that, although Castro doesn't remember, in those days they spoke with the guerrilla commander for the first time. They had just arrived at the airport in Camagüey—they both must have looked exhausted—when Fidel appeared. He looked at Gabo and asked "Have you eaten?," showing an interest in making sure they were comfortable during their stay on the island. Then they immediately attended the trial of Jesús Sosa Blanco, a colonel of Batista's army, accused of murdering various locals from a small rural area known as El Oro de Guisa who had supported the rebel army. He was sentenced to death. His wife and children asked many of the journalists to sign a document requesting a revised sentence. Plinio and Gabo signed it, but the petition was ignored. In any case, both were confident that the trial and sentence had been just, even though the political immaturity of the new Cuban government could have invalidated the result, or at least made it open to debate. When they returned to Colombia a few days later, the two friends were already a part of a group of intellectuals that were supportive of the Cuban Revolution. They had been fascinated by the triumph of the people, the charisma of their leader, the exuberant happiness shown by the blacks, whites, mulattos, guajiros, Havanans, the old and young alike; everyone, except Batista, until he departed on December 31, 1958. Ana Belén should have sung her song then, instead of thirty years later:

Existe un país en los trópicos	There's a country in the tropics
Donde el sol es un sol de verdad,	Where the sun is very strong
Y a la sombra de bosques exóticos	And in the shade of exotic jungles
Imagínate lo bien que se está.	Imagine how great it must be.
Los locos que el mundo no traga	The misfits that the world won't accept
Nos juntamos al anochecer	We come together at dawn
Dando vueltas a un sueño probable,	Spinning dreams that could come true,
A un amor que no ha podido ser.	A love that might have been.
Y mientras el mundo se queda	And while the world moves
Transitando por la misma vía,	In the same orbit as always
Aquí estamos, rueda que te rueda,	Here we are, spinning round you,
Ahuyentando la melancolía.	Warding off sadness.
Cazamos al vuelo las lágrimas,	We catch tears in mid-air,
Las bebemos con vino y con miel,	We drink them with wine and honey,
Y aprendemos la risa del cómico	We learn to laugh like a clown
Y salvamos así la piel.	And save our skins that way.[15]

THE SECOND OPERATION: THE LATIN PRESS (PRELA)

Soon after the Revolution erupted, a press agency was formed, called Prensa Latina, that would focus on events in Cuba. Jorge Ricardo Masetti, an Argentinian journalist, had commented on the rumors perpetuated by the media in the United States during a television interview: "Yes, this shows that the North American press agencies have a monopoly on information, and Latin America doesn't have any chance of replicating it because there is no Latin American news agency."[16] This observation was the catalyst for Prensa Latina ("Prela," as its members would later call it). After hearing Masetti on television, Che Guevara, who was a very close friend of his, called him up with a proposal. They had met in the Sierra Maestra; Masetti was the reporter who had interviewed Guevara and, since their very first conversation, they had begun a relationship that was far beyond merely cordial. Che suggested forming a press agency, promising to help make all the necessary arrangements to get it off the ground. When he said that one of the main objectives would be to counteract the imperialist propaganda spouted by the international agencies, especially the agencies in the United States, Masetti, thrilled, accepted the suggestion immediately.

One day, Apuleyo Mendoza happened to meet a Mexican man who was looking for a Colombian with some journalism experience to open a satellite office of Prela in Bogota. Apuleyo accepted, but with the condition that he would be allowed to hire another Colombian colleague to be the editor, receiving the same salary that he would get as the director. And that was how García Márquez moved with his whole family to Bogotá, to begin this exciting work with his friend. It was a double assignment: to objectively cover the situation in Colombia, and to report news from Cuba at the same time. His job consisted of writing and sending news stories to Cuba. It was the first real political journalism that García Márquez had ever done. In January 1960, the two friends launched a magazine, *Acción Liberal* (Liberal Action), where they were co-directors. It was to be a tri-monthly publication, in solidarity with Cuba, which aimed to combat the "official truths." It worked in tandem with Prela, and they had a passionate interest in it, but few issues were ever published.

Masetti traveled often, to personally meet his collaborators in other countries and to give them instructions. One day, he arrived in Bogotá and met the two friends. They had already been working for Prela for almost a year in the capital of Colombia. Masetti informed them that one of the two would have to leave the agency there, because journalists were needed in other places. So, in mid-1960, García Márquez moved to the office in Havana, to undergo intensive training so that he could then open up a new branch office in another location. During that stay, he met Fidel Castro for the second time. His first trip to the island in 1959 had been very brief, and there hadn't been enough time to fully process everything that was happening. This second stay in Havana was longer, but he still wasn't able to really explore the capital. He said later, "You know, fifteen days after the triumph of the Revolution, I was in Cuba. I was at 'Operation Truth.' Then I went to work in Bogotá, at the Prensa Latina office. In mid-1960 I returned to Havana. I worked there for six months, and I'll tell you what I got to see of Cuba: I saw the fifth floor of the Retiro Medico building, where the Prensa Latina offices were; I got to know the elevator of the Retiro Medico building; I had a partial view of the Rampa, and the Indochina store that was on the corner; I got to know an elevator on another side of the building that went up to the twentieth floor, where I lived with Aroldo Wall. Oh yeah! I also developed a familiarity with the Maracas restaurant, where we would eat, a block and a half away. We worked every single minute of the day and night. I said to Masetti: 'If anything's going to sink this Revolution, it's going to be the light bill.'"[17]

Angel Augier, a Cuban poet and journalist, told us in November 2002 that he had had a great relationship with Gabo when he was in Havana during those months in 1960, since Augier was also working for Prela. The Cuban poet always edited Gabo's writings, correcting the spelling that to this day continues to be a sore spot for the Colombian. Spelling is such a weak point that in 1997, the Nobel laureate even proposed retiring it (*jubilarla*) in a speech at an academic meeting in Mexico.[18] Augier was implacable, especially with regard to certain grammatical forms. During a visit Gabo paid to the nonagenarian in his house in Havana in the summer of 2001, he reminded Augier, "Your pencil was devastating. You were always taking away my gerunds in particular, which we Latin Americans are so fond of using."[19]

He met Rodolfo Walsh there, an author who he had always admired: Walsh was responsible for the agency's Special Services. Masetti, García Márquez, and Walsh quickly became close friends. They lived together during one of the happiest periods of their lives. Through an extraordinary coincidence, Masetti had stumbled across a coded message from the CIA. He gave it to Walsh, who succeeded in decoding it. It was about preparations for the Bay of Pigs invasion (Playa Giron, as it is known in Cuba). They came up with a plan to surprise the Americans, but the government told them that it already had its own plan. In spite of that rebuff, it was an unforgettable event in the lives of the three journalists, which Gabo would later immortalize in his "Recuerdos de periodista," published on December 16, 1981.[20]

After six months of training, Masetti sent García Márquez to Canada to open a new office there. First, he went to New York in early 1961, to apply for visas for himself and his family, but they were denied. For García Márquez, those months in New York were agonizing: "I stayed in New York, waiting for a visa to go to Canada. But I never got to Canada. And then . . . when was the Bay of Pigs? '60 or '61? April '61. In April of '61, I was in the worst place you could possibly be; because if I had been here or in Giron, fighting or not, I would have been much safer than in the Latin Press office in New York, where we were practically surrounded by *gusanos* [counterrevolutionary worms], who believed that they had already finished with this. We couldn't be armed because the police would have been all over us for having weapons. And if we didn't have any weapons, the *gusanos* would be all over us. We had some nails and pieces of pipe. Basically, [it was] the worst possible place to be at the time."[21]

In the United States, anti-Castro sentiment and the number of Cuban exiles continued to grow. For the Prela journalists, the danger was mounting. One day, someone whispered in García Márquez's ear, like something out of a movie about gangland Chicago in the thirties, that if he wanted his family and himself to be safe, he had better leave town. In spite of the threats, he continued working. This would, unfortunately, eventually result in his resignation, prompted by the other side, the communists in Cuba, where the influence of the Soviet Union was becoming increasingly prominent. A sect of communists and their leader, Anibal Escalante, were successfully insinuating themselves into certain areas of Cuban politics, gradually becoming virtually omnipresent. They understood very clearly that Masetti, Walsh, García Márquez, and Mendoza, as Leftist as they were, would never be members of their sectarian group. A pronounced hostility between the Prela journalists and these communists developed, as they gradually came to exert increasing control over Prela. Masetti tried to elicit some support from Che Guevara or Fidel Castro to remedy the situation, but with no success. García Márquez resigned. The others followed their director out the door. This was a crushing blow to Guevara, because in a sense Prela was his baby, and also because its demise was proof that there were factions within the Leftist Cuban Revolution, and the unity of the project begun in the Sierra Maestra could crumble.

After those months in New York, García Márquez went to Mexico with his family, without having set foot in Canada. A few years after García Márquez left Prela, Masetti and Walsh were assassinated by their own country's military government in Argentina.

During the time that García Márquez worked for Prela, he met Fidel Castro on various occasions, but their real friendship did not begin in that period.

At present, nothing remains of Prela. The communists, of the mindset that knowing is perhaps a right, but certainly not a left, destroyed everything related to Masetti's organization, and, sadly, a very important part of García Márquez's journalism would be lost forever, as was a part of the history of the Revolution's beginnings.

EARS OF THE WOLF

Gabo hadn't just lost a job, sending him plummeting into another period of financial instability. He also lost, and this is much more important, all contact with the Revolution. The doors of Cuba—or, more accurately, the ports of Cuba—remained closed, and García Márquez wouldn't set foot on Cuban soil again until 1975. The Prela situation not only did not play out in his favor, it would result in notoriety for the Colombian, rather than public adoration. In those years, he mainly lived in Mexico, and he published *La mala hora* (The Evil Hour) (1962). He began to work on screenplays, and, most notably, he locked himself up for eighteen months to write *One Hundred Years of Solitude*, which was published in 1967. While he wrote the novel, he told his friend Plinio Apuleyo Mendoza: "I'll have a big hit with this one or I'll lose my mind."[22]

Meanwhile, as Castro's Cuba began to mold itself into a socialist schematic, the first rifts between the intellectuals and those in power became apparent. The wolf pricked up its ears. The Revolution—which had promised a new life, far from the former dictatorship, which would respect fundamental human rights and promote democracy and freedom—very quickly began to act like a despotic regime. In June 1961, various writers and artists were summoned before the Tribunal in Havana to give their opinion on the magazine *Lunes*. In that magazine, Nestor Almendros, a cinematographer, had defended the film *P.M.*, directed by Saba Cabrera, the brother of Guillermo Cabrera Infante, which had been banned from Cuba for portraying Cuban nightlife instead of promoting revolutionary values,[23] when the real serious issue at the time was the Bay of Pigs.

Many of the intellectuals summoned defended the magazine and freedom of expression in general. Fidel Castro cut them off, giving the intellectuals a long lecture. He made a distinction between form and content. Regarding form, there was complete freedom; there were no restrictions. But that wasn't the case when it came to content: "For the Revolution, everything; against the Revolution, nothing." This was the key phrase of the speech, that none of the intellectuals present would ever forget. But, who would decide what was for the Revolution and what was against it? From that moment on, the intellectuals in Cuba began to censor themselves to avoid being exiled, imprisoned, or worse. In 1987, during another speech, Fidel Castro announced that from then on, the Revolution would have freedom of content too. Unfortunately, although there is more flexibility as this book is written, complete freedom of expression in Cuba remains elusive.

In 1968, the incident that would be the first serious indication of the dictatorship would take place: the Padilla case. This will be discussed in the next chapter. That was also the year the Soviets invaded Czechoslovakia, with the approval, support, and encouragement of Fidel Castro. At that moment, the wolf was all ears. Springtime in Prague. Although most Cubans assumed that Fidel Castro would condemn the Soviet invasion with tanks from the Warsaw Pact, he gave it his blessing, to the great surprise of many, including García Márquez: "To me," he said, "the world fell in on me, but now I think that we all go through the same thing: we come to the clear realization that we are caught between two imperialist states equally cruel and insatiable, and in a way this is liberating to the conscience."[24]

In an interview with Plinio Apuleyo Mendoza, he explains his position and contrasts it with Fidel's, as he tries to comprehend his friend's view while not sharing it: "[My position] was public, and one of protest, and if the same situation came up again, it wouldn't change. The only difference between my position and Fidel Castro's (since we don't have to always agree about everything) is that he ended up justifying the Soviet intervention, and I never will. But the analysis that he gave in his speeches on the internal situation of the popular democracies was much more critical and dramatic than anything I said in the travel pieces we were just talking about. In any case, the destiny of Latin America was not determined, and it won't be determined, in Hungary, Poland, or Czechoslovakia, it will only be determined in Latin America. Everything else is a European obsession, and that includes some of your questions on politics."[25]

This and other factors would definitely produce a certain wariness of the supreme leader on the writer's part during those years. The wolves sized each other up, marked their territories, adjusted their positions, and made their moves. Gabo would soon go from being a sometime journalist to a living symbol of magical realism, and his writing would become the paradigm of the wonderful literature written in Spanish in Latin America. For Cuba, he would have to wait just a little longer. Nothing comes without a price. And Fidel doesn't give anything away. There may be a right to know, but acting on that knowledge can only be a left.

CHAPTER THREE

★

FADE TO BLACK: THE PADILLA CASE

B Y 1968, GABO'S LIFE HAD CHANGED DRASTICALLY. THE YEAR before, his novel *One Hundred Years of Solitude* had circled the globe in many languages. It was a far cry from the hard-scrabble days of his youth, when he'd had to sleep in a different room every night in a certain fleabag hotel, in whichever bed the whores didn't happen to be using, in exchange for manuscripts of stories as payment when he didn't have any cash. It was quite a switch from the time he spent in Paris in the mid-fifties, when he had had to beg for change in the Métro and spend the cold winter nights on a park bench or huddled over a grating in a station, trying to dodge the police, who always mistook him for an Algerian. The last two years of struggle were still not far behind in Gabo's memory, right up until the publication of his novel. Between the dawn of the sixties and 1965, he hadn't written one word of fiction; and during that year, on a trip to Acapulco with his wife, he had suddenly stopped the car and said: "Mercedes, I've found the voice! I'm going to narrate the story in the same style my grandmother would use to tell me her incredible tales, starting with the day when the father takes his son to see the ice!"[1]

That year, there would barely be any vacation. Back in Colombia, García Márquez scraped together $5,000 (savings, proceeds from selling the car, and loans from friends, especially Álvaro Mutis) and shut himself away for fourteen months to write the story of the Buendia family and Macondo. Mercedes had to make lace to barter for meat from the butcher and bread from the bakery, and to placate the landlord while they were nine months behind in the rent. By the end of this period, their total household debt had climbed to over $10,000. But all that ended when the novel was published. From that point on, not only were his financial troubles gone forever, but García Márquez would also be able to navigate much more easily through the treacherous waters of the Latin American political scene. Among other things, he decided to commit himself more fully to the Cuban Revolution. His motivation was clear: Gabo firmly believed that Cuba's leader was different from the typical bosses, heroes, dictators, and thugs that had figured so prominently in Latin American history since the nineteenth century, and he sensed that the Revolution, still young, could only bear fruit in the rest of the countries in Latin America through his involvement. His political conviction stemmed from the belief that, in time, the entire world would be socialist, in spite of capitalism's advances in North America and Western Europe.

The year 1968 marked a milestone in Cuba's history. It was the year of the Warsaw Pact's intervention in Czechoslovakia and the beginning of the Padilla case. It was a convulsive time in Western society in general, since it also witnessed the start of student movements, touching off a general crisis in the universities. Protest songs were popularized as the Vietnam War intensified (and would last until 1975), and Che Guevara no longer lived to tell the tale. Against that backdrop, an event that initially seemed unremarkable within Cuban cultural politics would shake the Castrist monolith to its very core and would force García Márquez to pick a side in the Revolution.

THE CASE AGAINST PADILLA: A LOOK AT LATIN AMERICAN "INTELLIGENCE"

Taking into account all of the events of those years is necessary for fully understanding the sea change in how Latin American and European intellectuals viewed the Cuban Revolution and its leader. In 1968, *Fuera del juego*, a collection of poems by Heberto Padilla, won the Julian del Casal prize in poetry. The prize jury was made up of three Cubans—José Lezama Lima, José Z. Tallet, Manuel Díaz Martínez—and two foreigners: the Englishman J. M. Cohen and the Peruvian Cesar Calvo. Shortly before that, Padilla had harshly criticized the book *Pasión de Urbino* by the Cuban writer Lisandro Otero, in a piece published in the magazine *El Caimán Barbudo*. In 1964, Otero had hoped his book would win the Biblioteca Breve prize sponsored by the Spanish publishing house Seix Barral, but Guillermo Cabrera Infante had won with his book *Tres Tristes Tigres*. In his article, Padilla stated that it was a shame that, for political reasons, one couldn't discuss a novel of such high literary merit as Cabrera Infante's in Cuba, while a book as mediocre as Otero's would receive so much attention, since its author was then the Vice President of the National Council of Culture. Padilla concluded: "In Cuba, a writer can't openly criticize a novelist/Vice president without suffering the attacks of the writer/director and the poets/editors hiding behind the faceless label *The Editors*."[2]

Padilla lost his job as a result of that article, since he had publicly praised the work of Cabrera Infante, one of the Cuban authors who at the time was considered "a traitor to the revolution." Juan Goytisolo described how he found out about that accusation while in Paris: "On November 8, 1968, it was about two o'clock in the afternoon, I had gone down to Bonne Nouvelle Boulevard, as usual, to stretch my legs and pick up a copy of *Le Monde*, when a dispatch from the paper's correspondent in Cuba suddenly caught my eye: 'The Armed Forces committee denounce the counterrevolutionary activities of the poet Padilla.'" The article, signed with the initials of Saverio Tutino—special envoy from the *Paese Sera*—included some passages from the committee's denunciation of the poet, who was accused not only of a number of literary-political provocations, but also—which was much more serious—of having "happily squandered" public funds while he had been director of Cubartimpex. According to the article, Padilla was at the head of a group of Cuban writers who resorted to sensationalism and foreign exposure, "creating works which are a blend of weakness, pornography, and counterrevolution."[3]

Shortly before the winner of the UNEAC Prize (Union of Writers and Artists of Cuba) was publicly announced, Raúl Castro had spread the rumor that if Padilla, the counterrevolutionary writer, won the prize, there would be "very serious consequences."[4] Even *Los siete contra Tebas*, which won the UNEAC prize for drama, written by Anton Arrufat, a writer who had been very faithful to the regime to that point, was labeled counterrevolutionary. The jury for the prize, however, did not consider Padilla's book to be counterrevolutionary; they judged it to be a critique of extraordinary literary merit. It should be pointed out here (and this is often overlooked) that Padilla's book included some very heartfelt praise for much of what constituted the artistic world of the Revolution. That is how Manuel Vázquez Montalbán viewed it in his book *Y Dios entró en la Habana*, when he stated: "Padilla is not only critical, he also praises many Revolutionary works. To Fidel, Padilla can be summed up in two words: dishonest and disloyal."[5]

Finally, UNEAC accepted the jury's decision and published

Fuera del juego and *Los siete contra Tebas*, but they didn't give Padilla or Arrufat visas for the trip to Moscow or give them the 1,000 pesos that were supposed to be included with the prize. And they added a prologue to the poet's work that had nothing to do with the author or his ideas, in which they accused the writers of collaborating with the enemy to the north, claiming to base this judgment on *strictly artistic* grounds. "Our literary conviction permits us to point out that these works of poetry and drama serve our enemies, and its authors are just the artists they need to stow away in their Trojan horse for the time when imperialism puts into practice its politics of military aggression against Cuba."[6] These were considerations that later, paradoxically, would be combined with others less literary, never clearly defined. They only state: "The Directors determined that the prizes have been squandered on works built upon ideological elements that are completely opposed to Revolutionary thought."[7] And therefore, the prologue concludes grandiosely, "The directors of UNEAC reject the ideological content of the prize-winning book of poems and theater script."[8]

They reproached Padilla for "his lack of Revolutionary enthusiasm, his criticism, his disregard for history, his defense of the individual in the face of social needs,"[9] and also "his ignorance of the moral obligations inherent in the Revolutionary construct."[10] Of course, although the prize-winning works were, technically, "published," they were not circulated; they were not available in bookstores; and they could only be obtained clandestinely, passed around among the very few people who had somehow managed to get their hands on a copy.

After these events, some writers decided to react: "On Franqui's advice," Goytisolo explains, "I got in touch with Cortazar, Fuentes, Vargas Llosa, Semprun, and García Márquez, and through Ugné Karvelis's office in Gallimard, I tried to reach Heberto on the telephone. Since the phone calls were useless—no one ever answered that number—we decided to send a telegram, signed by all of us, to Haydee Santamaria, in which we stated we were 'alarmed by the slanderous accusations' leveled against the poet, we expressed our support for 'every action undertaken by the Casa de las Americas [headquarters of the National Council on Culture] in defense of intellectual freedom.' Haydee's reply—received by telegram two days later—completely stunned us."[11] Here is an excerpt from that reply: "It is impossible to determine from so far away whether an accusation against Padilla is slanderous or not. The cultural policy of the Casa de las Americas is the policy of our Revolution, the Cuban Revolution, and the Casa de las Americas will always be directed as Che had wished: with guns at the ready, shooting cannons into the field."[12]

PADILLA'S ARREST AND THE FIRST OPEN LETTER

In 1971, Padilla, with his wife, the poet Belkis Cuza Malé, was arrested, because he was "at the time what was popularly known as an 'incorrigible writer.'"[13] His wife only spent a few days in jail, but Heberto remained in prison for several weeks. The poet's arrest provoked strong responses and protests, especially among the intellectuals who had been supportive of Castro's Revolution up until then. A cry rose up warning of the imminent Stalinization of Cuba. Some writers immediately cut off all support for and ties with the Revolution forever, including Mario Vargas Llosa, Juan Goytisolo, Carlos Fuentes, Plinio Apuleyo Mendoza, Octavio Paz, Jean-Paul Sartre, and of course the revolutionary Carlos Franqui. He had been one of the main protagonists in the events that brought Castro to power in 1959, yet he had already abandoned the Revolution's inner circle by the early sixties because of the increasingly Marxist character of the movement (due to the growing influence of Raúl Castro and the radical faction of the Sierra Maestra, after Camilo Cienfuegos had died under suspicious circumstances).

Goytisolo recalls, "The author of *Rayuela* [Julio Cortázar] summoned me to his home at the Place du General Bueret, and between the two of us we composed what would eventually become known as 'the first letter to Fidel Castro,' a letter that won the approval of Franqui, who we had been in contact with as we wrote it. We decided that it should be a private letter, so that its recipient could address our concerns without the inevitable opposite effect that a public broadcast would have. Only in the event that, after a certain amount of time had passed and we got no response at all, would we then reserve the right to send a copy of the letter to the newspapers."[14] In the letter, the signers requested more information on Padilla's arrest in these terms: "The undersigned, supporters of the principles and objectives of the Cuban Revolution, address you in order to express our disquiet as a result of the imprisonment of the poet and writer Heberto Padilla, and to ask you to re-examine the situation which this arrest has created."[15] Gradually they collected more signatures for the first letter. They obtained fifty-four signatures in all. The only one missing was García Márquez. When all of this was going on, he had been in Barranquilla, Colombia, with his family. When the case had first blown up, he had been in Barcelona, where Plinio Apuleyo Mendoza lived. To avoid harassment from reporters, he decided to leave, along with Mercedes, for a prudent, indeterminate amount of time, retreating to a place somewhere in the Caribbean far away from a post office or a telephone, "to find the scent of ripe guava."[16] They stayed away for a long time. Apuleyo Mendoza tried to call him many times, but it was impossible to get in touch with him. He left several messages and sent a telegram, but never received a reply. He assumed that García Márquez had not received his messages, and since they had always shared the same opinions about Cuba, he decided to go ahead and sign his friend's name, holding himself personally responsible. He explained the decision later in his book *La llama y el hielo*:

We had talked about this subject so often, sharing the exact same point of view, because of which I had no doubt whatsoever of what his eventual reaction to Padilla's arrest would be. I honestly believed that. So when it was impossible to get in touch with him, and we were about to send the telegram, I said to Juan Goytisolo, calmly, without the slightest hesitation:

"Sign Gabo's name. I'll be responsible."

I thought that omitting his name, because of what seemed to me to be merely logistical problems, would give the wrong impression, when all of his friends, the writers of the *boom*, had already signed.[17]

But it seems that García Márquez *had* received the messages, and had answered, but his reply in the mail didn't arrive in time. Supposedly, he had asserted that he would not sign anything "until I have been fully informed on the subject."[18] Some of the people we interviewed, who would prefer to remain anonymous, assured us that Marbel Moreno, the wife of Plinio Mendoza, told them that Gabo had agreed to put his name on the letter, but later regretted it, and Plinio took the consequences of his friend's change of heart upon himself.

As Goytisolo observed, "With his consummate skill in avoiding confrontation, Gabo would discreetly distance himself from the critical position of his friends, without directly facing them: the new García Márquez, brilliant strategist of his enormous talent, coddled by fame, astute observer of the great ones in this world, advocate on an international stage of supposedly 'advanced' causes, was about to be born."[19] We'll never know the truth for sure, since Gabo insists that he did not sign, Mendoza covers his back, and other people closely involved attest that he did lend his name, but later wanted to obscure his earlier decision because of how Fidel would react. Vázquez Montalbán told us that it is a question that will always remain shrouded in mystery.

In early April, a letter of self-accusation written by the poet began to circulate, but the real intent of the author has been subject to debate. Most of the intellectuals agree that the letter was actually not written by Padilla. One of them, Manuel Díaz Martínez, states that "Our poet is as much the author of this letter as he is of *The Divine Comedy*."[20] Padilla probably did physically write it, but under threat, since methods of intimidation were prevalent in the Cuban Revolution's system of repression. Based on accounts from his closest friends, there were too many political errors to which Padilla confessed to make his sole authorship credible. In 1992, in a conversation with Carlos Verdecia, Padilla himself confirmed: "That self-accusation was written in part by the police, and in part by other people. There are some paragraphs in which I wanted to identify who had been the original writer. In some passages, the level of detail is so pronounced that the hand of Fidel Castro himself is clear. I wish I had the text here right now so I could show you."[21]

PADILLA'S HARA-KIRI: THE SELF-ACCUSATION

A few days after the crucial false confession, the poet was released— but with one condition, which led to the event that would erupt into the biggest scandal yet: the UNEAC organized a meeting where Padilla had to read his self-accusation aloud, in front of the members of that organization and many of his friends. The act took place on April 29, 1971, as a corollary to the letter itself. At that time, in addition to publicly admitting his own guilt, he accused other writers, his own friends, of "counterrevolutionary behavior" in their works. On this eclectic, substantial list, he included his own wife Belkis, Norberto Fuentes, Pablo Armando Fernández, César López, Manuel Díaz Martínez, José Yáñez, Virgilio Piñera, and José

Lezama Lima. Most of the people named got up to stand in front of the microphones to say something in their own defense. Diaz Martínez's chilling words on that portion of the meeting require no further explanation:"Padilla's self-accusation had been made public, but it's one thing to read it, and something else entirely to have heard it read that night. That moment was one of the very worst of my life. I'll never forget the expressions of total shock—while Padilla read—of those seated around me, much less the shadow of terror that glazed the faces of those Cuban intellectuals, young and old, when Padilla began to call out the names of his friends—several of us were of *corpore insepulto*—whom he presented as virtual enemies of the Revolution. I was sitting directly behind Roberto Branly. He compulsively turned and gave me a look of sheer horror, as if they were already carrying me off to the gallows."[22]

Spanish intellectuals like Félix Grande have weighed in on the event, with analyses focusing on the senselessness of repressing Padilla in particular, but also on the absurd spiraling effect that the case set off for other Cuban writers at the time—for example, with Norberto Fuentes, who, years later, outside of Cuba, has written works which bitterly recall those singular moments. "Could they have imagined," asked Grande,"on April 29, 1971, during that infamous self-accusation that the Cuban political authorities forced on Heberto Padilla, one of those pointed to by Padilla's finger (an imaginary finger, that hid the real finger of Castrist repression against intellectuals in Cuba, Latin America, and the entire planet) would just happen to be the writer Norberto Fuentes?"[23] As Nadia Lie explained in her article "Las malas memorias de Heberto Padilla,"[24] Norberto Fuentes was one of the few intellectuals present at the self-accusation who ventured to defend himself right then, rejecting the "counterrevolutionary" label, the magic word that then justified, and still does to this day, any kind of political repression. Fuentes was a young writer then, active within the

Revolution's cultural scene. Later, he would write *Hemingway in Cuba*,[25] which deeply resonated in Cuba and was lauded by Fidel Castro, prompting a closer relationship between them. After that, he covered several military campaigns as a war correspondent, along with other Cuban internationalists. With Fidel's support, in 1989 Fuentes received the trophy of the Order of San Luis and the "Medal of National Culture."

In his self-accusation, Padilla accused himself of introducing counterrevolutionary thought into literature, and thanked his friends, "responsible for the State and the healthy functioning of the Revolution," for the generosity shown him in giving him the opportunity to rectify his mistakes. The *new* Padilla confessed: "I have made many mistakes, really unforgivable, really censurable, really unspeakable, and I feel truly relieved, truly happy after the experience I have had, that I can now start my life over with a new spiritual approach. I requested this meeting. [. . .] I have defamed and constantly injured the Revolution, with Cubans and with foreigners. I have gone very far with my errors and counterrevolutionary activities. [. . .] That is to say, a counterrevolutionary is a man who acts against the Revolution, who hurts it. And I acted against and hurt the Revolution."[26]

The hara-kiri culminated in a histrionic display, when Padilla was obliged to confess his disloyalty to the island's leader and to make a public display of his pain, to inspire all the other counterrevolutionaries to reject their ideas, get back on the right track, and maintain unity (uniformity?) in the grand project to *save* the Cuban people. Like a lost sheep returning to the fold, staring at the ground with a chastised child's expression, he recited: "And we won't go into the times when I have been unfair with and ungrateful to Fidel, which I will never cease to regret."[27] The self-accusation not only dealt with the verses of his poetry that had won the unlucky prize, and the hurt Padilla had caused the Revolution's supreme leader; it also gave critical interpretations of some of his articles and literary essays, and declared the politically correct way that solidly Revolutionary figures should be treated in front of those who have deserted the cause. On that subject, he had to retract the criticism he had launched against Lisandro Otero, and completely reject the defense—literary only, of course—that he had once voiced for Cabrera Infante, at the time when he had been exiled in London: "The first thing I did when I returned to Cuba a few months later was take advantage of the opportunity that the literary magazine *El Caimán Barbudo* offered me to write about Lisandro Otero's *Pasión de Urbino*, unfairly, cruelly assailing a friend I had had for years, a true friend like Lisandro Otero. [. . .] The first thing I did was attack Lisandro. I said horrible things to Lisandro Otero. And who did I defend? I defended Guillermo Cabrera Infante. And who was Guillermo Cabrera Infante, whom we all know? Guillermo Cabrera Infante has always been a bitter, resentful man, no longer with the revolution, a social outcast, a man from the very humblest origins, a poor man, a man who for whatever reason has been deeply bitter since adolescence, and a man who has been an irreconcilable enemy of the Revolution from the very beginning."[28]

THE SECOND OPEN LETTER

Many intellectuals were incensed by Padilla's self-accusation, and increasingly distanced themselves from Castro and his Revolution. The number of open letters addressed to the leader grew, but the patriarch, not having yet slipped into the autumn of his reign, was as undaunted as ever. At the First Congress on Education and Culture, which took place just three days after Padilla's self-criticism, "Fidel Castro delivered the most vitriolic speech against the intellectuals that he has ever given."[29] That triggered the immediate division of the group of intellectuals that had been so unified in their support of Castro's Revolution until then. A second letter was later sent by the same general group that had sent the first open letter, written on May 4 in Mario Vargas Llosa's apartment. Harsher in tone than in their first letter, the more than sixty signers expressed their "shame and anger" in reaction to Padilla's self-accusation, and their alarm at the signs of radicalization, warning of isolationism and the negative repercussions for dialogue with the Cuban government. Vargas Llosa later confirmed that he had written the letter himself: "We believe we have a responsibility to make our shame and anger known. The damaging confession that Heberto Padilla signed could only have been obtained through methods which are the very negation of legality and Revolutionary justice. The content and form of that confession, with its absurd accusations and wild affirmations, and the act performed in UNEAC, in which Padilla himself and his friends Belkis Cuza Malé, Manuel Díaz Martínez, César López, and Pablo Armando Fernández were subjected to a painful charade of self-accusation, recall the most sordid events of the Stalinist era, with its show trials and witch-hunts. With the same vehemence with which we have defended the Cuban Revolution from the very beginning, as it seemed exemplary to us in its respect for the human being and in its fight for freedom, we now entreat Cuba to avoid the dogmatic fog, the cultural xenophobia, and the systematic repression that Stalinism imposed on the socialist states, from which manifested many flagrant examples of events similar to what is now taking place in Cuba."[30] He continued: "The disregard for human dignity presupposed in forcing a man to ridiculously accuse himself of the worst betrayals and infamy alarms us not because the person in question is a writer, but because any Cuban comrade—a peasant, laborer, technician, or intellectual—could also fall victim to similar acts of violence and humiliation."[31] With this letter, the group requested the Cuban regime to put an end to the violation of human rights, and to return to the original spirit of the Revolution, which "made us think of the Revolution as a model of socialism."[32] That is, it wasn't a question of enemies of the Revolution seizing on a moment of weakness to try to destabilize the system; rather, it was a group of political *comrades*, just as committed to socialism's future in Latin America, who couldn't ignore the obvious or condone gratuitous violence and the trampling of certain inalienable rights.

This time, Cortázar did not sign. After having read the first few lines, he exclaimed: "I can't sign this!"[33] Julio Cortázar was one of the strongest defenders of the Caribbean island's political and cultural aspirations. He had always actively participated in all the demonstrations of support for the Revolution, and he frequently traveled to Cuba. After the first open letter was sent, he tried to reconcile with the Cubans. At one point, when he was asked to write something in a magazine about Vargas Llosa, he politely declined the request in his strong Argentinian accent: "You know about all of the efforts I have made to make amends with the Cubans, constant efforts that have unfortunately been only minimally successful. . . ."[34] He had to give an explanation to Vargas Llosa, who reacted negatively. But Cortázar's most thoughtful overture of reconciliation was the letter he sent from Paris to Haydee Santamaria on February 4, 1972, in response to her letter expressing dismay at his inclusion in the list of signatures of the first open missive to Castro, and threatening that he should decide once and for all to be "with God" and not "with the devil."[35]

Cortázar seemed to harbor regrets because of the seeds of doubt that had been planted in Cuba over his signature on the first letter, asserting that it had been impossible for him to have made any other decision at the time, since the information available in Paris about events in Cuba described torture, concentration camps, prisons, Stalinism, Soviet domination, and so forth. Cortázar, who had taken the trouble to ask the staff at the Cuban embassy in Paris to provide him with an official version of events, and stalled so that

Goytisolo did not send the letter off to the Caribbean shores until they had the full truth, did not get any response from the Cuban diplomats other than silence, so circumstances had obliged him to sign that famous polemic text. He writes: "After weeks of waiting in vain, which was equivalent to Cuba ignoring or disparaging the love and concern of its supporters in France, it seemed impossible for me not to associate myself with a request for information, which a group of writers believed they had every right to make of Fidel. It was impossible; it was a friendly way, from comrade to comrade, to say: 'There are some things that can be endured up to a certain limit, but beyond that, there is a right to an explanation,' because the contrary implies disrespect or guilt. Eight or ten days passed after that, without anyone at the embassy being able to understand that, in spite of the warnings, the first letter had come to signify a right. [. . .] Cuba's image was tarnished, jeopardized by its regrettable conduct of consistently declining to address the issue."[36] He maintains that he chose the harder path: signing the first letter, then not putting his name to the second; as he explained in another essay, titled "Policrítica a la hora de los chacales" (Political criticism at the hour of the jackals), this was his way of sincerely continuing to support the Revolution and offering his help wherever it was most needed.

Goytisolo described how some others reacted to the second open letter to Fidel: "On my walk around Argel a few weeks before, I ran into Régis Debray, who, after having been released from his imprisonment in Bolivia thanks to pressure from Western Leftist intellectuals, had just made a quick visit to Cuba. When I asked him what he thought of Padilla, whom he had praised in particular as a 'beautiful example' of an intellectual revolutionary in an article published in *El Caimán Barbudo*, he replied that he was nothing more than a CIA agent and he deserved whatever he got. Later, in Paris, Simone de Beauvoir told me indignantly that she and Sartre had been walking down Raspail Boulevard and had seen Alejo Carpentier, and he, clearly rattled, panicked by the thought of merely being seen greeting them, turned in the other direction so abruptly that he smacked his nose against a shop window. According to some friends, the Cubans were spreading around the rumor that Sartre was a CIA agent too."[37]

Cortázar's reaction to the Padilla case was predictable, but García Márquez's reaction was much less clear, since it continues to be an enigma to this day, even for Plinio Apuleyo Mendoza, one of his closest friends. In Mendoza's previously cited book, *El caso perdido: La llama y el hielo*, phrases like the following frequently appear: "We had dinner on three occasions, always talking obsessively about Cuba and the Padilla case, never able to come to agreement."[38] At one point, Mendoza admits defeat: "Years ago, due to irreconcilable differences, we stopped discussing the subject altogether."[39] Curiously, most of the writings dealing with the Padilla case that have been published tend to assert that García Márquez signed the first letter to Castro. For example, in *Les quatre saisons de Fidel Castro*, Jean-Pierre Clerc writes: "An initial letter, respectful, is sent to the leader by fifty writers, French, Spanish, Italian, and Latin American, including Beauvoir, Calvino, Cortázar, Fuentes, García Márquez, Mandiargues, Moravia, Sartre, Vargas Llosa."[40] And one writer maintains that "while Blanco Amor—not differentiating among the various stars of the boom—implies that García Márquez denounced the Castrist regime on that occasion, Benedetti asserts that he only signed one of the two famous letters sent to Castro, and Collazos declares that he didn't sign either. The three conclusions cancel each other out; the lie is a sign of the case's importance."[41]

In our opinion, it's more a lack of reliable information than a lie, but it is certain that the ambiguity demonstrates the particular importance of the Nobel Prize winner's position in this matter. In an article published in Colombia in the magazine *Semana*, Jon Lee

Anderson lays all the responsibility on Plinio Apuleyo Mendoza, affirming that "since García Márquez was on a trip and there was no way of communicating with him, Plinio took the liberty of adding his name to the list of petitioners."[42] And regarding the second missive, he writes: "A second open letter of protest was signed by all of those who had signed the first one, except for Julio Cortázar and Gabriel García Márquez."[43]

THE "BOOM" GOES BOOM: THE BREAKUP

The success of the guerrillas in the Sierra Maestra and the triumphant march into Havana in those first days of 1959 had heralded the beginning of a time of hope unprecedented in the history of Western civilization. A small Caribbean island had faced off against international capitalism as symbolized by the United States, and in the following years had consolidated an alternative that could extend throughout Latin America, and that had begun to bear fruit with the Chilean elections bringing Allende to power. But the Padilla case signified the first crack in the system, resulting in a general disenchantment with the Revolution among a segment of the population that until then had been uniformly supportive of the Cuban project: the intellectuals. The political transcendence, the impact, and the prestige of the writer in question within the Spanish-speaking world was beyond doubt; and although the international profile of Heberto Padilla wasn't at the level of a Borges, a Darío, or a García Márquez, what's certain is that—as fate would have it—the international resonance of the case would deliver a harsh blow to the evolution of the Cuban Revolution.

The first consequence, disastrous for Fidel Castro and his followers, was the disintegration of the group of Latin American writers known as the *boom*, a breakdown in the group's unity that had been intimately tied with the Cuban experiment. José Donoso expressed it very well in his *Historia personal del boom*: "I think that if the boom was almost completely unified in anything, it was in the firm belief in the cause of the Cuban Revolution; I think the disillusion caused by the Padilla case destroyed that, and destroyed the boom's unity."[44] Many writers from many different countries, including Spain, shared Juan Goytisolo's view when he said that by 1968 Cuba had ceased to be a model for him.[45] Many personal relationships also came apart, many friendships, such as the intense, deep bond between Vargas Llosa and García Márquez. The wife of the Chilean writer José Donoso affirmed that, before those events, "Friendship, true friendship, with real affection, mutual respect, and admiration, was what bonded Mario Vargas Llosa and Gabriel García Márquez. [. . .] They admired each other, enjoyed each other's company, their endless conversations, the walks they would take together around the city, and Mario wrote about Gabo."[46] María Pilar Donoso was referring to the book that Vargas Llosa had published about the author of *One Hundred Years of Solitude*, titled *Gabriel García Márquez: historia de un deicidio*, which had been his doctoral dissertation at the Universidad Complutense de Madrid, and was one of the best essays ever written on the work representing the pinnacle of the Colombian's success, not reached again over the next thirty years of the twentieth century. However, the two great friends grew apart for political reasons, among other things. García Márquez remained loyal to Castro, but the writer from Peru deemed him, from that point on, to be "the great black beast to be battled."[47] García Márquez asserts that at one time the author of *La ciudad y los perros* "said that the Padilla case had separated him from his best friends, and the entire intellectual community of Latin America had been affected by the incident."[48]

Dasso Saldívar also refers to that friendship and its rupture in his biography of García Márquez, *Viaje a la semilla*: "Until circumstances in their life, friendship, and politics separated them, putting them on divergent, even diametrically opposed paths, the two had honored the extensive parallels in their lives and had cultivated an intense, deep friendship the likes of which has rarely been seen in the world of Latin American letters."[49] In fact, since then, the two have very rarely expressed an opinion about the other, in public or in private. It seems like a mutual pact of nonaggression, reflecting total respect for the other's literary work (the two best writers, in our opinion, of the *boom*), and for each other's opposing political views.

Since that time, García Márquez has been criticized by many, starting with his old friend. Vargas Llosa began to call him "Castro's courtesan," Lee Anderson comments, "[a]nd the Cuban-exile writer Guillermo Cabrera Infante accuses him of suffering from delirium totalitarium."[50] Fortunately, he did not break with all his friends. In spite of their different ideas about Cuba, García Márquez still maintains a friendship with Plinio Apuleyo Mendoza, and with some other Cuban dissidents or exiles such as Eliseo Alberto, author of a hair-raising story on ideological control of intellectuals in Cuba titled *Informe contra mí mismo* (1997).

A CARD UP HIS SLEEVE: THE LETTERS OF GARCÍA MÁRQUEZ

García Márquez explains his behavior regarding the Padilla case in terms of his direct, extensive knowledge of the Cuban Revolution, a knowledge drawn from channels that are not publicly recognized, a card up his sleeve that allows him to—as he puts it—judge more objectively. In *El olor de la guayaba*, Apuleyo Mendoza interviewed Gabo in 1982, and he explained then what his motivations were for not distancing himself from the Revolution. Cautious, and not a big fan of hard facts, García Márquez said that he had "much better, more direct information, and a political maturity that permits me a calmer, more patient, more human understanding of reality."[51] As on other occasions, Gabo's journalist friend went away without getting the answers he had sought. Also, Gabo could have credibly made that assertion in 1982, by which time he knew the Cuban situation and its leaders very well, but it's not a valid response for the year 1971, since at that time he had only indirect information on Cuba. In *El caso perdido*, Mendoza acknowledges the fruitlessness of his efforts, since many of their conversations on the subject went around in circles. Mendoza recalls one conversation:

> "The things I could tell you...." Gabo would sometimes sigh.
> "If you only knew...."
> Yes, he is definitely the repository of certain powerful secrets that he cannot reveal. He must know all about the contentious relationship between Castro and the Soviet Union. Maybe it's buried there, in secrets, the reasons for his allegiance.[52]

But the reality is more complex than it seems. García Márquez's unconditional allegiance to the Revolution—and, subsequently, his refusal to criticize the Padilla case and others that followed— cannot be viewed solely in light of possible consequences from the dictatorship, since there are social and economic factors that seem to trump the attacks on freedom of expression. Mendoza, who declares his opposition to Stalinist methods, nevertheless makes an effort to try to understand his friend's radical position when he says: "To put it in his own terms: there were only two soups on the menu. One soup probably included a certain amount of freedom, the possibility of writing editorials in the papers, giving speeches from the balconies, getting elected senator or councilman; but the children were starving and illiterate, and the sick suffered everywhere because they couldn't go to a hospital. The other soup on the menu didn't have the same kind of freedom that we had experienced before, but misery did not exist, the children ate, went to school, and had a roof over their heads, there were hospitals for the sick, and class differences were overcome. Between these two soups, between these two realities, the only ones on the table of the world, he had to choose. He made his choice. Of course I did not agree with him."[53]

Obviously, it's hard to justify acts of physical and psychological violence in the name of a regime that claims to be egalitarian and aims to solve the basic problems of survival of an enormous, desperately poor population, especially when it's well known that, basically, their system has failed to achieve equality among all the members of its society. Maybe that is why he has displayed such reticence regarding this case and has always avoided giving clear answers.

THE AFTERMATH: THE CASE AGAINST GABO

Having weathered the initial grief and scandal that resulted from the self-accusation, Heberto Padilla was released from prison. He worked as a translator until, after ten years had passed, he obtained permission to leave the island, thanks to none other than Gabriel García Márquez. We know that the Nobel laureate has used his influence over Fidel to help political prisoners leave the island on numerous occasions. Mendoza attests: "His friendship with Castro has allowed him to effectively intervene to win the freedom of a great number of political prisoners. Three thousand two hundred, it seems. Thanks to him, to Gabo, Heberto Padilla could leave Cuba. Padilla called him at the hotel where he was staying in Havana. He went to see him. He asked for his help; he got it."[54]

The last hurdle that Gabo had to get over was winning in the court of public opinion. Fidel Castro would never make very extensive statements on an issue of relatively minor importance at a time when the Cuban economy was in dire crisis because of the failure of the plan that Castro had formulated himself to radically increase sugar production, dubbed the "crop of ten million." On the other hand, for a time, as we've previously described, García Márquez avoided any public appearances while the Padilla case was being resolved, so he wouldn't be harassed by impertinent questions from a certain stripe of sensationalistic journalist. So the first time García Márquez discussed the subject at any length was during an interview he gave in Barranquilla to Julio Roca, a Colombian journalist from the *Diario del Caribe*. It was published in the magazine *Libre* at the end of 1971 as part of a compilation of writings (interviews, letters, texts from Castro's speeches, and so forth) related to the Padilla case. Almost perfectly coinciding with the final events of the case, Roca had the opportunity to pose some very specific questions. He went right to the heart of the matter and waited for García Márquez to lay his cards on the table.

In the first part of the interview, Roca asked García Márquez what his position was going to be within the group of Latin American intellectuals who had clearly separated themselves from Castro's Revolution. García Márquez, far from answering directly, denied that there had been any break. He ventured that "the conflict between a group of Latin American writers and Fidel Castro is an ephemeral triumph of the press agencies."[55] According to García Márquez, there was no conflict. It was the media that planted the seeds of the alleged problem and radicalized the positions, manipulating the speech that Castro gave at the First Congress on Education and Culture (from April 30 through May 6, 1971), only making the most inflammatory passages public. Still, he admitted that there were some strong statements in the speech, acknowledging that "actually there are some very harsh paragraphs."[56]

So the situation could be blamed completely on the press, according to García Márquez. "The foreign correspondents—he insists—picked a few disconnected phrases out of context and strung them together to make it seem like Fidel had said things that *in reality he did not say*,"[57] a blanket defense of the dictator that attempts to soften the general context of the confrontation with the intellectuals. Now, we know very well that Castro's words were crude and cruel and his intention clear. According to César Leante, specifically referring to this situation, "Castro's speech was one of the most vicious attacks on intellectuals that has ever been given."[58] In spite of his friendship with García Márquez, another of the implicated, Apuleyo Mendoza, in his book *El caso perdido: La llama y el hielo*, bitterly laments "that Fidel, in a speech delivered at the Congress on Culture in Havana, unleashed against the signers of the telegram [. . .] such a barrage of vilification, describing us as a privileged elite, who frequented 'the salons of Paris' (as if we were living in the times of Proust)."[59]

In that interview, García Márquez stated that he hadn't signed either of the two letters sent to Castro: "I didn't sign the letter of protest because I didn't think they should send it."[60] In the eighties—in 1982 and 1984, to be exact—he explained his constant support of the Cuban Revolution to Plinio Apuleyo Mendoza. However, at the time when the Padilla case had unfolded, Castro and García Márquez had not yet embarked upon the relationship, so much deeper than mere cordiality, that would bond them for so many years. In view of that, his explanation holds a certain mystery. How does he justify his faith in the revolution's "vitality" and "good health," and what really kept him from signing a letter of disagreement and protest? The ultimate motivation for those letters cannot be summarized as simply an abrupt criticism of the Revolution, but rather it represented above all an effort to guide the movement back onto the right political path, from which it had begun to stray. Also, at that time, especially regarding the first letter, the signers could not have predicted Castro's reaction; proof of this is Julio Cortázar's signature on the first letter.

In the last part of his explanation, García Márquez adds that "At no time would I ever question the intellectual honor and the revolutionary vocation of those who signed the letter."[61] García Márquez's gesture, supportive of Castro while simultaneously supportive of the signers, allows him to navigate between two loyalties: maintaining unconditional service to the Revolution while respecting his own position as a leading member of the *boom*, a phenomenon beyond mere literary importance that had taken on a significance previously unseen in Latin American culture, transporting the written narrative of *Nuestra America* to the pinnacles of world literature in the latter half of the twentieth century. Gabo was aware of the damage that a complete polarization of positions could do, both to the Revolution itself and to the future of socialism in Latin America. He believed in the signers, and still considered them Revolutionaries, perhaps to mitigate Castro's contempt for those who signed the letters of protest. The texts are very clear, and at no point do they indicate intent to destabilize the principles of the Revolution. In the first letter, for example, from the opening it is very clear that the signers are completely "supportive of the principles and goals of the Cuban Revolution";[62] and, in the second, the signers oppose Castro and his actions, but still consider themselves to be uncompromising Revolutionaries. And they concluded by expressing a sincere, transparent desire: "We would like the Cuban Revolution to go back to being once again what it had been at one time, and what made us consider it a very model of socialism."[63]

It was not they, but Castro's government, which was beginning to act in a manner completely opposed to the principles that originally drove the project. The signers of the letters did not understand this "Stalinist" infusion, nor were they about to accept it; and that is why they fought so emphatically for freedom of expression. Unfortunately, from then on, it became increasingly clear that what existed in Cuba was, as Manuel Díaz Martínez put it, "a government conspiracy against freedom of thought."[64] And, referring to

Castro's famous words "for the Revolution, everything; against the Revolution, nothing" from his speech to the intellectuals in 1961, he adds: "We finally knew, at last, that which was, in Castro's view, for the Revolution and that which was against."[65] When the dictator affirmed that "to be judges, here you have to be true Revolutionaries, true intellectuals, true fighters,"[66] he was clearly referring to those who are, in his opinion, false intermediaries, cloaking themselves in political and cultural authority, which only really belongs to him personally and his team of government, a small circle comprised exclusively of those who submissively follow the directives of their leader.

To complete the picture, the slant of García Márquez's position on freedom of expression in his 1975 article "Cuba de cabo a rabo"[67] is very revealing. In that text, Gabo expressed his hopes for the complete success of three upcoming events: the First Congress of the Communist Party; the exercise of the people's power through universal vote by secret ballot; and the enactment of the Socialist Constitution. He added that during this institutionalization process, he would pay "special attention to the problem of freedom of creative expression and free speech."[68] That is to say, García Márquez admitted that the issues of creative expression and free speech represented a serious problem on the island, but in a sense they wouldn't do so for long because "in their Constitution, the Cuban people have solved the problem with a stroke of the pen: all forms of artistic creativity are free."[69] However, when it came to content, the control was still as iron-handed and discouraging as it had been in the most difficult early days of the Revolutionary process. "But the next article," the Colombian writer added, "isn't quite as encouraging, as it refers to not the form, but the content of artistic creativity. This content—according to the proposed article—cannot oppose the principles of the Revolution in any way."[70] The following paragraph further accentuates the discord between García Márquez and the position of the Cuban government: "The limitation is alarming, especially since it assumes the existence of a functionary authorized to prejudge a work's viability. But it's also inconsequential, because it goes against the Constitution's overall spirit, which is open and human, and it also goes against the wonderful sense of creative liberation, of unbridled imagination and critical happiness that permeates every aspect of life in Cuba today."[71]

García Márquez was well aware of the role writers played within Latin American societies, and of freedom's importance in stimulating artistic creativity and of the esteemed position literature held throughout the continent at that particular point in time. Consequently, the restrictions at work within the heart of the Cuban Revolution led to what became known as "the gray period" in the literary scene, during the early seventies, due to the notable absence of high-quality works being produced then on the island, in contrast to the blossoming of contemporary literature in other places such as Mexico, Peru, and Argentina. García Márquez, in his zeal to protect writers in the face of censorship, but also out of respect for the Cuban leader's decisions, tried to identify positive aspects within some very alienating cultural policies. "The curious thing, and the most *unfair*," he muses, "is that at the root of these policies is not contempt for the artist, but just the opposite: an exaggerated estimation of his importance in the world."[72] That is, an intellectual's importance is relative because, since his mission to raise a country's critical consciousness is crucial, he will never be a decisive destabilizing factor in a political or social system, unless that system has already begun to unravel. Regarding the *exaggerated estimation* of the intellectual's role, Gabo stated: "This conviction implies the belief that a work of art can topple a social system and imperil the destiny of the world. If that had ever been or ever could be possible, it wouldn't have been because of the destructive power of the work of art, but because of the internal, invisible erosions of the social system itself. After traveling all over Cuba from one end to the other, I haven't the slightest doubt that the Revolution is safe from the subversive firestorms of the artists."[73] It seems that Fidel was not so sure, then or to this day, since there are still writers who are prohibited or censured on the island, the black sheep and the ostracized; and the repression has not stopped; but, in spite of that, internal dissidence continues to grow. García Márquez's faith in the Castrist political machine and in socialism's natural triumph in Latin America is such that any artificial control of the world of culture is simply unnecessary. If the Revolution works, the Revolution itself will naturally discharge any incongruous elements without violence. That is why, he insists, "any writer who dares to write a book against it, has no reason to run up against the Constitution. The Revolution will simply be mature enough to digest it."[74]

The conclusion is clear: if, back in 1971, he had not been equipped to defend Castro's Revolution and had disappeared for a time, and if his earlier answers had been vague, four years later, his faith in socialism in general, and in Castro's system in particular, had been consolidated. He believed it was a viable system, because it would not only succeed in liberating the lower classes from the oppression they had been subjected to, but it could also assimilate internal criticisms, incorporating them into the various forces that comprised the framework of social balance, and even use them as opportunities to strengthen the island's development and progress.

GARCÍA MÁRQUEZ ON CASTRO AND "THE PADILLA CASE"

The question about the Padilla case from the 1971 interview with Julio Roca could not have been more clear: "Do you agree or disagree with Castro with regard to the poet Padilla's case?"[75] As was by now the norm in public opinion, Cuba-related issues were always framed in a way that did not allow for any nuance. To the Cuban traveling abroad or living in exile in any country, his next-door neighbor, his seatmate on the train, his thesis adviser, someone he sees every morning having breakfast at the same coffee shop, someone behind him in line at the movies, and so on, everyone always instinctively asks him, "Are you from Cuba, or from Miami?" This gross simplification always, understandably, provokes Cubans' anger in knowing that, at the outset of a conversation, before they have even opened their mouths, an ill-fitting label has already been slapped on them, no matter which side they are on. García Márquez, who has a special affinity for Cuba, is, nevertheless, incapable of expressing a solidly decisive opinion on *the case*, either due to a genuine lack of detailed information, or to an inability to openly oppose Castro on a matter that, in the harsh light of day, was a significant political error and an abuse of power. With his response "I, personally, am not convinced of the spontaneity and sincerity of Heberto Padilla's self-accusation,"[76] or when he says "the tone of his self-accusation is so exaggerated, so abject, that it seems as if it had been obtained by devious methods,"[77] or when he acknowledges that Padilla cannot be properly defined as a counterrevolutionary writer, his position seems clear and his discordance with Castro obvious. He would never refer directly to who was ultimately responsible for the process, much less would he insinuate that there was a failure in the ideological system that sustains the Revolution. He would only venture to allude to the negative effect that the censured poet's position could have on the future of the country: "I don't know if Heberto Padilla's attitude is actually damaging the Revolution," he said, "but his self-accusation is damaging it, very seriously."[78] That is to say, Padilla, according to García Márquez, while not an enemy of the Revolution, was perhaps the cause, unconsciously, of certain prejudices that could damage, in untold ways, Castro's ability to construct a better society.

Then, as an almost direct outgrowth of what they had just talked about, the interviewer asked if García Márquez could comment on suspected Stalinist influence within Cuba's domestic politics, to which García Márquez replies that this would all become clear soon because, if that were the case, "Fidel himself will admit it."[79] His total confidence in the supreme leader is made clear once again, but the most revealing thing here is that he does not deny Stalinism's possible presence within Cuba. He could have offered his own opinion, issued a flat denial, or sidestepped the question. Still, his answer shows how Gabo believed that he had extensive insight into Castro's strategy to emerge unscathed from the serious problem that had been growing over time. So when Roca asked if García Márquez was going to break with the Revolution, his answer could not have been more clear: "Of course not."[80] He went on to insist, once again, that there had not been any rupture between the Latin American intellectuals and the Cuban government: "Of the writers who protested the Padilla case," he assured, "none have made a break from the Cuban Revolution, as far as I know."[81] With the advantage of hindsight, thirty years later, we can analyze these texts within the context of knowing how events actually unfolded. We know, for example, that in the wake of the Padilla case, a considerable disbandment of the intellectuals as a group did take place. Perhaps it was not so obvious at that time, but neither could it be credibly said that nothing at all had happened that could indicate a possible disbandment. So it is reasonable to assume that Gabo was aware of the consequences his decision could have and, although his position was not entirely without criticism, the interview ended with a vote of confidence for the Revolution and a clear expression of his continuing solidarity with it, which "cannot be affected by a glitch in cultural politics, even if that glitch is as considerable and serious as Heberto Padilla's supposed self-accusation."[82] He played his hand, but the bluffs went around the table so much that public opinion had no idea what he was holding—like a suspenseful scene out of *The Sting*. García Márquez, who had not set foot on Cuban soil since his stint working at Prensa Latina, tried to draw closer to the bearded men in power, through his public statements and using his personal contacts. Over time, Gabo has become one of the best ambassadors of the Revolution and socialism on the world stage, while Castro has gradually become one of the most decisive literary critics for the Nobel Prize winner's work.

PART TWO

★

THE POWER AND THE GLORY

CHAPTER FOUR

★

THE LURE OF POWER

"**A**LL OF THIS I WILL GIVE TO YOU IF, KNEELING BEFORE ME, you adore me," the Devil said to Jesus. Power and the ability to rule a land and its people is possibly one of the greatest temptations known to man. In Barcelona, they like to think that this biblical scene must have taken place on Mount Tibidabo (from the Latin *tibi* "to you," *dabo* "I will give"), because everything that could be seen from the view from there—Barcelona and its surroundings—was well worth having. In García Márquez's *Chronicle of a Death Foretold*, Bayardo San Roman sets his sights on marrying Angela Vicario, and uses his influence to buy the most attractive, most expensive house in town, and the one Angela likes the most. He humiliates its owner, the widower Xius, in the process. Even though he doesn't want to sell the house for anything in the world since everything in it reminds him of a whole life he shared with his wife, Xius ends up giving in when Bayardo offers a sum at least twenty times the house's actual worth. The tears Xius sheds on accepting the offer are sad proof that he has succumbed to the power of Bayardo's money.

The exercise of power is one of the greatest pleasures known to man. The simple knowledge of owning something or controlling someone is a pleasing sensation that everyone wants to have. The pleasure is heightened when one's life experience has previously systematically denied it. The first volume of Gabo's memoir, *To Live to Tell the Tale*, makes clear that that had been the case in his own life, up until mature adulthood. He had an impoverished childhood, growing up in a large family with little money, first jobs that didn't even pay a living wage, the constant necessity of having to ask for money or barter with his manuscripts, and so forth. Later, he led a vagabond's life in Europe, and his nomadic family couldn't settle down in one place with even a minimum of financial security until after *One Hundred Years of Solitude* was published.

But by 1967, García Márquez was forty years old. Life until then had been comprised of more disappointments than pleasures, and only now would he begin to enjoy the sweet fruits of power, but he would do it in his own way.

FASCINATED BY POWER

You can be for him or against him, but it's almost impossible to be indifferent to a personality as overwhelming as Castro's. It's not just his power and the way he wields it; it's also his ability to seduce, his unquestionable talents and gifts, his bravery, all factors that can inspire unconditional allegiance but also visceral hatred. Anyone who visits Cuba will come across people who, in spite of having lived their whole lives in abject poverty and fairly miserable circumstances, regard Castro as some kind of deity, although, admittedly, one who is past his prime. And there are also those who, while living rather comfortably, cannot help but make obscene gestures at the television every time Castro appears on the screen. These attitudes are presented in especially stark contrast whenever the media on the island and the media in Miami cover the same news story. According to popular legend in Cuba, when the Pope visited the island, he and Castro went for a walk together along the beach. It was a windy day, and the Holy Father's customary white skull cap flew off his head, landed in the water, and was almost swept away by the current. Quickly, in a show of diplomatic courtesy, but also of friendship and unity, Fidel went to the water's edge and chased after the cap, without venturing into the water, until he reached it. He bent down and grabbed it, turning and stepping back, still without getting wet, and he returned the cap to the Pope, safe and sound. The next day, the GRANMA in Cuba ran the following headline: A NEW MIRACLE: FIDEL WALKS OVER WATER LIKE JESUS CHRIST. On the other hand, a headline in the *Miami Herald* proclaimed: THE CUBAN DICTATOR'S DEATH IS NEAR: HE DOESN'T EVEN KNOW HOW TO SWIM ANY MORE.[1]

Everyone closely follows the state of their ruler's health on the island, some because they don't want anyone or anything to change, others because they do want a regime change, and that will not be possible until Castro is permanently out of the picture. Joaquín Navarro-Valls, head of the Press Office at the Vatican, who accompanied Pope John Paul II on all of his trips, told us in the summer of 2001, at his family's estate in Cartagena, Spain, that he had had to go on several preparatory visits to Cuba before the Pope's trip. On one of these, he met with the heads of the Catholic clergy in Havana before meeting with Castro. Someone mentioned some rumors were going around that Fidel was gravely ill with prostate cancer, and he asked if Navarro-Valls could try to tell from his appearance if that was true. Navarro-Valls didn't give it much thought, but then it came time to have dinner with Castro, and he served his guest a magnificent Spanish wine. After several hours of friendly conversation, free-flowing wine, and a wonderful meal, the spokesperson for the Vatican wasn't quite sure how to interrupt his host's animated conversation to indicate that he needed to go to the restroom. At the end of the evening, he was finally able to answer nature's call, but Fidel didn't show any sign of needing to do the same. The next day, Navarro-Valls went back to see the clergy to tell them about some of the events being planned for the Pope's upcoming visit, and, amused, he told them, "I can assure you, as far as the Commander's health goes, I don't know if he might have some type of cancer; but I do know it's definitely not of the prostate."[2]

García Márquez falls into the camp that deeply admires Cuba's leader, and many believe that the constant support that he has shown Cuba and its president is a result of his infatuation with power. Jorge Masetti says that García Márquez "is a man who likes to be in power's kitchen"; and Jon Lee Anderson, who talked with him over several months in 1999 about many aspects of politics and literature in Latin America, concludes that his fascination could be rooted in "an emotional response to his own dramatic rise from such humble origins."[3] In fact, after asking a woman in Bogotá what she thought, she replied: "Remember that Gabo came from a real hellhole of a town on the coast, and he very easily could have ended up as one of those guys selling sunglasses on the beach."[4] This comment, while vividly demonstrating the contempt the country's inland residents harbor for the people on the coast, still pays tribute to the author. Jon Lee asserts that, for the vast majority of Colombians, García Márquez is a national treasure, and the regional rivalries reflected only confirm the sincere affection for him.

But the writer's attraction to the power that he never had where he came from goes deeper, since it has to do with everything related to its exercise. Most of the authors that look at this particular fascination base it on his novels. It's clear that many of his works are stories about dictators, colonels, and generals. The most obvious examples are *No One Writes to the Colonel*, *The General in His Labyrinth*, *The Autumn of the Patriarch*, and *One Hundred Years of Solitude*. And this particular interest can be linked to his friendship with Fidel Castro and other Leftist leaders, dating from when he decided to become more actively involved in politics, again, in his own way. In an interview with Plinio Apuleyo Mendoza in 1972, he remarked: "I am a communist that can't find a place to sit down. But in spite of this I continue to believe that socialism is a real possibility, that it is a good solution for Latin America, and that there needs to be more active militancy. I tried to be militant at the beginning of the Revolution in Cuba, I worked within it, you'll recall, for two years, until a fleeting conflict forced me out the door. That didn't affect my solidarity with Cuba one bit, which remains constant, comprehensive, and is not always easy, but it turned me into a scatter-shot, harmless sniper."[5]

But these affinities, which began bearing their first fruits in the second half of the seventies, had been brewing for much longer. On April 18, 1958, García Márquez published an article in *Momento*, titled "My Brother Fidel," which contrasted the bearded revolutionary leader with the unacceptable attitude of the dictator Fulgencio Batista, who is, basically, "a target inside the Presidential Palace."[6] He still had not yet met the man who would eventually be his best friend, but there were already certain signs of consanguinity, which presaged a future encounter. His admiration is blatant in this first text, and he uses a quote from Fidel's sister—"I don't admire Fidel as a sister. I admire him as a Cuban."[7]—to compliment the Cuban leader. He writes: "This deep concern for his countrymen's problems, combined with an unbreakable will, seems to form the essence of his personality."[8] Plinio Apuleyo Mendoza, the Colombian friend García Márquez would distance himself from politically after the Padilla case, tried to understand the Nobel Prize winner's attitude toward Cuba in terms of his peculiar fascination. In his book *El caso perdido: La llama y el hielo*, he comments on García Márquez's admiration for the Latin American *caudillo*, the archetypal political boss. He asserts that García Márquez has no interest whatsoever in bureaucracy, but in the man who holds power in his hands: "Obviously, García Márquez's sympathies lean toward the *caudillo* and not the bureaucracy. [. . .] To him, I'm sure, bureaucracy doesn't mean a thing. [. . .] The boss, on the other hand, forms a part of his geographical and historical landscape; he conjures up the myths of his childhood, evokes ancestral memories, and is present in all of his books. Gabo relates to him, to the quintessential strongman, with his romantic adventure of solitude and power, his awesome, sad destiny as a dispenser of good fortune and tragedy (so much like God)."[9]

Establishing a link between this affinity for the *caudillo* and his friendship with Castro, Mendoza adds: "His attraction to Fidel must be viewed from this perspective. Fidel resembles his most common literary creations, the phantoms he conjures around himself, the ones he identifies with his own destiny as the humble telegraph operator's son who rose to the highest pinnacles of glory; Fidel is the living realization of a myth from his early childhood; a new interpretation of Aureliano Buendia. If you're looking for the key to his Castrist fervor, there you have it in solid gold."[10]

Cesar Leante, a Cuban writer-in-exile who is the director of Pliegos, a publishing house in Madrid, makes several references to García Márquez's admiration for the Latin American *caudillos* in his book *García Márquez, el hechicero*, and he considers it something of an obsession, in light of the ample space García Márquez devotes to the subject in his works, and as reflected in his political choices: "García Márquez's unconditional support for Fidel Castro falls within the realm of psychoanalysis [. . .] which is the constant, immeasurable admiration that the creator of The Patriarch has always felt for the Latin American *caudillos* heading up the guerrilla armies. For example, the colonel Aureliano Buendia, but especially the unnamed Caribbean dictator who, like Fidel Castro, grows old in power."[11] However, García Márquez insists that the tie that binds them is strictly friendship, and that that can be accounted for by their natural affinities, completely independent of political leadership qualities or ideology: "Friendships are formed," he observes in Juan Luis Cebrián's book, "out of human affinities. Writers are my friends not because they are writers or intellectuals, but because of that special connection that one feels, with respect to another. Fame gives one access to the possibility of all sorts of friendships, including with heads of state. It's just that with some, there is a genuine connection, and with others there's not. Friendships with them also grow out of certain human or literary affinities."[12] He makes it clear that he doesn't see those friendships originating in an attraction for the hero archetype of his childhood, but resulting more from a merely coincidental commonality of interests. Jon Lee Anderson wrote in an article that "of course, García Márquez denies having an obsession with power. 'It's not my fascination with power,' he told me. 'It's the fascination that those in power have for me. They are the ones who seek me out and confide in me.'"[13] Anderson continued: "When I repeated this assertion to one of García Márquez's best friends in Bogotá, he burst out laughing. 'All right, that's what he says, but there is some truth in it. All of the Latin American presidents want to be his friends, but he wants to be their friend too. For as long as I've known him, he's always had this desire to be close to power. Gabo loves presidents. My wife loves to tease him, telling him he even gets a thrill out of just seeing a vice-minister.'"[14]

FLY, FLY, LITTLE KITE

García Márquez's attitudes toward Latin American politics and the role he has played in Cuba from the late seventies on are more easily understood from this perspective. Cesar Leante signals that "In Cuba, he is considered a type of minister of culture, chief of cinematography, and supreme ambassador, not representing the

Ministry of Foreign Relations but Castro directly, who entrusts him with delicate, confidential missions that he doesn't assign to his official diplomats."[15] In one of his articles, Juan Luis Cebrián called García Márquez "a political messenger." He maintains that "actually, he's nothing more than a friend of some very powerful people to and for whom he delivers messages; some that could potentially save lives, set people free, or dramatically improve someone's luck. He enjoys handling these types of secrets, whispered in the ears of heads of state. He's enthralled by the strictly confidential nature of the messages, and he moves in this world like a fish in water."[16] In 1977, García Márquez answered a questionnaire for the Mexican magazine *Hombre Mundo*, with over thirty questions about his personality, likes, and dislikes. Responding to a question asking what his favorite occupation was, he answered simply: "Conspiring."[17]

It would seem that certain friendships offer some personal satisfaction that goes beyond mere companionship: García Márquez is truly a good friend of Fidel Castro's. This has allowed him to, at times, carry out tasks for the state, make deliveries, carry messages back and forth with the utmost discretion, which is something he loves doing and has done with Mikhail Gorbachev, Felipe González, Belisario Betancur, and Carlos Andrés Pérez.[18] For that reason, Cesar Leante refers to Gabo as "Castro's gopher, messenger, and go-between,"[19] and he tells of some of Gabo's well-known tendencies: "Curiously, to go to the Far East, as a journalist revealed, he chose the longest route: from Mexico to Madrid, then Paris, then Moscow, and, finally, Tokyo. The novelist says flying makes him 'panicky'; he plans his trips in short segments. Still, on this trip, some suspect that there may have been other reasons. He had barely set foot in Barajas when he called . . . Felipe González. If he had called Cela, or Delibes, or Torrente Ballester, or any other writer, it wouldn't have attracted any attention, since they are his colleagues. But he immediately made contact with the president of the Spanish government (before, when Solana had been minister of Culture, he called him too; it seems that Gabo prefers politicians to writers, and that may be why he doesn't call up Semprun)."[20]

García Márquez performs this function because he feels it is necessary, given the situations that Cuba and the rest of the Latin American countries are in. He doesn't see himself as a servant doing his master's bidding, or as a carrier pigeon that instinctively delivers his king's messages to wherever they need to go; he regards what he is doing as a task mandated by his Latin American conscience: "It is my duty to serve the Latin American revolution however I can, and, concretely, to serve the defense of the Cuban Revolution, which is one of the most basic obligations for any Latin American revolutionary right now."[21] In an interview he gave to the journalist Juan Luis Cebrián, García Márquez clearly underscores the close relationship between Castro and the future of Latin America: "Over the last ten years, much has been accomplished by dissimilar governments acting in conjunction from a common Latin American consciousness. There is increasing unity of action every day; and, no matter what they say, the champion in this is Fidel."[22]

One of the texts that best illustrates the image Gabo has of his friend is the introduction he wrote to Gianni Minà's book *Habla Fidel*, where he presents a person of almost mythic proportions. He describes a disconcerting, imposing physical presence: "Maybe he is not conscious of the power he exudes, which seems to immediately fill up the whole space, in spite of the fact that he is not as tall or as corpulent as he seems at first sight."[23] Later, Castro is a *caudillo* (García Márquez uses that word himself in the introduction[24]) who cares about individual people: "The essence of his personal thought could be the certainty that working for the masses is, fundamentally, taking care of the individuals."[25]

According to García Márquez, Castro goes out to face the problems that need to be solved directly; he doesn't just hide away in his office, ignoring the issues: "Since he is not an academic politician, stuck in his office, he goes out to uncover the problems wherever they are; at any hour his car can be seen prowling around, unaccompanied by any motorcade, rolling through the deserted streets of Havana in the wee hours of the morning, or on a remote highway."[26]

He is also a man with a taste for risk and adventure: "The most stimulating thing in his life is the feeling of taking a risk."[27] And his only goal is to win.[28] García Márquez also explains that Castro's intentions are honorable, and that he is interested in knowing the objective reality of events, before falling into the subjective traps of the shadowy halls of power: "I've often wondered if his love of conversation doesn't fall under an intrinsic necessity to stay in touch with the truth, in the midst of power's mesmerizing illusions."[29]

Then García Márquez pays him one of the highest compliments, suggesting that Castro's concept of history and political community emulate two of the great inspirations for Latin America's idiosyncratic identity: "His vision of the Latin America to come is the same as Bolívar's and Martí's: an integral, autonomous community, capable of changing the destiny of the world."[30]

The conclusion of the introduction could not be more apologetic. García Márquez describes a man very near to perfection, practically a saint, and a new messiah: "This is the Fidel Castro I know, from countless hours of conversation which don't often allude to the specter of politics. A man of austere habits, limitless dreams, with a formal, traditional education, simple manners, careful in his speech, who is incapable of conceiving an idea that isn't extraordinary. He dreams of a day when his scientists will find a cure for cancer, and he has created a foreign policy befitting a world power on an island with no fresh water, 84 times smaller than its main enemy. He protects his privacy so fiercely that his personal life has become the most inscrutably enigmatic part of his legend. He has the almost mystical conviction that man's highest achievement is the proper formation of his conscience, and that moral stimulants, more than material ones, are capable of changing the world and moving history forward. I believe that he is one of the greatest idealists of our time, and that is perhaps his principal virtue, although it is also his main weakness."[31]

These words, written at the end of the 1980s, further corroborate the praise García Márquez had been offering to the Cuban leader in his writings since the mid-seventies. In 1975, after his first trip around the entire island, he said that Fidel "has been able to evoke within the people the simplest—but most sought-after and elusive—sentiment that, throughout history, the greatest governing leaders down to the lowliest have all wanted to inspire: affection. He has done it, of course, through his political intelligence, his instincts and honor, his almost animalistic capacity for work, with his profound identification with the people, and his complete faith in the wisdom of the masses, and with the universal vision with which he faces even the most seemingly insignificant issues of day-to-day political power."[32] García Márquez's personal connection to Castro grows so close over the years that in the late 1990s he said to Manuel Vázquez Montalbán: "Probably, if Fidel passes away before me, I won't go back to Cuba. For me, that island is like the land of a friendship."[33]

THE NARROW PATH

To reach paradise, one must not forget that the path is narrow and the door heavy. The pilgrim only forgets about the hardships along the way at the journey's end. Gabo set off on his pilgrimage in 1958. Maybe he thought differently then; in any case, merely starting to walk wasn't enough. With his first articles about Fidel the revolutionary, camped out on the Sierra Maestra, waiting for Batista to make his move, the doors didn't spring open. García Márquez seemed sympathetic, positive, interested, acquiescent; but he still hadn't thrown in his lot completely, nor was his support uncondi-tional. Years later, as Vázquez Montalbán would tell it, Fidel had observed ironically that in García Márquez's early writings at the end of the fifties, "he went swimming without getting his hair wet."[34]

The following year, his participation in Operation Truth played in his favor, and his role at Prensa Latina seemed to catapult him directly into the idyllic territory he so longed to inhabit; but that went awry. From her apartment in the Latin Quarter in Paris, Elis-abeth Burgos, a Venezuelan writer and activist and the biographer of Ribogerta Menchu, told us that in the mid-1960s Gabo asked her to get him inside the difficult-to-penetrate, tangled inner circle of the Revolutionary elite. Burgos had joined the Communist Party in Venezuela in 1958 to fight against the dictatorship of Pérez Jiménez. At that time, Gabo was living in Venezuela and got to know her. Just as the Venezuelan dictator fell, García Márquez got the idea to write a novel dealing with power and dictators. Later, Elisabeth moved to Cuba and experienced the Revolution's first steps. She was very close to the Revolution's inner circle, especially Che Guevara, and, along with Régis Debray, she helped plan the expedition to Bolivia where the revolutionary from Argentina would meet his death. In 1966, she served as a delegate to the Tri-continental Conference, an effort on the part of the worldwide Leftist community to support the Latin American revolutionaries' struggle against imperialism. During those years, she wasn't able to get her writer friend into contact with the Cuban Revolutionary elite, and in the early 1970s she left for Chile to support Allende.

Having lost that link, Gabo tried to go through Régis Debray, who was Burgos's husband at the time, although he had some con-ditions. This French intellectual and politician was also involved in the Cuban Revolution right from the start. He arrived in Cuba in 1961, traveled with Che Guevara to Bolivia, and was imprisoned there. After Che's death, Debray was sentenced to thirty years in prison, but in 1971 he was released, thanks to the efforts of Charles de Gaulle, the novelist André Malraux, and the philosopher Jean-Paul Sartre, who had also supported the Cuban Revolution from the beginning but had distanced himself from it in the wake of the Padilla case. In the 1980s, Debray was an adviser to Mitterrand on Latin America. When Gabo approached him, he had just been released from prison. In Havana, during a meeting with Fidel Castro and Carlos Rafael Rodríguez, director of the powerful National Institute of Agricultural Reform, Debray, an "old communist" who had risen as far as the vice-presidency of the State Council, suggested that it might be a good idea to invite the writer García Márquez to Cuba, maybe to the Casa de las Americas, as they had done before with other writers committed to the cause, like Cortázar and Vargas Llosa. Debray told us all this on a cold January day, in his apartment on the Rue de l'Odéon in Paris. In this very civilized setting, with high ceilings, parquet floors, books everywhere, and some very valuable paintings adorning the walls, we knew that the man in front of us still bore the scars from the torture he had endured in the jail in Camiri thirty-five years earlier. Neither Castro nor Rodriguez had shown any interest in extending an invitation to the Colombian writer, because they were unsure of his level of commitment. It seemed to them that his articles defending the Revolution and Fidel were unclear. But some statements he had made that year were beyond question, especially when he expressed his desire to visit the island and get to know Cuba, the tropical paradise. In the magazine *Triunfo* in November 1971, González Bermejo asked García Márquez:

"You recently said in an interview that the things that interest you in the world are the Rolling Stones' music, the Cuban Revolution, and four friends. Summarize your involvement with the Cuban Revolution."

"I believe in the Cuban Revolution every day."

"What aspect of the Cuban Revolution is most important to you?"

"That it creates its version of socialism keeping in mind its own conditions, a socialism that seems like Cuba and nothing but Cuba: humane, imaginative, and happy, without bureaucratic corrosion. This is a serious challenge for all of Latin America, which has conditions very similar to Cuba's."

"When are you going to Cuba?"

"At any time now. I'll have the first draft of my book done by December, and I hope to go to Cuba early next year. If I haven't gone to Cuba by then, it will be for a strictly practical reason: I need to finish my book."[35]

★ ★ ★

If Gabo didn't go to Cuba then, now we know why not, and it wasn't just for practical reasons, but for very speculative ones. Gabo must have received Castro's earlier message as conveyed to Debray, but he didn't act, or he couldn't act, until 1975. Having finished his second novel, *The Autumn of the Patriarch*, he tried again. The matter of the "first draft" masks a more bitter truth for him. But that's another subject, for another time.

CHAPTER FIVE

★

THE PATRIARCH IN HIS AUTUMN

WITHOUT DOUBT, ONE OF THE MOST INTRIGUING PERIODS in García Márquez's life is the span of time between the publication of *The Autumn of the Patriarch* in 1975 and the awarding of the Nobel Prize in Literature in 1982. His friendship with Castro was consolidated in that time, as were friendships with presidents of other Latin American and European countries, on a smaller scale. The cultural panorama in Cuba took on a new tone, far removed from the first blow to the Revolution dealt by the Padilla case and the "Gray Period"—the early seventies—when many works of marginal quality had been published. The Ministry of Culture was created in this period, and its first director was Armando Hart, who had had a strong presence in the regime from the outset. Through this institution, Cuba would put a strategy in place to nurture a national culture. Politically, Cuba would solidify its position in the Soviet bloc through the approval of a constitution—about a third of which was based on Stalin's model of 1936[1]—which was accepted in a referendum by 95% of Cuban voters in 1976.

In the economic sphere, the seventies had opened with the failure to reach the goal of producing 10 million tons of sugar, a plan Castro had pushed to jump-start the national economy. While 8.5 million tons were produced, the myopic focus on sugar production resulted in neglecting production of a great many other staple products. To correct this, in the mid-seventies the USSR began to send aid in the amount of four billion dollars annually. On top of that, Cuban sugar and nickel were exported to Eastern bloc countries, and Russian oil was sold to Cuba at special reduced prices, which was then resold on the world market at prevailing international rates. And finally, the 300 million dollars in credit granted by Western countries from the end of the sixties through the mid-seventies must be taken into account. A revitalized Castro emerged from this landscape, stronger than ever. From then on, he would hold a level of power unimaginable until then: he would be the president of the Council of State; he would continue as the supreme chief of the Armed Forces (with these two posts he could control the direction of any centralized entity, since he controlled the judicial system and the military); he would preside over the Council of Ministers and the Committee on the Council of Ministers (this enabled him to decide urgent matters with no possibility of being vetoed); and he was still the first secretary of the Communist Party of Cuba (the only party that controls all of the political power on the island), as he had been since the beginning of the Revolution. To make sure that the system was completely ironclad, Raúl Castro, Fidel's brother, was the regime's de facto number-two man, occupying the second-from-the-top position in the hierarchy of each of the aforementioned governmental bodies.[2]

With Castro effectively assuming the role of all-powerful, omnipresent patriarch in a country whose recovery was supported by Eastern as well as Western countries (with the exception of the United States) in terms that any other country of the Third World would have readily accepted, the situation on the island markedly improved, thanks to a more efficient economic organization, a more intelligent approach to production, a more efficient use of investments, and an emphasis on managerial training, a political approach with greater deference to economic realities, rising sugar prices, and an extension for repaying the debt to the USSR, coupled with new loans and credits from the market economy. At this time, *The Autumn of the Patriarch* was published, and García Márquez finally, definitively penetrated the inner circle of Cuban Revolutionaries.

One day in May 1975, all the bookstores throughout Colombia were flooded by Gabo's book, which tells the story of a Latin American dictator who has just died. That same day, as if it were Christmas Eve, the stores stayed open, until the hundreds of thousands of copies were all sold. The books were gone by about ten o'clock that night.[3] Shortly thereafter, a similar scene would play out in other Hispanic countries. Gabo had not published a novel since *One Hundred Years of Solitude*, so the new book's publication was a highly anticipated event, not just to Colombians but to half the world. After an eight-year absence, the author of the most highly praised novel in the Spanish language published a new story about Caribbean militants, heads of state, a certain breed of powerful men headed toward extinction.

But what had García Márquez been up to before that date, between the events we've already discussed at the time of the Czech invasion, when his overtures to Fidel were essentially rebuffed, and the events of the Padilla case, which ended in 1971? Those were years of militant journalism and intensive research into the history of dictators. He wasn't in Cuba at all during that period, nor was he there in the sixties after he stopped working for Prela, although one publication, the *Expreso* of Lima, stated in its July 10, 1975 edition that he did take a trip to Cuba at the end of 1967 and beginning of 1968. He probably would have gone there to promote his recently published novel, but there is nothing in any of the Cuban newspapers of those years to corroborate that a trip took place. Some very close friends of the writer, like Roberto Fernández Retamar, president of the Casa de las Americas, and Dasso Saldívar, Gabo's biographer, have talked in personal interviews about García Márquez's prolonged absence from Cuba spanning from the early sixties up until 1975.[4] Between the Padilla case and his first trip back to the island in 1975, two important periods must be highlighted that illustrate a growing sympathy for revolutionary ideology: García Márquez's defense of Allende and the criticism of Pinochet, and his involvement with the magazine *Alternativa*.

Salvador Allende was the first radical Leftist leader to win an election in Latin America. Up until then, all the socialist or communist presidents had come to power, like Fidel Castro, by force. This event evoked a surge of optimism among Leftists throughout Latin America, who saw a gateway to the possible dissolution of the United States' imperialist terrorism in the countries of "Our America," thanks to the opening of a North–South front in the seventies through the consolidation of Castro's regime and the triumph of the Left in the southern cone. Unfortunately for the Leftists, their hopes were cut short by Augusto Pinochet's coup in 1973, which ended the life of the communist president and the Chilean regime.

At that time, García Márquez, who had always been inclined toward the Latin American Left, banged his fist on the table, stood up, and decided to become a political activist from his position as a famous writer. When he found out about the bombing of Moneda Palace, he firmly decided that he would not publish any more works of fiction until the new Chilean dictator fell (a decision which led to the 1975 publication of nothing less than a novel about a dictator, which ridiculed Pinochet's image and other leaders like him); and he even took the trouble to send Pinochet a telegram, which wasn't exactly to congratulate him: "The Chilean people will never let themselves be governed by a gang of criminals like you, who are on the payroll of the North American imperialists."[5]

In 1974, motivated by a need to counteract the poisonous effects he thought the Chilean regime was having, he published the book *Chile, el golpe y los gringos* ("Chile, the Coup, and the Gringos"), a work that has since fallen into obscurity despite being widely read during those tumultuous years. In the opening pages, he discussed in very strong terms the blockade that the United States had imposed on Chile during Allende's rule, and how Cuba had collaborated with their allied country by sending a shipment of free sugar, just as street demonstrations were beginning to break out in Chile because of food shortages. He also lavishly praises Fidel Castro's visit to Chile around that time, for expressing solidarity with Allende's regime and sending a message of hope to the people of that country who were suffering from the effects of chronic shortages.[6] Thankfully, Gabo did not succeed in following through on his initial threats: during Pinochet's long reign, the Nobel Prize winner published two of his most important works: *Chronicle of a Death Foretold* (1981) and *Love in the Time of Cholera* (1985), as well as a novel of lesser importance, but equally fine, *The General in his Labyrinth* (1989), just as Pinochet's government was in its death throes. In 1975, García Márquez decided to "spend his fame in politics," living out his ideological commitment no matter the consequences: "In one way or another," he later confessed, "I think I've always held a very strong position. But now, it's much more active, much more militant, probably because of a problem of conscience, after the military coup in Chile [. . .]. At that moment, and frankly for the first time in my life, I began to think that what I needed to do in politics was more important than what I could do with literature." In an issue of *Prensa Latina*, he was even clearer: "What can I do with this fame? Shit! I said to myself. I'll spend it in politics. I mean, I'll place it at the service of the Latin American revolution."[7] Issue Number 188 of *Alternativa*, dated November, 1978, published an interview with García Márquez titled "Reality has gone Populist." At first, all the questions have to do with politics, until the interviewer abruptly changes the subject:

ALT: All right, enough about politics. Why don't you tell us how your writing is going?

GGM: Yeah, hell, you guys seem to forget that I'm actually a writer. And I'm trying to find the time to write. I'm still keeping my promise to not publish any fiction until Pinochet falls. But twenty-four hours after his fall—and he is going to fall—I'll publish a book of stories about Latin Americans in Europe, which I've been working on for a while. [p. 6]

Gabo was referring to *Doce cuentos peregrinos*, which actually came to light a little later than the promised twenty-four hours, since it wasn't published until 1992. But we've already mentioned that there were three novels published before that. In any case, there were still allusions to his vow in interviews in the eighties. In 1983, when his work *Chronicle of a Death Foretold* was already a classic, he defended himself, responding to a question about that old promise he had made: "I made those declarations after the publication of *The Autumn of the Patriarch*. Honestly, I was furious. I had been working on that book for seven years, and the first thing everybody asked me was what plans I had for the next one. When people ask me those kinds of questions, I make up all kinds of answers, just to make them happy. Actually, I didn't have any immediate plans to write another novel, and that answer eliminated that repugnant question from later interviews."[8] His decision couldn't have been very firm. Maybe he thought Pinochet wouldn't last as long as he did. Some say Gabo is a great poker player, just like his friend Fidel. We don't know, but we can definitely call his vow a big bluff. What is clear is the huge publicity his stated promise generated, which may have, on the one hand, inspired opposition to the Chilean dictatorship, and, on the other, fomented expectations for whatever his next book would be. So it should come as no surprise that the first edition of *Chronicle of a Death Foretold* (1981) would mark a new, almost unthinkable record in publishing, with 999,999 copies distributed simultaneously throughout all the countries in the Spanish-speaking world, and they vanished from the shelves in the blink of an eye. A book that, as he himself described it, was written "in my underwear, from nine in the morning until three in the afternoon for fourteen weeks without a break, sweating buckets in the rooming house for single men where Bayardo San Roman stayed for six months while he was in town."[9] And the "anti-Pinochet" effect would have later repercussions, in 1986, on the publication of a new book focusing on Chile, *La aventura clandestine de Miguel Littin en Chile*, about a film director who goes to that country to make a movie critical of the government.

Pinochet ordered Gabo's book to be publicly burned, along with other titles, in Valparaíso in 1987. The civilized world had not witnessed such a spectacle since the fall of Nazi Germany. Later, Gabo would talk about this peculiar demonstration ironically, with humor and even a certain pride, concluding that a decision of that magnitude must have meant that the book's effect had surpassed his wildest expectations.

The other phenomenon we referred to as a sign of growing ideological commitment which preceded the publication of *The Autumn of the Patriarch* was García Márquez's involvement with the magazine *Alternativa*. In 1974, that publication was launched in Bogotá, as a weekly for radical Leftists, focusing on relatively general information, successfully breaking the mold of the almost clandestinely circulated publications in that arena, which had been distributed on an almost personal level until that point, relegated to an ephemeral existence. Finally, a radical magazine broke into the Colombian kiosks, thanks to the help of certain "militant" financial backers, since many radicals gave generous amounts of money to ensure that the publication would have a respectable circulation. García Márquez supported the initiative from its inception, heading up the board of advisers and publishing his most revolutionary writings within its pages—some of which, not surprisingly, dealt with Cuba and its problems. Headings like "Cuba from One End to the Other," "The Months of Gloom: Che in the Congo," and "A Whole Nation in Elementary School" seemed more like apologetic texts written for survivors of the Sierra Maestra than articles written by a foreign journalist without national interests in Cuba. With those credentials, the year marking the publication of *The Autumn of the Patriarch* also marked the long-anticipated return to Cuban soil of the man who, in five or six years, would become the most powerful unofficial politician in Latin America, and perhaps even the entire Western world.

PATRIARCHS FOR ALL SEASONS

Gabo's novel, which examines the dictator archetype, relates to his fascination with power. In postmodern lexicology, expressions like "drunk with power" illustrate the vice that people can fall into once they have experienced the profound pleasure that can come from ruling any sort of organization. In general, those who have ruled with absolute power do not consider relinquishing that power, and they feel very comfortable in their role as master of everything around them, because they can be arbitrary and exercise complete self-determination in their actions. It's an attraction that feeds upon itself, and it is insatiable. García Márquez, who has a very sensitive nose for detecting political animals with enormous appetites for power, created a work that could incarnate the prototypical, time-less dictator, and it took him almost twenty years to finish the task.

In an article dated September 30, 1981, titled "The Ides of March," he explained what led to his fascination for secrets and the agony and ecstasy of power: "My preoccupation for the mysteries of power can be traced to something I saw when I was in Caracas, around when I was reading *The Ides of March* for the first time, and now I'm not totally sure which of the two things happened first. It was in early 1958. General Marcos Pérez Jiménez, who had been the dictator of Venezuela for ten years, had fled for Santo Domingo at daybreak. His men had to hoist him onto the plane with a rope, since there hadn't been time to find a portable stairway, and in the rush to flee, he had forgotten his briefcase, where he had put his spending money: thirteen million dollars in cash. A few hours later, all of the credentialed foreign journalists in Caracas, myself included, gathered to wait for the formation of the new government in one of the sumptuous salons of Miraflores Palace. Suddenly, an official from the army, dressed in battle fatigues, burst out of the office of the assembly and, brandishing a machine gun, ready to fire, he walked backwards through the salon. At the front entrance to the palace, he got into a taxi, which took him to the airport, and fled the country. The only traces of him remaining were the dirty foot-prints left by his boots on the immaculate rugs in the salon. I under-went a sort of shock: in a strange way, as if a forbidden capsule had been ingested in my soul, I understood that that particular scene embodied power's entire essence. Some fifteen years later, ever since that event, and always carrying it somewhere in my mind, I wrote *The Autumn of the Patriarch*."[10]

In an interview with Jon Lee Anderson, Gabo explained that what impressed him most about that scene was how quickly they had decided who the successor would be, as if power, this sacred reality, could be dealt with in such a natural way. "Within minutes of the general's exit," Jon Lee recalled, "they had reached an agreement in that room: the new Venezuelan leader would be Rear Admiral Wolfgang Larrazábal." And Gabo comments: "I couldn't believe that power could be defined in that way. In that moment, something happened."[11] Another interview, with the newspaper *El País* in 1978, produced the following exchange:

> *El País:* Finally, I would like you to explain what attracts you so much to dictators, powerful men like Franco, Torrijos, Fidel. . . .

> **García Márquez:** Torrijos, laughing his head off, has told me many times that I have a thing for dictators. Every government is a group of people, but the personality of the individuals has huge importance, particularly in Latin America. There, *caudillismo* is ingrained in the purest historical traditions, and it will be a very long time before it will be completely extinguished. That doesn't mean that you can't have a revolution with a *caudillo*, in the same way that you here seem to think that you could with a king.[12]

A few months after García Márquez received the Nobel Prize, in March 1983, *Playboy* magazine published one of the best, most extensive interviews the Colombian writer has ever given, although the article's existence is now little-known. We found out about it thanks to a Colombian man we met at a reception in New York. We had gone to the Graduate Center of New York University for a conference, held in a wonderful building at the corner of 34th Street and Fifth Avenue in Manhattan, right across from the Empire State Building; and at the reception after our presentation, we were discussing our research with this man, who was studying for his doctorate at the university. He told us about the article, and we went off in search of a copy, which wasn't easy, since when we asked the university department director where we could find back issues of *Playboy*, her face contorted with disgust. "I wouldn't have expected that from you," she said, aghast. When we explained why we wanted it, she helped us to locate *Playboy*'s offices in New York, but they had already closed by that time, and the next morning we had to depart very early for Boston. More than a year went by, asking for help on our quest from journalist friends in Peru, the United States, and Puerto Rico, but the text of the interview did not surface. And *Playboy*'s Web site only contained the sort of images to be expected from an illustrated magazine of that nature . . . until someone finally had the bright idea to simply call up information in Spain and ask for the company headquarters here. They gave us a number in Barcelona, and three days later we had the article, thanks to that organization's fastidious dedication to serving their clientele. But they had only sent us a photocopy of the article itself, not the whole magazine. Toward the end of the article (on pages 25 and 26 of that issue of the magazine), the following dialogue appears:

Playboy: We've heard that you did one draft of *The Autumn of the Patriarch* and threw it away because it read too much like a clone of *One Hundred Years*. True?

García Márquez: Partly true. I tried the book three times. The first time I wrote it, I based it on a memory I had of Havana in 1959. I had been covering the trial of one of Batista's big generals. He was being tried for war crimes in a large baseball stadium. What interested me, as I watched him, were the literary possibilities in his situation. So when I sat down to write *The Autumn of the Patriarch*, I thought I could use the form of a monologue by the dictator as he sat in the middle of the stadium. However, as I began writing, the idea quickly fell apart. It wasn't real. Latin American dictators, the great ones, all either died in bed or escaped with huge fortunes. For a second try, I decided to write the novel as if it were a fake biography—that version did turn out to be, stylistically, more like *One Hundred Years*. So, sadly, this version was eliminated. Honestly, I don't understand why so many people wanted *The Autumn of the Patriarch* to be like *One Hundred Years*. I suspect that if I wanted commercial success, I could go on writing *One Hundred Years* for the rest of my life. I could cheat, as they do in Hollywood: *The Return of Colonel Aureliano Buendia*. What I finally decided to go with was a structure based on multiple monologues—which is very much the way life is under a dictatorship. There are different voices which tell the same thing in different ways.

Then, after some time, I reached another block. I personally had never lived under one of the old dictatorships. To make the novel work, I wanted to know what daily life was like in a very old dictatorship. While I was writing, there were two [cases] of interest: in Spain and in Portugal. So what Mercedes and I did was move to Franco's Spain, to Barcelona. But even in Spain, after a certain moment, I realized that something was still missing in the atmosphere of the book; things were too cold. So, again, to get the right mood, we moved. This time to the Caribbean—we'd been away a long time. When I arrived in Colombia, the press asked me, "What have you come here to do?" I said, "To try to remember what the guava fruit smells like." Mercedes and I traveled to all the Caribbean islands—not taking notes, simply living. When we returned to Barcelona, the book just streamed forth.

From around this time, one anecdote crystallizes, talking about how Gabo had succumbed to an obsession for power in all its unfathomable depth and mystery. His friend Teodoro Petkoff remembers how one day in Barcelona, after discussing the still-unpublished manuscript of *The Autumn of the Patriarch*, the subject turned to Franco. Suddenly, García Márquez said to Petkoff, pensively, "What is power? It's as if it's a little ball that some people hold in their hands, and they're constantly caressing it."[13]

García Márquez does not write quickly, or superficially. Each text that he sends off to the presses is thoughtful, carefully labored, very deliberate, and exhaustively rewritten. It is a well-known fact that *No One Writes to the Colonel* went through eleven drafts before the final version was published, and García Márquez is known to have used five hundred sheets of paper to produce a short story of eleven pages. So it's unsurprising that a novel of such importance in terms of its author's personal obsessions and ideological and political interests would represent such a long journey, spanning many years and many drafts. *The Autumn of the Patriarch* aims to present a complete dissection of power, specifically absolute power, held by a solitary individual, like that experienced by the most illustrious dictators. To prepare, García Márquez first assigned himself a disciplined research regimen, reading biographies of dictators and novels featuring characters that have exercised absolute power, and gathering information on contemporary *caudillos*, some of them still active. The figure that interested him most from the classical period was Julius Caesar. One of the books that was the most help to him was Thornton Wilder's *The Ides of March*, which he read several times on different occasions, especially while he was rewriting *The Autumn of the Patriarch*, "like a dazzling look into the agonies and ecstasies of power."[14] That historic personality had such a seductive effect that García Márquez was prompted to delve into other sources: "Before *The Ides of March*," he explained, "the only things I had read about Julius Caesar were in high school textbooks, written by the Christian brothers, and Shakespeare's plays, which seem to be more grounded in imagination than historical fact. But after that, I immersed myself in essential resources: the inevitable Plutarch, the gossiping, incorrigible Sueton, the dry Carcopino, and the essays and battle memoirs of Julius Caesar himself."[15]

Another classical personality with traces in the Caribbean dictator is Oedipus Rex, who has several things in common with the Patriarch: Oedipus governs a closed world, where events take place in a fatalistic way and man ends up being a victim of his own destiny. The real locale of Tebas, masterfully recreated by Sophocles, becomes a mythic, undefined place, ready to bear witness to the tragic conclusion. Also, the population is depicted as anonymous and depersonalized, a mass that is really a chorus. "It's as if they were a Greek chorus. Although the narrative molds utilized are very different, as they belong to very disparate periods of literature, both works are in the same spirit: the dialectic between supreme power, represented by a sole individual, and the people, represented by the anonymous throng."[16]

Still, the most important examples were drawn from modern Latin America. Starting with figures like Montezuma and Juan Manuel de Rosas, the most familiar dictators are those that the author himself identifies as being the most direct inspirations for his work. In an article from the summer of 1981, he expressed that "The hardest time I ever had as a writer was doing the research for *The Autumn of the Patriarch*. Over almost ten years, I read everything I possibly could about the dictators in Latin America—especially in the Caribbean—with the goal of making sure that the book I was thinking about writing would bear as little resemblance as possible to actual reality. Each step was disillusioning. Juan Vicente Gómez's intuition was more insightful than a team of psychics. Dr. Duvalier, in Haiti, had ordered all of the black dogs in the country to be slaughtered, because one of his enemies, trying to escape the tyrant's persecution, had shed himself of his human condition to take the form of a black dog. Dr. Francia, whose reputation as a philosopher was so respected that he was the subject of a Carlyle study, locked up the Republic of Paraguay as if it were a private house, only leaving a window cracked open to let the mail come in. Antonio López de Santa Anna gave his own leg a magnificent funeral. The severed hand of Lope de Aguirre floated in a river downstream for several days, and whoever saw it pass by was horrified, thinking that even in that state, that murderous hand could still brandish a dagger. Anastasio Somoza García, in Nicaragua, had a cage with two compartments in a garden in his yard: one side of the cage was for wild animals, and the other, separated only by an iron bar, was reserved for his political enemies. Martínez, the theosophical dictator in El Salvador, ordered that all the public light fixtures be covered in red paper to combat an epidemic of measles, and he invented a pendulum to be held over food to detect if it had been poisoned. [. . .] Overall, we writers of Latin America and the Caribbean have to swear, with a hand over our hearts, that reality is a better writer than we are. Our destiny, and maybe our glory, is to try to humbly imitate it, as best we can."[17]

In the end, other names to add to the list are Melgarejo of Bolivia, Trujillo in the Dominican Republic, Machado and Batista in Cuba, Porfirio Díaz in Mexico, Estrada Cabrera in Guatemala, Oscar Benavides in Peru, and Maximiliano Hernández in El Salvador—basically, patriarchs of every season: some had already passed through their winter and rested in their tombs, some were embarking on the springtime of their power, others were in their high summer, and there were some who, after many long years of reign, were still in their autumn. García Márquez reserved a place at the table of his tyrants' banquet for Franco, as he had witnessed his autumn and long winter, almost mistaken for eternity. In 1978, he responded to Angel Harguindey's questions during an interview for *El País* in the following terms:

AH: Everything that has been written about Franco's death almost unanimously concludes that in terms of sordidness and high drama, it surpassed the death described in your novel. As the author of *The Autumn of the Patriarch*, what thoughts did Franco's long suffering and death inspire?

GGM: It's likely that in this case, talking specifically about the process of Franco's death, I think the reality surpassed the fiction, but you have to realize that the fiction came first, and that Franco's people didn't leave that reality up to God's will: they took it upon themselves to manipulate it. Franco had a death that would have been unbelievable in literature [. . .]. When I started to plan *The Autumn of the Patriarch*, I understood that, first, I didn't want to miss out on the experience the Spanish people had had under a dictatorial regime like Franco's, and then I didn't want to deprive myself of this experience of living under an old-style dictatorship to work on the book. The pact I had made with myself not to go to Spain got turned around completely: to come to Spain and wait for Franco to die. I thought I would be there around three years, and I stayed for seven. I finally concluded that Franco would never die, and I started to fear that it was an experiment in eternity.[18]

Certainly, within the Spanish-speaking world, and especially in Latin America, the figure of the *caudillo* predominates, a real "mythic creature of Latin America," as García Márquez put it,[19] since "individual personalities have such great importance, especially in Latin America. There, *caudillismo* is part of the purest historical tradition, and it will be a very long time before it can be rooted out."[20] That's why "the theme of the dictator has been a constant within the Latin American world of letters since its beginnings," Gabo affirms, "and it will continue to be so while greater historical perspective is gained regarding that archetype."[21]

With all of these elements, García Márquez tries to present a generalized vision of power as a political posture of control, but also as a universal tendency. The dictator is only a public manifestation of the little tyrant we all have inside ourselves, which goes unnoticed until it springs into action. It is one of the great mysteries of humanity, impossible to decipher. The intellectual can only describe it, marvel at its existence, and uncover the general factors that activate this tendency, but nothing more. In García Márquez's work, we get a glimpse of certain behavioral patterns that characterize these mythic creatures, which seem amazingly accurate. In general, "they tend to be very close to their mothers, are incredibly ambitious and vain, they are megalomaniacs, eccentric, prone to a debauched existence in many cases, and to a Spartan existence in others, making work into a veritable religion. They are egocentric to unimaginable extremes, leading to all kinds of messianic practices. Most of them view themselves as immortal, and live on the edge. Almost all [. . .] are conscious of the division between power and government, which is why they tend to delegate the exercise of government to people they trust implicitly, and reserve all of the mechanisms to control society for themselves. They also practice nepotism, and tend to shamelessly blur the lines between public and private, governing the country as if it were just one more of their many personal properties."[22]

Don't go anywhere just yet; there's more. We've gone out for a minute to find some photos of the Nobel laureate from Colombia, posing, like Forrest Gump, with some very interesting presidents.

CHAPTER SIX

★

WHO'S NOT IN THE FAMILY PHOTO?

N OT ONLY THE MOST VIGILANT READERS, BUT ANYONE AT ALL who has read García Márquez's work—and this book's previous chapter—would have noticed one glaring omission: the Latin American dictator who was in power the longest during the twentieth century, and who was still in power, relatively young and healthy, at the dawn of the twenty-first century, and who made the Guinness Book of World Records for giving the longest speech in history (more than nine hours), was not included in the group photo of the patriarchs. There are only two possible explanations: either he is not a dictator at all, or the person who took the snapshot deliberately left him out for some reason.

In general terms, Latin American and European Leftists refuse to call Castro a dictator, arguing that, for the forty-plus years he has been in power, he has resisted a trade blockade and successfully stood up to the most powerful country in the world. That is true, and to be commended; but struggling against a blockade and battling the great monster are not synonymous with respecting fundamental human rights, nor do they guarantee democracy. What's more, facing that challenge has resulted in the most inflexible, insular, *caudillista* regime that Latin America has ever produced.

And, although García Márquez tries not to step on anybody's toes, keeping the patriarch of his novel far removed from the bearded guerrillas of the Cuban Revolution, the unintentional similarities between the protagonist of *The Autumn of the Patriarch* and Castro are obvious, bearing in mind García Márquez's exaggerated, apocalyptic style, since his book deals with a man from a Caribbean country who "governed as if he knew he was predestined never to die,"[1] and "when they left him alone with his nation and his power again he did not poison his blood again with the sluggishness of written law, but governed orally and physically, present at every moment and everywhere with a flinty parsimony but also with a diligence inconceivable at his age" (7–8), he was omnipresent "for it always seemed that he was in two places at once, they would see him playing dominoes at seven o'clock at night and at the same time he had been seen lighting cow chips to drive the mosquitoes out of the reception room" (8), he was more feared than loved, since "no one has ever told you what he really thinks but everyone tells you what he knows you want to hear while he bows to your face and thumbs his nose at you from behind" (24), and "the more certain the rumors of his death seemed, he would appear even more alive and authoritarian at the least expected moment to impose other unforeseen directions to our destiny" (41–42); "It was calculated that over the course of his life he must have sired five thousand children, all seven-monthers, by the countless number of loveless beloveds he had who succeeded each other in his seraglio" (44), and very few had—and this was also the case with García Márquez himself—"enough of his confidence to ask him to free a prisoner or pardon someone condemned to death" (60); and, the propaganda machine of power would interpret historical, political, and even natural events as triumphs of the regime, "for the official organs proclaimed the passage of the comet as a victory of the regime over the forces of evil" (77); he always wore his uniform, even when he slept, and they found him wearing it when he died.

The patriarch in García Márquez's novel always showed up in places at the most unexpected times: "during the beginnings of his regime he would appear in towns when least expected with no other escort but a barefooted Guajiro Indian with a cane-cutting machete and a small entourage of congressmen and senators whom he had appointed himself with his finger according to the whims of his digestion, he informed himself about the crop figures and the state of health of the livestock and the behavior of the people [. . .] and even though he seemed to be dozing because of the heat he would not let a single detail go by without some explanation in his talks with the men and women he had called together" (82); he had rapidly become a myth: "his legend had begun much earlier than he believed himself master of all his power" (84); sometimes the narrator remembers times long since past when the patriarch "still thought himself mortal and had the virtue of doubt and knew how to make mistakes" (86); sometimes it wasn't easy to tell his faithful subjects and the counterrevolutionaries apart: "without being able to distinguish in that thicket of ovations who were the real patriots and who were the tricky ones because we still hadn't discovered that the shadiest ones were those who shout loudest long live the stud, God damn it, long live the general" (92); once in a while he made sure "that nobody would be left without proof that he was once more the master of all his power with the fierce support of armed forces that had become once more the same as before since he had distributed the shipments of food and medicine and the material for public relief from foreign aid" (99); the regime always scrupulously protected the public image of the revolution, by lying:

"who finally bore public witness to the fact that they had found the jails closed down, the nation in peace, everything in its place, and they had not found any indication to confirm the public suspicion that there had been or might have been a violation by intent or by action or by omission of the principles of human rights, rest easy, general" (103).

As is the case with all known dictators, he expelled whomever bothered him: "he gave orders for the nuncio to be placed on a life raft with provisions for three days and they cast him adrift on the lane that cruise ships took to Europe so that the whole world will know what happens to foreigners who lift their hands against the majesty of the national, and the Pope will learn now and forever that he may be Pope in Rome with his ring on his finger sitting on his golden throne, but here I am what I am, God damn it, them and their shitty petticoats" (135); and he didn't think about who would succeed him, and he didn't let anybody else worry about it either: "he had refused in his senile insistence to take any decision concerning the destiny of the nation after he was gone, with the invincible stubbornness of an old man he had resisted all suggestions made to him" (158); because "when I finally die the politicians will come back and divide up the mess the way it was during the times of the Goths, you'll see, he said, they'll go back to dividing everything up among the priests, the gringos and the rich, and nothing for the poor, naturally, because they've always been so fucked up that the day shit is worth money, poor people will be born without an asshole" (159). "...there was no other nation except the one that had been made by him in his own image and likeness where space was changed and time corrected by the designs of his absolute will" (159); the lessons on how to exercise power had been learned very well: "he made him repeat it as many times as he thought necessary so that the boy would never forget that the only mistake that a man invested with authority and power cannot make even once in his lifetime is to issue an order which he is not sure will be carried out" (180), with an impressive understanding of the psychology of those he shares some scraps of power with: "no one had any need or desire to kill me, you people are the only ones, my useless ministers, my lazy commanders, except that you don't dare and never will dare kill me because you know that afterward you'll have to kill each other" (236); occasionally he felt the urge to remember that he had been "proclaimed supreme commander of the three branches of the armed forces and president of the republic for such a time as was necessary for the reestablishment of order and the economic balance of the nation" (239), and so on.

Unsurprisingly, many critics have focused on these parallels. Plinio Apuleyo Mendoza, for example, wrote that "Fidel seems like one of García Márquez's most constant literary archetypes."[2] As a child, García Márquez constructed the image of a hero who, guided by his grandfather's influence, would become a Latin American *caudillo*. This *caudillo*, as Apuleyo Mendoza asserts, appears in most of his novels in one form or another, including in *The Autumn of the Patriarch*. César Leante not only discusses this in greater detail, he also points out that this was the only novel by García Márquez that was not immediately published in Cuba. He posits that "Castro initially vetoed it,"[3] although we have not been able to locate the document he cites to support this. Leante wrote: "When in 1981 the Cuban edition of *Chronicle of a Death Foretold* was published, the book's back cover read as follows: '*La Casa de las Américas* has published *One Hundred Years of Solitude*, *No One Writes to the Colonel*, *The Evil Hour*, *Leaf Storm* and all of his short stories. His novel *The Autumn of the Patriarch* has enjoyed great success all over the world.' That is to say, they are disingenuously confessing that all of García Márquez's works have been published in Cuba, except for *The Autumn of the Patriarch*."[4]

In that sense, it's possible that the obvious similarities did not go undetected by Castro either. That's what César Leante concludes: "Why the exclusion of a novel of such importance in his body of work? Simply, because Fidel Castro didn't like it; he didn't like it because he saw in the novel's protagonist, that is, in the Patriarch, traces of himself."[5] And he adds that Fidel Castro "suspects that his personality and his behavior hadn't been far from García Márquez's mind when he composed the character. Or if it hadn't been intentional, there were still some very uncanny similarities. Personality traits and, especially, behaviors of the *caudillo* could very easily be attributed to Castro, and the Cuban reader would see this. So he decided to silence the work."[6] Finally, he asserts: "Castro wasn't wrong to recognize certain characteristics in the Patriarch that could have been—or really were—his. In the same way that García Márquez thought that 'absolute power embodies all of human greatness, and all of human depravity,' he, Castro, as an absolute dictator, personified that greatness as well as those depravities. He had accomplished the great feat of conquering Batista, to install himself in power in perpetuity, and in that aspect far surpassing the previous tyrannical regime."[7]

César Leante also mentions the fact that when a review of the novel was published in the magazine *Casa de las Américas*, they chose a Colombian journalist, Manuel Mejía Vallejo, whose critique was not entirely positive, and that "casts doubt on the quality of the great novel."[8] The Cuban poet and critic not only mentions the common circumstances of the two personalities; he also describes the characteristics and behaviors that they both share. One of those is assuming the typical dictator's role as protector and benefactor, an image aggressively promoted throughout all the communication outlets under his control: "The Patriarch uses his own propaganda machine to maintain his power and the public's faith in him. His highest priority is to protect his public image and his position of authority. The deluge of slogans ('Fidel, Fidel,

Fidel!', 'Commander-in-Chief, at your service!', Maximum Leader); the publication and broadcast of all of his speeches through all media outlets; [and the display of] statues and portraits of him everywhere in every corner of the country, constitute [further examples of] the symmetry between Castro and the Patriarch."[9] And there are intriguing similarities of the aforementioned and the unnamed Patriarchs in their attitudes toward intellectuals. The world of culture, especially at the highest levels, has always tilted toward dissidence, independence, a spirit of open challenge. So, naturally, dictators do not feel comfortable in this world, and they can adopt one of two positions: they can denigrate the intellectuals or try to control them. The Padilla case was just one of the thousands of examples that could be cited. Every Cuban intellectual has a story to tell, or has told it to Eliseo Alberto so it could be included in the revised edition of *Informe contra mí mismo*, recently published by Alfaguara. There's a passage from *The Autumn of the Patriarch* that speaks for itself:

We never heard that expression again until after the cyclone when he proclaimed a new amnesty for political prisoners and authorized the return of all exiles except for men of letters, of course, for them, never any amnesty, he said, they've got fever in their quills like thoroughbred roosters when they're molting so that they're no good for anything except when they're good for something, he said, worse than politicians, worse than priests, just imagine, but let the others come back without distinction of color so that the rebuilding of the nation can be the task of all, so that nobody would be left without proof that he was once more the master of all his power with the fierce support of the armed forces that had become once more the same as before . . . (99).

Aside from the Padilla case and other personal stories, a large-scale event of 1980 illustrates the same concept: the Mariel Boatlift. In that year, thousands of Cubans sought refuge in the Peruvian embassy in Havana, waiting for authorization to emigrate from the island. Finally, Fidel Castro allowed most of them to leave. Of those that did leave, the majority were delinquents, criminals, homosexuals, secret agents who wanted to infiltrate Miami, or the mentally ill . . . in other words, people who wouldn't do any harm to the government's image. But it wasn't so easy for intellectuals and university professors to emigrate, although some professionals did manage to get out. The person most commonly associated with this event was the writer Reinaldo Arenas, who took advantage of some confusion regarding his name to slip onto a boat that would spirit him away, not exactly to paradise. In his autobiographical work *Before Night Falls*, not entirely devoid of exaggerations and fantasies on the author's part, Arenas recalls this event, which was also featured in Julian Schnabel's movie based on the book, featuring a brilliant performance by the actor Javier Bardem, who almost won an Oscar for Best Actor for his portrayal of the Cuban writer.

To these common points, César Leante adds the importance of politics and power to García Márquez's dictator as well as to his friend Fidel Castro: "García Márquez presents his dictator as, above all, a political animal, and if anybody lives for, from, and through politics, it is Fidel Castro. They are not only his passion, but his whole reason for being. Politics are as essential as his internal organs. Some people love money and living well. Not Fidel Castro, Fidel Castro only loves power."[10]

In spite of this, César Leante thinks that it would be a mistake to interpret the novel as an indirect criticism of the Cuban leader on the author's part: "García Márquez's intention was never to condemn his hero."[11] It's true that over the course of reading the whole novel, one begins to feel the sympathy and the admiration that Gabo has for him. "He is an intractable *caudillo*, mythic, like the Patriarch, like Aureliano Buendia, and because of this mythic stature he is ready to forgive all of his horrors, all of his crimes."[12] This last observation is conclusive, because repeated readings of the books alluded to strongly suggest that García Márquez would never openly criticize Castro. It stands to reason that a man who has decided to politicize his life to the very core could not start out on his personal campaign by provoking the man who would spearhead not only the interests of his people, but also of all Latin American people, determined to not give an inch in the face of the enemy to the North. But the similarities are there for all to see, and they are obvious.

In his interview with Jon Lee Anderson, García Márquez said that another one of his close friends (also a dictator), General Omar Torrijos of Panama, not a big reader at all, had enthusiastically read *The Autumn of the Patriarch* from cover to cover. "He told me," García Márquez recalled, "that it was my best book. When I asked why he thought that, he leaned toward me and said: 'Because it's true, we're all like that.'"[13] It's logical to assume, and some data would suggest, that Fidel had the same opinion, and shared it with the author of the magnificent work. No dictator is exempt. The similarities go as far as Stalin. In his articles of 1957 (published in 1958) where he wrote about the Iron Curtain, after having traveled in the Soviet Union, García Márquez mentions a visit to Stalin's tomb in Red Square, where he could see the tyrant's delicate, girlish hands. Coincidentally, the Caribbean dictator in the novel appears dead in the book's opening pages, and the collective narrator focuses on "the smooth maiden hands with the ring of power on the bone of the third finger" (5–6), while, toward the middle of the book, another narrator, someone very close to the action, sees "the unavoidable eyes, the hand of a sleeping maiden that plucked a banana from the nearest bunch and ate it with anxiety" (90); when he reaches a very advanced, though indefinite, age, the narrator affirms that "he was older and more remote than anyone had been able to imagine, except for the languid hands without the velvet gloves which did not look like his natural soldier's hands but those of someone much younger and more compassionate" (183–184).

SOMETHING FOR NOTHING?

In hard times, it's not unusual to ask people to give of their time, their laborer's hands, their eyes that once held tears, their old wanderer's legs, their chests, their hearts, even their tongues. So far, so good; because in hard times, everything one can give is needed. The problem comes when, after this tremendous sacrifice, they tell a man to get up and walk.[14] The writer and intellectual are left with two options: to crumple under the pressure of power, or to subtly present different points of view. When Silvio Rodriguez is asked if his most emblematic song, *Ojalá*, is subversive or critical when read between the lines, he always answers that the song is about a frustrated love relationship, but even doctoral theses have suggested a possible challenge to the political system, especially in the second half of the song, which says: "I hope that my desire goes after you / after your old government of corpses and flowers." Then comes the chorus, one of the best musical passages out of all the singer-songwriter's works, which, in this line of interpretation, could be referring to the omnipresence that naturally goes along with all dictators, and that we've seen reflected in García Márquez's works:

I hope your constant look goes away,
The precise word, the perfect smile.
I hope something happens to make you disappear:
A blinding light, a sudden snowfall.
I hope at least death takes me away,
To not see you so much, to not see you always

In every second, in every look
I hope you can't even be touched in song.

Silvio wrote those lyrics in 1969, when he was a young song-writer who had already gotten into trouble with authority. Gradually, thanks to his indisputable talent and his use of revolutionary propaganda, he would become the most widely renowned artist of his generation and the one who contributed the most to exporting the revolution, from an ideological and artistic standpoint. His musical genius is beyond question, and he became a musical as well as political icon for youth in Latin America and Europe in the seventies and eighties. Apparently he could not jeopardize his career by making direct references to the regime, so any allusion had to be made strictly within the confines of subtle ambiguity. We'll never know if those verses have an ideological bite, but the text's versatility is clear. The same phenomenon can be seen in *The Autumn of the Patriarch*, prompting García Márquez to reflexively demonstrate in his words and actions his loyalty to the principles of the struggle against imperialism and his strictly revolutionary stance. He took two important steps in this regard after 1975: he wrote a book about the blockade's devastating consequences in Cuba, and he gave an orthodox, apologetic interpretation of Cuba's intervention in Angola. We will discuss this further shortly, but first, a final thought: did Gabo need to convince Fidel, although he doesn't demand it, of his *fidelity* to the leader, of the purity of his intentions, once *The Autumn of the Patriarch* had been published? Probably not; but something to that effect may be seen in *The General in His Labyrinth*. Some critics assert that the writing of this book, and its publication in 1989, was an attempt to make up for *The Autumn of the Patriarch*. Elisabeth Burgos and Jacques Gilard, whom we interviewed all over France over a two-year period, are convinced that it was "a consolation prize" for Fidel, and only for him, although the text about the Patriarch could have offended other presidents on familiar terms with García Márquez. Vázquez Montalbán told us that, although the references are never direct, it's possible that *The General in His Labyrinth* has that intention, since, even within Cuban politics, the previous novel about the Patriarch had been viewed by some people as a warning to Castro, so that he wouldn't decide to stay in power until the end of the world as we know it. And, as Gabo said in his interview with Jon Lee Anderson, "Fidel isn't like the rest of us. He thinks he has all the time in the world. Death is simply not in his plans."[15]

Simón Bolívar is, along with Martí and a Soviet leader like Lenin, the true inspiration for the revolution launched by the bearded guerrillas in the Sierra Maestra. Traces of the different strains of Marxism, communism, and socialism are less clear and have evolved in Cuba according to the level of involvement with the Eastern bloc countries over the course of the Revolution's first thirty years, or the amount of power and influence that leaders surrounding Castro have had over him, such as his brother Raúl, Che Guevara, or Carlos Rafael Rodríguez. Nevertheless, the indigenous paradigm is always constant and beyond question. In Cuba, Martí is the focal point of any political or cultural proposal, while Bolívar acts as the continental model. If Castro used the Cuban icon to unify all the islanders in the face of outside threats, Bolívar is the touchstone of the Revolution as an experiment of the entire Latin American continent. We have seen how, at different stages, Fidel has conceived of a future that involves not only Cuba, but the entire universe of *Our America*. His activity as a student leader in 1948 in Bogotá demonstrates this view, and later his support of Allende in Chile, and of the guerrillas in conservative countries, and, finally, the government democratically elected in Venezuela, bringing Hugo Chávez to power. The American utopia, the concept of a South America politically united to quash the imperialist instincts of *yanqui* capitalism, has always been a dream, an elusive unicorn that Fidel has chased after relentlessly. Gabo has always defended Fidel against those who criticize his excessively radical, personal positions, because he believes in the utopia too, as Bolívar did. In an interview with Gianni Minà, García Márquez talks about his Cuban friend:

> I criticize him in private, but not in public. At this stage, those who have been Stalinists think they have the right to settle accounts with us for something we never were. For our countries, the problem is national independence, autonomy, and Cuba has it. Cuba has been a barrier against the United States' expansion. Castro is a Utopian dreamer, like Bolívar.[16]

Alfredo Bryce Echenique talks about the same thing in his *Antimemorias*, after having spent some time in Cuba and with García Márquez: "If anyone criticized Cuba, in Cuba, and Fidel, right to Fidel's face, it was Gabo. And, if this extraordinary, exuberant writer [. . .] has always been considered the pro-Castrist *par excellence,* maybe the last one left standing, I think that Gabo also lived in Cuba because they left him alone there, he could work in peace, make decisions in peace, be alone when he wanted to be, and because the Caribbean was always his cup of tea, as the Brits would say."[17]

Vázquez Montalbán notes that although many have associated Fidel with Bolívar's iconic image, one could read *The General in his Labyrinth* "as if he were Bolívar, or as if he had nothing at all to do with Bolívar,"[18] and he points out that Gabo himself discounts those who were preoccupied with that sort of speculation, since García Márquez had given Castro the text to read before it was published, as he usually has with all of his novels since the eighties.

Still, the continental, anti-imperial flavor of the revolution Castro started has a decided tint of Bolívar. Both Gabo and Fidel have at one time or another expressed one desire: the unity of the Latin American world around a great socialist experiment. For Bolívar, that unity—minus the socialism component, of course, for purely historical reasons—was an obsession, as García Márquez observes in his novel of 1989: "His ultimate hope was to extend the war into the south in order to realize the fantastic dream of creating the largest country in the world: one nation, free and unified, from Mexico to Cape Horn."[19] And pages later, he recalls the glory of that February 8, 1826, with that triumphant entrance into Lima, and a reception where Bolívar repeatedly stated: "there is not a single Spaniard left in the vast territory of Peru." "That day," García Márquez continues, "confirmed the independence of the huge continent which he proposed to turn, according to his own words, into the most immense, or most extraordinary, or most invincible league of nations the world had ever seen" (80). To be sure, this is only one example of historical inspiration, since the same could be said of other Latin American leaders who came after Bolívar, like Martí; and in general, that vision is something that many of us would like to see realized, although we may not be politicians, or even Latin American necessarily, but we want to guard against the global encroachment of the United States' Anglo-Saxon power structure, and any assertion of Hispanic culture seems as if it were our own.

But the similarities between the two leaders go beyond the desire for a united, powerful Latin America. Within the vast twenty-story apartment building in Havana between Infanta and Manglar streets, Virgilio López Lemus turned on a small light and we found ourselves in a large room, looking out over the horizon. This Cuban poet and scholar, who authored one of the first books published in Cuba about García Márquez, *Gabriel García Márquez, una vocación incontenible*, had invited us over to his apartment, and with the help of some good strong coffee he guided us through the mysteries of astrology. García Márquez is extremely superstitious. He is also very familiar with the lives of Bolívar and Castro. Therefore, it is not likely that he would have failed to notice that they were both Leos. That wouldn't be significant if it weren't for the fact that many of the personality traits they share are ones that any book about the various signs of the zodiac would characterize as typically Leo, and they are also the ones that García Márquez emphasizes the most in his work. The lion is always proud, arrogant, and unusually ambitious, with excellent leadership skills. A Leo is not timid or introverted; he tends to captivate his friends and family with his virtues until they are almost totally dominated. Leos have enviably unshakable convictions, a gift for management, a majestic presence; they tend to cast a disdainful eye on the mediocre, vulgar, or lazy; with an air of superiority, they tell those around them how they should act, and that's why many Leos are educators, politicians, or psychiatrists; they are good public speakers and pay close attention to the image they project, choreographing their gestures and movements in public, making themselves seem almost theatrical; they are or try to be the center of attention almost all the time, wherever they are; they are vain and enjoy being flattered; they have a special sense of organization, and know how to delegate wisely; they have an acute sense of responsibility to care for the disadvantaged or disabled; their behavior is almost always polite and generous; they place an extremely high value on friendship; they are very astute and have a marked ability for coldly rationalizing everything.

So, it doesn't seem so arbitrary that García Márquez emphasizes Bolívar's determination to overcome problems, even triumphing over his own state of decrepitude, since "his resolute gestures appeared to be those of a man less damaged by life" (12), or that he has a philosophy of life as a constant struggle to get what he wants, with no fear of death: "He always considered death an unavoidable professional hazard. He had fought all his wars in the front lines, without suffering a scratch, and he had moved through enemy fire with such thoughtless serenity that even his officers accepted the easy explanation that he believed himself invulnerable. He had emerged unharmed from every assassination plot against him, and on several occasions his life had been saved because he was not sleeping in his own bed" (16). At some points, *The General in His Labyrinth* reads almost like a biography of Fidel, especially when it talks about the ultimate consequences of his revolutionary or political decisions, thwarting his enemies' assassination attempts, ever-brave and optimistic, like someone who doesn't see the dangers in front of him—or doesn't want to see them. The novel talks about Bolívar's "eyes of a happy madman" (26), "intoxicated with glory" (17), about how those who "knew him best asked themselves the reason for his high spirits" (26), or how, when he was at death's door, he overcame his illness: "the General's state of mind did not correspond to his prostration, for he behaved as if the diseases that were killing him were no more than trivial annoyances" (250), and so on, signs of tenacity and courage that we always see in Fidel's public appearances, even in the most difficult times.

But the similarities don't end there. These Leos, full of pride and a fighting spirit, have no stomach for admitting defeat. That word is not in their vocabulary. Bolívar "did not possess the patience good gamblers have, he was aggressive and a poor loser, but he was also astute and fast and knew how to put himself on equal footing with his subordinates" (63). Gabo describes Fidel in the same way: "One thing's for sure: no matter where he is, or when, or with whom, Fidel Castro has come to win. I don't think there's a sorer loser in the whole world. His behavior in the face of a defeat, even when it comes to the smallest things of everyday life, seems to follow an immutable personal law: simply, he won't accept it, and he won't rest until he has turned the tables and made it into a victory."[20] "I never wanted to lose," the Cuban stated in the magazine *Revolución*, "and I almost always fix things so I win."[21]

Just like Bolívar cheated, or celebrated his victories a little too loudly, with too much fanfare (like in the description of the chess game on page 201), or forced his adversaries to keep on playing until he showed them up, Fidel would manipulate any type of competition. Vázquez Montalbán notes: "His sisters say that when he was a little boy, their father, Ángel, bought them baseball equipment so that Fidel could play his favorite sport at the time, but when his team was losing, relying on his authority as the son of the owner of the bats and ball, he would end the game. Some early mornings Fidel has been at the closing of *Granma*, and would start up a game of ping-pong at the newspaper, up to 11 points, but if his opponent reached 11 first, the game would be extended to 21, or even 31 sometimes."[22]

Finally, in addition to the references identifying them with the most typical Leos, García Márquez provides some especially entertaining details about Bolívar, which have much in common with Fidel's likes and characteristics, such as possessing a great memory (71), the habit of showing up someplace completely unannounced, greeting the townspeople and talking with everyone, asking about their everyday concerns (40), the way he would insist that his subordinates be totally with him or totally against him, with nothing in between (73), his knowledge of good cooking and his passion for excellent cuisine (45), and, above all, his love of literature. Gabo has frequently said that his own friendship with Fidel grew out of common tastes in literature, and the Cuban leader's fascination with historical texts is well known, especially the biographies of great historical figures, military history, popular political theory, and so forth.

This is a recurring theme in *The General in His Labyrinth*, and it's likely that when he read the work, Fidel would have seen himself reflected in the description of the general. In the novel's opening pages, reference is made to the book *A Reading of News and Gossip Circulating in Lima in the Year of Our Lord 1826* (7), which is a text about the time and place when Bolívar reached an almost absolute level of power, fame, and glory. The general "had been a reader of imperturbable voracity during the respites after battles and the rests after love, but a reader without order or method. He read at any hour, in whatever light was available, sometimes strolling under the trees, sometimes on horseback under the equatorial sun, sometimes in dim coaches rattling over cobbled pavements, sometimes swaying in the hammock as he dictated a letter" (92–93). When Bolívar, in his autumn, goes into exile, he takes with him a first-aid kit, a few valuables, and books like "Rousseau's *Social Contract* and *The Art of War* by the Italian general Raimondo Montecuccoli, two bibliographical treasures that had belonged to Napoleon Bonaparte and had been given to him by Sir Robert Wilson, the father of his aide-de-camp" (31). The same page makes reference to the six hundred books he had carried with him three years before, at the beginning of his decrepitude, which he had been forced to leave in Quito. And Bolívar also wrote poetry (58), composed metered verses (79), and so on.

Was the publishing of *The General in His Labyrinth*, to García Márquez, an old debt paid? Or something for nothing? We'll never know. What's certain is that the similarities between his friend Fidel and the admirable old hero-general Bolívar are there. *The Autumn of the Patriarch* was published at a time when García Márquez was moving closer to the eye of the hurricane, where power never stops churning, and his two subsequent books would be payment on debts he owed himself: *Chronicle of a Death Foretold* (1981) had been buried in his drawer of ideas for thirty years, waiting for a push, and *Love in the Time of Cholera* (1985) had been another goal of his. On the one hand, it exorcised the image—as he remembered it—of the relationship that bound his parents together; and on the other, it let him experiment with the oldest, most common narrative form in world literature. With those two tasks completed, and before finishing the book of pilgrim's stories that he had been promising since the seventies, 1989 would be García Márquez's year of tribute to two revolutionary icons. As fate would have it, that winter would mark the demise of the benevolent parent gods, battered and defeated by raging, bitter easterly winds.

CHAPTER SEVEN

★

THE "QUEEN OF THE CARIBBEAN": ALL ASHORE

THE FIRST TIME WE HEARD IT, WE THOUGHT THE SONG WAS about a woman: "I want to do it again; I want to be your king. I am your slave, your servant, your protector . . . I have fun with you, and playing, you showed me how to love you, Caribbean Queen." But Málaga is very close to Granada, and a friend informed us that the members of the group Danza Invisible, aside from being great admirers of Cuban culture and performing a pop version of the Cuban song "Yolanda," used to hang out in a bar in their native Málaga and spend hours playing the pinball machine there. They would catapult the ball up to the top of the inclined surface, and as it descended, it would bounce off of objects representing real places in the Caribbean, each assigned a point value. If they succeeded in hitting each target enough times before the ball fell through the flippers at the bottom of the table and disappeared, the screen at the top would total up the points, and if the score was high enough they would win a free game. The name of that pinball machine was "Reina del Caribe" (Queen of the

Caribbean), and whoever got the highest score was the "King of the Caribbean." The members of Danza Invisible, each of whom had probably been crowned King of the Caribbean hundreds of times, wrote that song in its honor.

García Márquez did something comparable in the mid-seventies: Cuba, the "Queen of the Caribbean," bowed down at his feet not only because of his wonderful literature, but also because of his commitment to "spend part of his fame" on Cuban politics. In July 1975, he made a brief trip to the island, and in October of that year, he visited again with his son Rodrigo for six weeks. As a paradoxical counterpoint to the resounding failure of the *yanqui* landing at the Bay of Pigs in the early sixties, which also coincided with Gabo's resignation from Prensa Latina, his landing on Cuban shores fifteen years later would result in an indestructible marriage.

The Hotel Nacional, now renovated and luxurious, was then very modest. It was the first place in which he stayed, and the Diego family, with a reputation for cultivating intellectuals and artists, were his first friends. Eliseo Diego, the father in this illustrious family, is without a doubt one of the best poets to come out of Cuba. He was part of the *Orígenes* generation, along with other acclaimed poets such as José Lezama Lima, Cintio Vitier, and Gastón Baquero. In 1993 he won the international Juan Rulfo Prize, considered the "Latin American Nobel," and death, that little glass jar with hand-etched flowers that's in every home but no one ever stops to look at, surprised him a few months later, in early 1994. Lichi Diego, the best known of his children, would become a close friend of Gabo's, and they collaborated on film projects, first at the Film School of San Antonio de los Baños in Cuba, and later in Mexico. We talked with Lichi in Huelva, Spain, during a summer course at the International University of Andalusia in August 1999; but it was Fefe, one of Eliseo's daughters, who gave us the best peek into Gabo's world in the seventies when she invited us to the

Diego family house in El Vedado, the neighborhood in Havana between Coppelia and the river.

During one of those first trips to Cuba, in the summer of 1975, Gabo showed up at the Diego home, rang the bell, and said, still standing on the doorstep, "I've heard that a really good writer lives here . . . I'm sure I'll be at this house a lot." Theirs were definitely the first friendships Gabo would form in Cuba. Prior to his departure, once he had decided to make the trip, two of his friends in Mexico, Maria Luisa Elio and Jomi García Ascot, to whom he had dedicated *One Hundred Years of Solitude*, told him that they knew some Cuban writers, who could be his first contacts on the island. Said and done! García Márquez and the Diegos hit it off. Eliseo's erudition and warmth immediately connected with Gabo's irony and humor. García Márquez made frequent trips to the island, several each year. Although he stayed at the Hotel Nacional, he would show up at the house in El Vedado every day. Their discussions carried on late into the night, the whiskey flowed freely, and they talked about literature. "Papa liked little-known, unusual novels, about strange themes and esoteric subjects," Fefe recalled. "Gabo knew them all; he had read everything. His knowledge of literature was stunning. And they competed to see who knew the most books." And they talked about their own works too, discussing Eliseo's poetry as well as Gabo's novels.

One evening, the topic of conversation turned to the degree of realism in Gabo's stories. "Papa asked him if that were the case, how could he explain passages like the one where Remedios la Bella ascends to heaven in a sheet," Fefe remembered. "He replied that it was real too, because the townspeople said that a girl from the village had gone to heaven. So, if anyone talked about it, it was because it had really happened." The conversations on those evenings took place in a very relaxed, laid-back, happy atmosphere, full of trust. Gabo was just another member of the family in that house, not the great writer deserving any special treatment. "I would get home from work in the afternoon," Fefe told us, "and I would find Gabo and Mercedes there. They were always together; he almost never came alone. So she was always the one who called first to let us know they were coming. When I saw them there, for me, it was just like seeing my brothers or sisters, or aunts and uncles."

Some others who helped Gabo along in his gradual advance toward Fidel and his inner circle were Norberto Fuentes and Conchita Dumois. In the early seventies, as a young writer, Fuentes had been very close to the highest spheres of power, and he was protected by Raúl Castro. His book *Condenados de Condado*, about the Cuban counterrevolution in the Sierra del Escambray, won the Casa de las Americas Prize in 1968. He continued publishing stories and articles, and he was given access to confidential information to write a piece about the intervention in Angola, coincidentally around the same time that Gabo met Fidel, who suggested that he write some reports on the same subject. Finally, his book *Hemingway en Cuba* (1985) marked a turning point in Norberto's relationship with Fidel, until he was allowed to go into exile, with Gabo's help. Conchita Dumois, on the other hand, had met Gabo fifteen years earlier, when he had been with Prensa Latina. She had worked at the press agency too, and was Ricardo Masetti's second wife. When Masetti and Gabo resigned from the agency and left the island, she stayed behind in Cuba and continued to have a positive relationship with the government. Masetti died in a guerrilla attack in Salta, Argentina; Gabo moved to Mexico. When he came back to Cuba in 1975, he made contact with Dumois again, and she introduced him to Piñeyro, a key figure in the Cuban government who had had a very close friendship with Ricardo Masetti and his son Jorge, and who worked very closely with General Ochoa and General De la Guardia. But what finally got Fidel to notice Gabo was the latter's great report on the island, an excerpt from a book that still has yet to see the light of day.

GOING NATIVE

As his life began to take shape on the "Queen of the Caribbean," our man in Havana returned to publishing journalistic pieces on Cuban subjects. He had done this at the end of the fifties and in the early sixties. Later, he broke ties with the island. Now, especially with his collaboration with *Alternativa*, his position of political support and personal identification with the island became increasingly clear. One of those articles, perhaps the best known, is "Cuba de cabo a rabo" (Cuba from one end to the other). It was originally published in three parts: "The Blockade Nightmare," in issue number 51 of that magazine, dated August 1975; "Why We Need to Have Twins," in issue number 52, also in August; and "If You Don't Believe It, Come See for Yourself," number 53, of September 1975. In 1999, Editorial Mondadori published the fourth volume of García Márquez's collected journalistic work, *Por la libre*, which includes pieces published from 1975 to 1995.

The beginning of the triptych is spectacular; it sets the tone, apologetic and completely supportive, that will dominate the thirty pages of the combined three parts: "The simple truth, ladies and gentlemen, is that in Cuba today, there is not one unemployed person, not one child that doesn't go to school, not one human being without shoes, a place to live, or three square meals a day. There are no beggars or illiterates; there is no one of any age without access to a free education at any level; there's no one without access to free, timely medical care, free medicines, and free hospital services at any level; there is not one single case of malaria, tetanus, polio, or smallpox; and there is no prostitution, no vagrancy, no street crime, no people with special privileges, no police oppression, no discrimination of any kind; there is no one who doesn't have the chance to go where anyone else can go, to see a movie or attend a sporting or artistic event; there is no one who doesn't have the immediate possibility to make sure these rights are honored through means of protest and making a claim which will arrive without rebuff wherever it needs to, all the way up to the highest levels of the state."[1]

Like a modern-day version of the Spanish colonist Bartolomé de las Casas, who has gone over every inch of the island, seen everything there is to see and more, and even has witnesses, García Márquez asserts that no one has told him anything; his conclusions were based on an extensive six-week trip, with a guide and a driver who accompanied him so he would be free to roam around the whole country, from one end of the long verdant island to the other. His level of commitment to the expedition seems to have grown as the days passed: "I went over every square centimeter of the country, from the incredibly beautiful and mysterious Viñales Valley, where the clouds appeared at dawn under the palm trees, to the silent, rambling houses of Santiago de Cuba, whose jasmine-perfumed patios reached the Sierra Maestra, to Pinos Island, which was once a hellish penal colony, where the median age is now fifteen years old, to the spectacular sea of Matanzas, where popular power is awakening. I have talked with workers and soldiers, with peasants and housewives, with schoolchildren and with some of the most powerful leaders of the state, and I believe I have seen for myself that there is not one place on the island which the revolution has not reached with the same intensity, and there isn't one person who doesn't feel responsible for their common destiny. Every Cuban seems to think that if, one day, no one else was left in Cuba, he could, by himself and under Fidel Castro's direction, still go forward with the Revolution until it would reach its happiest phase. For me, this validation has simply been the most emotional, decisive experience of my entire life" (62).

Too perfect to be true. These initial descriptions of the island read as if they were about paradise on earth, and not just in the romanticized style typical of classic Castilian literature. It's not for nothing that a joke has circulated all around Cuba comparing that country with the place inhabited by the very first man and woman:

"You know, I think Adam and Eve must have been Cuban."

"What makes you think so?"

"Well, they didn't have any clothes, they walked around barefoot, they weren't allowed to eat the apples, and they were told that they were in Paradise."

The dramatic oversimplification of life in Cuba found within García Márquez's writings is beyond comprehension. It seems that, judging from his words, absolutely everyone on the island has equal access to all kinds of services and benefits; they are all perfectly happy and are totally committed to the system that has been put in place (not exactly through the ballot box), and they also enjoy complete freedom of movement and liberty of expression. This scenario, which has never occurred anywhere in the history of the universe, not even in societies most faithful to the ideals of Plato, Aristotle, or Rousseau, or in any communist, capitalist, Christian, Protestant, Eastern, or Western government, ladies and gentlemen, is apparently exemplified in Cuba, from top to bottom. When Bartolomé de Las Casas wrote his *Historia de las Indias*, after spending a few decades (somewhat longer than six weeks) living in American territory, he concludes that in Indian cultures there is no theft, no violence against women, no violent death, no heated arguments, no insults, and that, in a real sense, everyone is happy, that is, they are content, while all of the Spanish that have come to the New World are exploiters, uncivilized, and so forth. There is nothing in between. Gabo, the new Bartolomé, doesn't seem to realize that he's not doing the island any favors by presenting only one small slice of what constitutes true, objective information on Cuba. With that beginning, either he's let himself get carried away by his own passion, blinding him to reason, or he wanted to get in good with the Cuban power structure. García Márquez, who in his fiction shuns dull realism and never falls into one-sided, simplistic characterizations, in this instance talks about the good and the bad in absolute terms, cowboys and Indians, those who have stayed on the island and are revolutionaries to the core, and the ones that left and are a bunch of deserters, lured by a big tantalizing piece of capitalist pie.

In the following pages of his article, García Márquez goes on to discuss the blockade and the cowardice of those who have left to go live in the United States or other countries where there are more economic opportunities and higher standards of living, as if it were inexplicable and unacceptable that someone would feel badly when he is persecuted, imprisoned for his way of thinking, fired from his job because he doesn't agree with the government, or simply wants to leave because he doesn't feel free in a country with a one-party political system with obligatory membership, where the means of production are controlled 100% by the state, and where radical equality for all is strictly enforced while the party rulers live in luxury, and friends of the party rulers (including some foreigners) enjoy those advantages too, while the vast majority of the population has no chance whatsoever to improve their social and economic status, unless they leave the country. In the height of simplicity, everything positive in Cuba is because of Fidel and the Revolution, and everything negative that may occur at one time or another, like poverty, shortages, a racial conflict, any public disturbance or challenge to authority, and so on, is a result of the blockade. No one would say otherwise, and we are all aware of the effort represented by a small, weak country's resistance in the face of the imperialism of a world power, but it serves no purpose to adopt an infantile, overly simplified position where everything is the enemy's fault. This three-part report, which is certainly broad in scope and with a commendable level of supporting documentation, loses force, as any argument does, when it becomes a propaganda piece, an apologia for something considered perfect and faultless.

Toward the end of the piece, García Márquez devotes a few pages to Fidel Castro; his undeniable, enviable charisma, his strong public speaking skills, and his intelligence. At that time, they still had not yet formally met, and had yet to form the deep friendship that would unite them from the late seventies onward. But García Márquez was preparing the way. "This maturity," he wrote, "is apparent in every area of daily life in Cuba, and in a very special way, of course, in the person of Fidel Castro himself. The first time I saw him with my own sympathetic eyes was in that great, uncertain year of 1959, and he was telling an employee at the airport to make sure they always had a chicken in the refrigerator, so that the gringo tourists wouldn't believe the imperialist propaganda that the Cubans were starving. He was thirty-two years old then, and he looked bony and pale, with the same sparse adolescent beard that never filled out, and he gave off the impression of physical strength and an iron will that was too big for his body, but something in his eyes revealed the vulnerable heart of a child [. . .]. Those were the times of relentless, obsessive analysis, when he would go on television, unannounced, to explain a specific, challenging problem of the brand-new Revolution, and he spoke without a pause from four o'clock in the afternoon until midnight, without a drink of water, without taking a break to let anybody go to the bathroom, and he sifted through the matter, turning it over and over until he wore it down to its elemental simplicity" (84). In 1975, sixteen years had passed since the triumph of the Revolution, almost the length of time that Gabo had stayed away from the island, and his reflections on the Maximum Leader have to do with another of his literary and personal obsessions: power. Gabo believed that Castro was not the typical Latin American dictator blinded by his own power. We have seen how in *The Autumn of the Patriarch*, there are no indications of direct allusions to the Castrist system, or to the person who holds the keys to all the houses. In an interview in

1975, García Márquez clearly stated that he admired Castro because he had run the risk of power for all those sixteen years, and he hadn't been seduced by it.[2]

BLOCKING THE BLOCKADE: THE FIRST MEETING WITH CASTRO

What truly catapulted García Márquez into the realm of the Revolutionary elite and marked the real beginning of his friendship with Castro were his writings on the embargo, and on the Cuban intervention in Angola. The idea to write a book about the U.S. embargo, to thwart its dire consequences, at least in terms of public opinion, probably began to take shape during his first travels around the island, maybe even earlier. On July 30, 1977, the Cuban newspaper *Granma* affirmed that García Márquez had been working on that subject for three years, since 1974. However, Fefe told us that Gabo didn't talk about the project at first, and it only became a common topic of conversation during his visits to the Diego house in 1976. It was, no doubt, one of his most enjoyable tasks of that time. As research for this journalistic work, Gabo roamed the streets of Havana with a tape recorder or a notepad and pen, and interviewed whomever he came across. His idea was to demonstrate how most of the problems that Cubans faced every day in their work, family, and social lives were consequences of the shortages caused by the *yanqui* embargo. He collected people's anecdotes, and in the evenings he would recount them to the Diego family. He explained, with a great sense of humor and a talent for narrative, how a man tried to force an engine part from a truck into his car's engine, or how a mother could prepare a delicious, seemingly sophisticated meal for her family from poor-quality, limited ingredients, how passengers managed to squeeze themselves into buses and taxis when they were in short supply, how people improvised ropes for clotheslines and hung them up from one wall to the other, trying to keep them taut, and so on.

One story that Fefe shared with us made a striking impression: it was when expensive, imported women's nylon stockings with seams running down the back of the leg were all the rage. Since seamed nylons were not manufactured in Cuba, women would draw a fake seam onto their own nylons with a black felt-tip pen. In the retelling of this ample collection of anecdotes, Gabo found a goldmine of magical, fantastic narrative elements, since he would exaggerate, embellish, and reinterpret, often for humorous effect, the stories that, albeit without quite as much *magical realism*, had actually happened.

Gradually, the project began to take shape, and word of it was getting around Cuba and Latin America. In an exclusive report for Prensa Latina by Bernardo Marqués in June 1976, to be published in *Alternativa* in August of that year, the reporter sat down with the author, who had "come to Havana to continue work on a book about the Cuban revolution: *Cuba: Daily Life Under the Embargo.*"[3] García Márquez first sounds a protective note in response to the questions: "I really don't like talking about books that I'm working on; it seems that the most important thing is to write them. However, I will say this: I'm very wary of historians (I hope they'll forgive me) and I know that they're going to use statistics and data to summarize this period, but the secret battle waged by the Cuban people every day, their imaginative solutions to problems, their moral strength to overcome the embargo without altering their temperament one bit, or losing their sense of humor, I know that will be lost, and I'm trying to make sure that it doesn't get lost."[4] In response to a question about the literary genre of the work, he says that it's "a report, no, it's more like a novel, but you don't have to make anything up here: the reality hands you everything. It's an old dream that I'm finally realizing now. These are a fighting people, a people who know how to defend their rights. If you spend some time waiting in the lines here, or you ride on a city bus or walk around the streets here, you'll know exactly what life will be like once power goes to the people. And now that there are going to be elections in Cuba, elections where all of the people will really take part, the enemy will do whatever it can to silence them. And it's laughable because they've always been talking about the repression in Cuba and the lack of freedoms and lots of other nonsense, and now not a word."[5]

So, it is a work that not only presents some occasionally humorous anecdotes about coping with shortages; it's also an endorsement of the entrenched political system in Cuba in the face of U.S. imperialism. For García Márquez, Cuba is not only a land of optimists; it is also *free*, where all of its inhabitants are apparently satisfied with the regime that governs over them. This contrasts with the proliferation of anecdotes and stories going around the island. For example, on one of the last trips we made to Havana, we ran into an old friend, and asked him:

"So, Oscar, how have things been going, around here lately?"

"Well, we can't complain."

"Great. Things must be going pretty well then."

"No, no, it's that *we can't complain!!*"

Censorship has affected even the intellectuals most committed to the Revolution, including Gabo. In a letter he sent to the Colombian writer Roberto Fernández Retamar from Mexico on November 2, 1976, inviting him to collaborate on an article for issue number 100 of the magazine *Casa de las Américas*, he indicates some of the shifts his research on Cuba and the blockade had gone through; how his vision of the country had changed since the first time he visited in 1959, and what "priorities" his narrative efforts should focus on:

Dear, patient Roberto Fernández Retamar, who Haydee protects in her Blessed Kingdom:

Fayad Jamis told me that it's still not too late, but I'm afraid that it is, although I hope not. In any case, here it is:

it's an excerpt from my book about Cuba that I've selected for you maybe because it's the most personal. I couldn't send it earlier because I wasn't satisfied with my first Baby-lonian vision of the Havana of 1959, and, in trying to create the truest, loveliest evocation, the months have passed, exacerbated by the Colombian communists' ridiculous idea to present me as a candidate for the presidency of the republic: what insanity! So, already having the glory, I left Colombia last week, fleeing from the power, and I've tried hard to fix what I don't like about the article, so far without success. I'm sending it to you a little mutilated, but I'm convinced that the mutilation won't be noticed in an *avant-premiére* of la Casa.

The book still isn't done: first, because the powers-that-be there got me involved in other things of a higher pri-ority, and second, because my hopes that it would be a quick piece of journalism have vanished in a morass of lyri-cism that's like a part of my memories now. In any case, I will be in Havana on November 30, for two weeks, for the installation of the National Assembly.[6]

The "powers that be." By late 1976, Gabo had someone telling him which things were important and which could wait or *should* wait. And he had waited so long that the book still hadn't been published, although it was finished. Waiting. For what? Dasso Saldívar thinks that it will be published posthumously, but he's not sure if it will be after Fidel's death, or after Gabo's, or both. In 1977, García Márquez returned to the task and decided to finish it for good. But he ran into another snag, this time a personal, obsessive problem that surfaced in the writing of every work: the structure. If we briefly review all of his novels, stories, and articles, we will find that they are almost always perfectly designed: the chapter lengths are perfectly proportional, there is uniformity in the passage of time, there are circular structures in the general narrative formats, and so forth. It would be the same with *this* book. He needed to give it the right form to complement its themes, and he couldn't come up with it. In an interview published on November 4, 1977, he explained that he had enough research material to draw from, but that this wasn't enough to actually get him to start: "I have all the material I need, since I have visited the island many times and the Cubans have given me the information I asked for, but I haven't sat down to write it yet because I still don't have— same as usual—the structure. I only have a model: *A Journal of the Plague Year*, by Daniel Defoe, one of the writers who has influenced me the most. It will be a report where I will talk not only about Cuba, about how it knew how to create a culture in the face of adversity, about how it tried a way of life necessitated by the blockade, but also—and more than anything—I will talk about myself and my generation. Because I am tied to Cuba not just for ideological reasons; there are also very strong sentimental, emotional ties."[7]

However, aside from the structural dilemma, Gabo found himself with other vicissitudes that he had mentioned the previous year: "My book will be critical; it won't be simply singing rapturous praises. I believe that by this point, Cuba has done all the damage it could ever do to Latin America, and now comes the time when it will show off its positive achievements. [...] There is much to explain, and, especially, there is much to clear up once and for all."[8] In another interview in 1977, he touched on the same subjects, but in addition to a critical gaze, he adds another ingredient: the quantity of material gathered surpassed his expectations, and now the problem with the structure is even greater because of an excess of information. "My work started out as a report, but it has been expanding, it's branched out and decimated the original structure, and now I'm not really sure what to do with it. I had figured that it would be a book of about three hundred pages, and I've written seven hundred. As I found out about things, my appetite was whetted, to get to the root of certain problems. And the truth is that the book has taken on a life of its own, and it's turned out to be much longer, and even much more critical than how I originally envisioned it. So I've gathered a huge amount of material on various subjects that historians don't tend to focus on, and for that reason alone I think this project was worthwhile."[9] He sometimes makes specific reference to what those subjects are that the historians tend to overlook: "The blockade has developed a real culture of scarcity in Cuba, which is reflected in new ways of raising children, cooking, sewing, and in a thousand little details like, for example, the fact that a woman there will not say to her neighbor, 'let me borrow a needle,' but 'let me borrow the needle.'"[10] A culture of scarcity plus a new mocking sense of humor manifested in the number of jokes going around the island that deal with these themes, like the one about the signs posted at the zoo in Havana. At the start of the Revolution, there was a sign posted at the zoo's entrance that said: "Feeding the animals is prohibited." A little while later, they substituted a new sign which read: "Eating the animals' food is prohibited." Finally, when the real shortages set in, a new sign warned: "Eating the animals is prohibited."

In this interview and others given over the course of that year, Gabo gave similar, consistent answers, giving the impression that, on the one hand, he wanted this material to be published as soon as possible, to help to explain the Revolution from the inside, but also from the point of view of a foreign observer, fully committed to the Revolution. On the other hand, there was one serious problem that made its immediate publication impossible; perhaps its critical tone. For Fidel and the champions of the Revolution, no criticism was constructive if it was made public, because "the enemies could use it" against the imperfect organization. In July 1978, in an interview with Frank MacShane in the *New York Times*, García Márquez said: "It is a critical work, because I am ethically committed to presenting the good things as well as the bad. But I don't want it to be used against the revolution, by people who take quotes out of context. Naturally, some day it will be published, but first I have to finish it."[11] In the interview with *Playboy* in the early eighties, he explained his decision to postpone this book's publication: "It's true. It's a very honest, frank book. It would be very easy for someone to take phrases out of context to attack Cuba. I really don't want that to happen, but that's not why I've postponed publishing the book. Actually, I'm waiting for something big to happen—maybe the lifting of the U.S. embargo—before completely finishing it."[12]

This process we've been following, in relation to the book which tries to block the blockade, is surprisingly similar to what has frequently taken place within Castro's Cuba when the powerful elite deems an intellectual's work to be counterrevolutionary. First of all, the writer does not have to be an enemy of the Revolution (remember the Padilla case). Secondly, the regime judges the work's validity and imposes censorship. In Gabo's case, the censorship came first, because the book never made it to the presses. Almost thirty years have passed since he began writing the book, and more than twenty have passed since its completion. The Colombian writer's loyalty to Castro is, it would seem, indestructible. In addition, the self-criticism (the third step in the process of silencing any intellectual) is, in this case, an example of supreme docility. Gabo, who has always published whatever he wanted, when he wanted and where it seemed best, has a book he has spent years working on buried away in a drawer, produced at a time when he was being considered for a Nobel Prize, between *The Autumn of the Patriarch* and *Chronicle of a Death Foretold*, waiting for Fidel to give him the word and let him continue on in his career, something he, Fidel, will never do.

Apparently, to not directly involve his new, powerful friend in the interview with *Playboy*, Gabo focused attention elsewhere: first, he says that the book could be misinterpreted by the enemy; but then he alludes to some "magical" element, or destiny, or some intuition or act of fate that will ultimately decide when it gets published. Maybe the lifting of the embargo, he suggests. García Márquez knows that the embargo will not be lifted until Fidel leaves power or dies. Basically, he seems to offer any answer instead of revealing the secrets of his relationship with Fidel and the associated limitations it places on him. It is no coincidence that, just as Gabo begins to say that his book is critical and that he "has decided" to postpone its publication, that is, from 1977 on, it is also just around the time when he meets Castro personally and begins to cultivate a friendship with him. Around this time, the Diego family members are not the only ones who are informed beforehand of the writer's visits to the island, of where he will stay and what he will do. By that point, the press, as we have seen, also has that information, and they eagerly await his arrival.

Along with the book about the blockade and the usual questions about his novels, except for *The Autumn of the Patriarch*, a new theme becomes recurring: his written collaborations in relation to the Cuban intervention in Angola. In those efforts, as we shall see, Gabo once again assumes the role of a defender of the Revolutionary cause in Cuba and of its most effective spokesperson in the international public-opinion arena. Fidel, who had been apprised of everything Gabo had been doing around the island, and of all of his declarations regarding the Revolution from previous years, beginning in 1958, and of his unconditional support of the regime, showed up unannounced one day at the writer's hotel for a visit. Interested in the potential international repercussions that opinions voiced by an intellectual of Gabo's stature could have, it was the Cuban leader who sought him out and welcomed him into the fold. Something that Gabo had tried to accomplish for such a long time, with no luck, finally materialized effortlessly, and almost involuntarily. He had become the new king of "The Caribbean Queen." He himself described it at length in the interview with *Playboy*:

García Márquez: But let me really tell you about my friendship with Fidel, because perhaps this is the place to clear up the misunderstandings about it. I'll begin with a story I think is typical.

In 1976 and 1977, I went to Angola to do a series of articles that was published in the *Washington Post*. On the way back from Angola, I stopped in Cuba. Well, in Havana, reporters from Reuters and Agence France Presse asked me for an interview. I told them that I had a seven o'clock plane to Mexico but that they should come by the hotel at four. Around 3:30, Fidel unexpectedly arrived for a talk. So when the journalists dropped by at four, the hotel staff told them they couldn't see me because I was with Fidel.

I told Fidel my impressions of Angola for ten minutes, and then, I don't know why—perhaps because we were discussing the food shortages in Angola—he asked me if I'd eaten poorly there. "It wasn't bad for me," I said. "I managed to find a tin of caviar somehow and I was very happy." So Fidel asked if I liked caviar. And I said, "Very much." He told me that that was a purely cultural, intellectual prejudice and that he didn't think caviar was such an exquisite dish. Well, one thing led to another, and we continued talking for hours about food—lobsters, fish, fish recipes. The man knows everything there is to know about seafood. So when it came time for me to leave for my plane, he said, "I'll take you to the airport." At the airport,

Fidel and I sat in the VIP lounge and talked more about fish—while the plane was held up.

Playboy: A VIP lounge at Havana's airport? Doesn't sound very socialist.

García Márquez: It *is* socialist. There are *two* VIP lounges, as a matter of fact. Anyway, the reporters caught up with us at the airport and apparently said to each other, "If García Márquez has just come from Angola and Fidel has taken him to the airport, then they must be having an extremely important conversation!" So, when I left, the journalists came to the door of the plane and said, "Don't leave without telling us: what were you talking to Fidel about for all these hours?" I said, "I'd better not answer you. If I told you the truth, you'd never believe me."[13]

A personal letter Gabo wrote to the director of the Casa de las Americas on May 21, 1977 corroborates the story he told during the *Playboy* interview. In the letter, he apologized for not having called that Sunday before he left, since that day he went to his hotel and in the afternoon had "a very pleasant, very special visitor" who later accompanied him to the airport.

Having sailed into port, with his boat securely moored, blocking his attempt to "unblock the blockade," Gabo doesn't spend his fame on politics: he invests it. First, we'll see how he does it in Angola, and then we'll circle the globe to see how he approaches other tempestuous political leaders. Having conquered its most daunting island, the Caribbean seems small. America and Europe will be his next targets, with his ship's bow pointing north-northeast, where he would disembark, wearing a traditional Colombian suit, in the hottest winter of his life: 1982.

CHAPTER EIGHT

★

CUBANS IN ANGOLA:
"OPERATION CARLOTA"

ERTRUDIS GÓMEZ DE AVELLANEDA (1814–1873) WAS THE best female Cuban writer of the nineteenth century. A poet, novelist, playwright, and essayist, she was also a noted feminist. In 1853, the year of Martí's birth in Havana, Gómez de Avellaneda petitioned the Academia Española in Madrid to admit her as a member, since her ample body of work had been sufficiently praised by critics and lauded by the public, something which did not happen simply because she was a woman. In 1841, she had published her first narrative work, *Sab*, a novel condemning slavery. Cuba was one of the few countries where slavery was still legal. With this book, Avellaneda did her part in the struggle to end the inhuman, antiquated practice. Two years earlier, another Cuban writer, Cirilo Villaverde, published the first part of his definitive work, *Cecilia Valdes*, in Havana, the completed version of which would not come to light until 1882 in New York. Both novels launched ferocious attacks against a system of government that maintained obsolete structures, because the blacks represented cheap labor for producing sugar and tobacco crops, reaping huge economic benefits for the country. While slavery had already been abolished on the continent, the Caribbean became a rich source of testimonial and activist literature. On November 5, 1854, when Martí was cutting his first teeth, a slave woman in the Matanzas region of Cuba known as "la Negra Carlota" led a group of slaves in a rebellion, in which she lost her life. In tribute to that slave, the Cuban intervention in Angola was dubbed "Operation Carlota." On another November 5, this one in 1975, the Cuban government made the official decision to help the African country.

ANGOLA IS NOT ALONE

In the heart of equatorial Africa, next to Zambia, Namibia, and the Democratic Republic of the Congo, the Angolan people won their independence on November 11, 1975, after five hundred years of colonization by the Portuguese. Unfortunately, in a country where rival political factions wanted power at any price, the situation was far from simple. Civil war broke out.

The three main parties were the MPLA, the FNLA, and the UNITA. The first (Popular Movement for the Liberation of Angola) was led by Agostinho Neto and was supported by Cuba and the USSR. The second (National Front for the Liberation of Angola) had Holden Roberto as its leader and received support from South Africa, China, and the United States. The last (National Union for the Total Independence of Angola) was headed by Jonas Savimbi and was under Zambia's support.

These were the Cold War years, and the two great superpowers wanted to face off in Africa too. Cuba had already been suffering the consequences of the United States' blockade for many years. In early February 1961, the legislation that would establish the trade embargo against Cuba was signed into law in Washington, D.C. This measure represented a very serious problem for Cuba, and it was only able to cope with the situation thanks to the USSR, who proposed buying Cuban sugar at a good price, and also selling Soviet oil to Cuba. With that arrangement, total disaster was averted, and what could have been an even more serious economic crisis was avoided. After that, relations between Cuba and the USSR took on a tone of outright dependence. Without the USSR, Cuba would simply not have been able to survive.

In January 1975, feeling the pressure from the Portuguese and Africans, Neto, Roberto, and Savimbi held a meeting in Alvor, Portugal, where they signed an agreement to establish a transitional government that would represent all three groups. Their intentions were no doubt good; but, unfortunately, outside forces goaded them into continuing the conflict.

In May 1975, Agostinho Neto sought help from Flavio Bravo, a Cuban commander whom he had met in Brazzaville, transporting a shipment of arms. At that time, Neto had raised the possibility of a broader level of assistance and a more specific commitment in the future. Three months later, he was more explicit, asking that a group of military advisers be sent to start up four military training centers.

Cuba sent 50,000 men to support the MPLA, and they stayed in Angola until 1988. Over the course of those thirteen years, 300,000 Cubans would fight in the name of international solidarity.

FIERY WARRIOR: FIDEL WAS THE FIRST

In January 1977, García Márquez published an article titled "Operation Carlota: Cuba in Angola"[1] in the Colombian newspaper *El Espectador*, just as his relationship with Castro's government was becoming more active and intimate. In the piece, he adopted a tone striving for objectivity in describing historic events. In the first lines, García Márquez introduces the different parties fighting for power in Angola, and their respective leaders. Although many insist that the war in Angola is merely a manifestation of Cuba's dependence on the Soviet Union, the author presents it as a struggle to come to the aid of the Angolan party, the MPLA. It's an ideological battle to foment socialism in Angola, a "popular" war,[2] between various groups of people, and unfortunately it's also a "big," "modern," "atrocious" war.[3] In reference to Cuba's participation in the conflict, he utilizes expressions like "assistance of solidarity,"[4] "an action of solidarity,"[5] "political solidarity,"[6] and "international solidarity,"[7] and he emphasizes his favorable impression of the role played by the Cuban people, where, in spite of the serious economic problems caused by the U.S. trade embargo, the "Queen of the Caribbean" rushes to the aid of an African country, with altruism as the sole motivation.

First of all, the Cubans had done even more than Agostinho Neto asked for: "When the Cuban leaders received Neto's request, they did not follow his strict terms; instead, they decided to immediately send a contingent of four hundred and eighty specialists [. . .]. In addition, they sent a team of doctors, one hundred and fifteen vehicles, and adequate communications equipment."[8] Later on, referring to the official decision made on November 5 to help Angola, García Márquez notes that "it was a decision with irreversible consequences, and a huge, complex problem to solve in twenty-four hours. Complexity notwithstanding, the directors of the Communist Party of Cuba did not have over twenty-four hours to decide, so they made a decision without wavering, on November 5th, in a long, calm meeting."[9] He then mentions Cuba's aid to Algeria in the first years of the Cuban Revolution, and then the aid given to Mozambique, to Guinea-Bissau, to Cameroon, and to Sierra Leone, all of which had been taking place since the sixties. "The Cubans' international spirit is a historic virtue,"[10] García Márquez asserts, and he alludes to the Cubans' willingness to volunteer to fight in Angola, explaining the rigors of the selection process, in terms of physical and technical training, as well as "political training."[11] It's very likely that the Cuban government took care to select soldiers of impeccable Revolutionary profiles, to minimize possible criticism of the Cubans in the outside world. Still, "none went by force,"[12] although the peer pressure was almost worse, according to Gabo, than the orders from the top: "Some declined to go after having been selected, and they were subject to all kinds of humiliation and contempt by their peers in public and private."[13]

However, Domingo del Pino, journalist, expresses skepticism regarding this supposed Cuban solidarity, and "the spirit of volunteerism that García Márquez wants to make it seem 'Operation Carlota' had."[14]

In the last part of the article, García Márquez steps up his apocalyptic, sensationalistic tone. He had returned to Cuba after the intervention in Angola began, and he noted that he had been able to observe an almost miraculous transformation in life on the island, even in nature itself: "There has been a striking change not only in the spirit of the people, but also in the nature of things, in the animals, and the ocean, and in the very essence of Cuban life. [. . .] But the most amazing thing is that the repatriated seem aware of the fact that they have contributed to changing world history, yet they act with the natural dignity of somebody who has simply done his duty."[15]

The accolade ends, of course, with Fidel Castro, the superb director of the operation, the very personification of the fighting spirit: "And at that time [early 1975] there wasn't one point on the map of Angola that he couldn't personally identify, not one inch of terrain that he didn't know by heart. His focus on the war was so intense, so meticulous, that he could rattle off any statistic about Angola as if it were Cuba, and he talked about its cities, its customs and people as if he had lived there his whole life."[16] This sort of exaggeration, typical only of writings on the saints, contrasts with the research of Argentinian writer Andres Oppenheimer, presented in his excellent book *La hora final de Castro*, which suggests that Fidel didn't have that kind of knowledge of the African nation he was "helping" and explains how, with the passing of the years, relations between Fidel and Arnaldo Ochoa, the general in charge of operations in Angola, began to cool, because Ochoa began to act on his own. Oppenheimer notes: "Like the other officials in high command in Angola, Division General Ochoa tore his hair out in exasperation every time a new order arrived from Havana. What did Fidel Castro know about battle conditions in Angola, from his air-conditioned offices more than 10,000 kilometers away?"[17]

CUBAN AID, OR SOVIET AID?

García Márquez, as we have noted, presents this Cuban intervention as a mere act of altruism, of solidarity: "In spite of what so many have said, it was a completely independent, sovereign act on Cuba's part, and it was only after the decision was made to help, not before, that the Soviet Union was notified."[18] It was the Cuban people who decided to help the Angolan people, because they needed it. He affirms that Cuba's decision was made completely independently of the USSR, thus obediently confirming what Fidel Castro had himself asserted in his speech given on April 16, 1976, titled "The Twentieth Anniversary Year of Granma." "The Cuban decision was completely under its own responsibility. The USSR, which always helped the peoples of the Portuguese colonies in their fight for independence, and aided Angola by providing basic military equipment, and collaborated with our efforts when imperialism had cut off almost all of our access to Africa by air, never asked for one single Cuban to be sent to that country. The USSR is extremely respectful and careful in their relations with Cuba. A decision of this type could only be made by our own party."[19]

And referring to the U.S. president Gerald Ford and his secretary of state Henry Kissinger, Castro adds that "they lie to the North American people and to the world when they try to make the USSR responsible for the Cuban actions in solidarity with Angola."[20] In his interview with Plinio Apuleyo Mendoza in *El olor de la guayaba*, García Márquez comments: "In analyzing this, the problem is in the point of view: yours is based on the assumption that Cuba is a Soviet satellite, and I believe that it isn't. You only have to deal with Fidel Castro for one minute to realize that he doesn't take orders from anybody."[21]

However, Domingo del Pino reveals a certain skepticism when he asks: "Is it proletarian internationalism in practice on a global scale by a small country of nine million inhabitants, like the regime in Havana, or a service given to the USSR in exchange for their economic support of the Cuban Revolution? Has Cuba become the gendarme of the Soviet Union, as critics of this long-term intervention on the Black Continent charge?"[22] The answer is clear; that's why Castro needed someone from outside of Cuba to support the official version of the Revolution, "and García Márquez did this brilliantly with his unquestionable writer's talent: he tried to show that the Cuban intervention in Africa is an act of pure proletarian internationalism; that Cuba has not become a gendarme of the USSR and that the interests they are defending are of Africa, not of the Soviet Union. [. . .] Nothing to better legitimize this kind of psychological campaign than to attribute an intellectual source [here he clearly refers to García Márquez] to this Cuban political activist who died with her revolutionary reputation intact. This, wrapped up in a pile of secret, wildly imaginative data on the details of 'Operation Carlota,' should give the reader a good idea of Fidel Castro's altruism."[23]

For Gabo, Angola represented payback for all the problems the island had suffered through since the triumph of the Revolution:

"Maybe they themselves were not even aware of the fact that on another, perhaps less generous but more human level, even the less politically passionate Cubans felt rewarded for having lived for so long under unfair setbacks [. . .]. In 1970, when the ten million tons of sugar crops failed, Fidel Castro asked the people to turn the defeat into a victory. But in reality, the Cubans had already been doing that for a very long time, with a determined political consciousness and an unfailing moral strength. Ever since the victory at Playa Giron, some fifteen years earlier, they had had to witness with clenched teeth Che Guevara's assassination in Bolivia, and Salvador Allende's in the midst of the catastrophe in Chile, and they had watched as Latin American guerrillas were slaughtered, and the interminable night that was the blockade, and the accumulated damage of so many past internal errors that brought them to the brink of disaster."[24] Finally, the time had come when they could raise up their hands, forming a "V" for victory with their fingers, smiling from ear to ear: "All of that, aside from the irreversible but slow and arduous victories of the Revolution, must have given the Cubans a feeling of accumulated, undeserved penance. Angola finally gave them the gratification of a major victory, which they had needed so badly."[25]

AFRICA AND CHE GUEVARA: THE ART OF THE RESIGNATION

Che Guevara, the doctor from Argentina, who, his asthma notwithstanding, traveled to any place where a revolution needed to be started, leaving a legacy that history has only served to further idealize, also made his mark in Africa. He had expressed opposition to Soviet systems many times and was not in favor of an overly intense collaboration with the USSR. In an article by García Márquez, Che's presence signifies the first step of Cuba's struggle in Africa. From April through December 1965, the revolutionary was fighting in the Congo for that country's independence. Some of his men went to Brazzaville to form guerrilla units for the PAIGC (African Party for the Independence of Guinea and Cape Verde) and for the MPLA. One of those guerrilla groups clandestinely entered Angola and took part in the fight against the Portuguese. Later, another group would be formed in Dembo, Agostinho Neto's birthplace.

García Márquez considered this fight to be the first step marking Cuba's assistance to Africa, and he established a connection between the two actions, spanning ten years. Beginning in 1965, the ties between Angola and Cuba had begun to strengthen; but Gabo failed to mention one critically important detail, which is that "the man who Cuba accuses of being a pawn of South Africa, Savimbi, was the leader whom Che Guevara supported during his time there to head a revolutionary government in Angola."[26] Gabo, expertly directed by Fidel, seizes on the opportunity to criticize Che's man: "In the west, under Zambia's support, there was UNITA, led by Jonas Savimbi, an adventurer with no principles who had been in constant collaboration with the Portuguese military and the exploitative foreign companies."[27] As César Leante clarifies, "Cuban troops did not go to Africa to combat any imperialism—on the part of Portugal or South Africa—but to support Agostinho Neto against Jonas Savimbi; that is, to decide which of the two major liberation movements in Angola should be in power."[28] With this in mind, it wouldn't seem particularly appropriate to make reference to Che in this context, unless certain facts were not known, or, as is more likely, unless Fidel was guiding the content of the writer's article to affirm and consolidate his leadership and clarify the context in which actual assistance was given. So the Spanish writer Domingo del Pino's affirmation seems plausible when he wrote: "Maybe the most interesting thing about the article published by García Márquez last year in *Triunfo* magazine, titled 'Los cubanos en Angola: Operación

Carlota,' is the association—subtly, indirectly suggested—of Che Guevara with this Cuban military deployment in Africa. Apparently García Márquez, whether he knew what Che Guevara thought about the African guerrillas or not, didn't see anything strange about the fact that it took Cuba so long—exactly eleven years—to get around to fulfilling this moral obligation that Guevara supposedly started in 1964."[29]

Che's experience in Africa had been extremely disappointing, since he had not encountered in the Africans the requisite levels of enthusiasm and maturity necessary to sustain a revolution, another fact that also seems to not warrant mention in another of Gabo's articles, "Los meses de tinieblas: El Che en el Congo." Consequently, as Domingo del Pino writes, "It's surprising that the Colombian writer García Márquez [. . .] has suggested, probably inspired by Fidel Castro, that Cuba, in committing troops to Angola, wasn't doing anything more than fulfilling the moral obligation that had begun with Che Guevara and the African revolution."[30] It's likely that Castro's intention, in suggesting these parameters to Gabo, was to dispel any suspicions about a rupture between him and Guevara, while also confirming Cuba's supposed independence from the Soviet Union.

Before departing Cuba for good, Ernesto "Che" Guevara wrote a letter to Fidel Castro, in which he took his leave from him. In his article "Operación Carlota," García Márquez refers to this historic moment and mentions the date of Che's departure for the Congo, April 25, 1965, the same day the letter was dated, in which he "renounced his rank of commander and everything that legally bound him to the Cuban government."[31] Later in the piece, García Márquez insists that "his [Che's] personal ties with Fidel Castro, which have been subject to great speculation, were never weakened at any time."[32] Once again, Gabo is one of the few "Revolutionaries" authorized to address taboo subjects. Castro wants to project an image of absolute unity between the two colossal leaders (himself and Che), since by that time the Argentine was an unassailable revolutionary icon to the Cuban people. Fidel was aware of the serious repercussions the rupture with Guevara could have on the Cuban Revolution in terms of politics and public morale. As a result, anyone traveling around the island will see posters of Che with provocative Revolutionary slogans all over the place and images that often depict the two leaders in peace and harmony, united by the Revolution. The clearest example of this image appropriation is the monument, comparable to the statue of Martí in the Plaza of the Revolution, which was erected in Santa Clara, the same place where Guevara's remains were eventually buried. Around the gigantic statue of Guevara are other objects, most notably a large rectangular stone slab which has the text of Che's letter to Fidel carved into its front face—which offers, as we shall see, proof of Fidel's betrayal. Domingo del Pino discusses the rupture and tries to shed some light on circumstances and intentions. To him, it's very clear that in Africa, Che "had established great communications with Algerians who shared his thesis on Soviet 'neoimperialism,' a position that he initially formulated at the School of Economics in Algiers in 1964 and was probably the last argument to be added on to his list of discrepancies with Castro."[33] Divergences that extended into deeper, less immediately apparent areas: "This pessimism concerning Africa, and some basic deformities in the Cuban Revolution which he seemed to anticipate, like the growing influence of the USSR, the role of the unions, [...] were his last, almost desperate efforts to support the Cuban Revolution."[34]

But the definitive rupture between Fidel and Che would play out in a much more dramatic scene. One of the people we interviewed, who wished to remain anonymous, a person who is very close to Gabo and to many of the main protagonists of the Cuban Revolution, assured us that Che knew he was being pushed aside in Fidel's experiment much earlier, when Castro unabashedly took cover under the protective wing of the USSR. Che was not only a nuisance: in the end, he was treated as "the foreigner." When he returned from his trip to Algeria, he met with Fidel, Raúl, and other high functionaries of the Revolution. He gave them a detailed, comprehensive report on what he had seen. Suddenly, he spit and said: "I don't want this shit for Cuba and Latin America. Substituting one unjust system for another is not the point of the Revolution; exchanging a system of plutocrats and oligarchs for another where the privileged lead the Party and its bureaucracy, while the people are drowning in poverty and problems, forget it." After he spoke these words, there was a very heated argument, with very strong words and insults exchanged between Che, Fidel, and Raúl. Biographers of Che like Castañeda and Taibo II talk about a meeting that went on for forty hours, starting at the airport on March 15, 1965, when Fidel and Raúl went to pick up Che, arriving from Algeria, and that the meeting was very violent, almost to the point of physical aggression. From then on, Che completely disappeared from the realm of Cuban politics.

Regarding Che's final days in Cuba, del Pino maintains that "Che was busy training his Bolivian guerrillas, arguing exhaustively with the Cuban regime leaders, with Castro, over their serious disagreements, and to the extent possible trying to repair the damage, relying on his unquestionable authority, from the abuse committed by the regime on the Cuban Trotskyites who had been arrested because of the polemic stirred up in Cuba stemming from Che Guevara's intervention in the Algerian School of Economics, which the Trotskyites supported. In a final exercise of his authority with the Cuban Revolutionaries, Che Guevara managed to secure the release of a good number of those detained, although he was not successful in getting them permission to return to their jobs."[35]

To make sure that the "Guevara epidemic" had been permanently stamped out, Castro decided to read Che's personal letter to him in public. With that, Pierre Kalfon, Che Guevara's biographer, asserts: "Castro definitely takes the pressure off [he is referring to the pressure exerted by the Cuban people, who don't understand Che's abrupt disappearance] [. . .] but at the same time—his action is very savvy—he in effect prevents Che's open return to Cuba. That is how Guevara interprets it, deep in the jungle."[36] Che himself described his profound disappointment: "That letter should only have been read after my death. Being buried alive is no fun."[37] Pierre Kalfon's reflections are clear: "If the aforementioned quote from Che is authentic—and it seems that it is, judging from the various testimonials verified by Alarcón himself—it represents a radical transformation in Guevara's mental attitude toward his mentor. Had Castor just sacrificed Pollux? Had the beautiful, wondrous friendship between the Argentine and the Cuban been dealt a death blow that day? From that moment, the general perspective on the relations between the two men demands a revision. Although Castro would not openly abandon Guevara, Cuba's doors would be closed to him."[38] With that, the High Commander assured his solitary rule, dissimulating any rupture, and simultaneously disguised his very real dependence on the Soviets, convincing his people that a small island, so strategically located, could somehow rise above international political winds, in the middle of a cold war, when the entire world was either capitalist or socialist. Gabo, who from that point was becoming just another member of the regime, was once again Castro's messenger. The carrier pigeon flew swiftly, but there were still many kingdoms to be reached.

★

CHAPTER NINE

FLYING HIGH

"THE SUPPER WAS AT THE HOME OF DANILO BARTULIN and his wife, Maria Jose, and there's an old story about them and a few kilos of chorizo. Knowing that I was going on a trip to Cuba, Carmen Balcells, my literary agent, once gave me some chorizos to give to Maria Jose and Danilo, chorizos that were confiscated by customs, news I relayed by telephone to my sausage-deprived hosts whom I had yet to meet. Now I have met them. She is descended from that excellent race of Spanish women, tall and slender like her mother, as the song goes, and he had been chief of security under Allende, fleeing the Palacio de la Moneda at the last minute, by express orders from the president, who wanted to be left alone with his death. Now, Bartulin imports elevators, and once in a while he manages to import Iberian sausages, which customs don't have a problem with any more, an effective strategy to eat chorizo in Cuba without anybody hassling you. We ate and drank, enough to bust a gut; and Gabriel García Márquez, Mercedes, his wife, one of Gabo's brothers, Jaime, and his wife, Jesus Aznarez, a correspondent from El País in Mexico, Mauricio Vicent, Jesus Quintero, El Loco de la Colina, the hosts and I talked about everything, and Gabo was reminded that just after he won the Nobel Prize, having some rice and beans that Nieves Muñoz Suay had made for lunch, and Ricardo was there, Gabo had said that since he had won the Nobel Prize, from now on he would only talk to dukes and secretary generals. I warned him of the increasing problems he's going to have in a world where fewer and fewer dukes are appointed, and secretary generals are a race on the way to extinction."[1]

In early 2003, we told Manuel Vázquez Montalbán, who wrote the previous words, that our dream would have been to have written the book he had authored about Cuba, one of the most vivid renderings of the last half century of Cuban history and its supreme leader, with all the associated politics, culture, economics, and personalities from the worlds of religion, academics, et cetera, using the Pope's visit as the backdrop. We envy him partly because of his large supply of colorful anecdotes, like the one we just cited, which featured Gabo and the Cardinal of Havana, and Cuban and Spanish government ministers. But what intrigues us the most is what García Márquez said as soon as he had won the Nobel Prize, about the dukes and secretary generals. Certainly, within the time frame between the events we discussed in the previous chapter and when he won the coveted award, some years passed during which García Márquez indeed prepared himself politically for that honor. It came as a surprise to no one that the Nobel laureate was also wrapped up in politics. In 1980, Gabo himself talked about "the political criteria that predominate in the heart of the Swedish academy."[2] And to demonstrate this, he recalled that in 1938, Hitler had barred any German from receiving the prize, because its founder was a Jew; and that the Academy awarded the Nobel Prize in Literature to Winston Churchill, simply because he was a greatly admired man of prestige, and there was no other more appropriate way for them to honor him; and that Pasternak refused to accept the prize in 1958 for fear that he would not be allowed to return to his country. On the subject of political injustice, in our Latin culture, just ask Vargas Llosa or Borges. In 1980, referring to the former, García Márquez wrote that "he is the writer of the highest artistic merit in the Spanish language, and they can't claim to exclude him, out of pity, from the annual predictions. The bad part is that the final result isn't based on the actual worthiness of the candidate, or even on divine justice, but on the inscrutable will of the members of the Swedish Academy."[3] To wit, the justification offered for why Borges would never receive a Nobel Prize and why Artur Lundkvist, a permanent secretary of the Academy, said as long as he lived, the Argentine would never get it, was very well explained by Gabo in the same article:

What's certain is that on September 22 of that year [1976]—one month before the vote—Borges had done something that had nothing to do with his masterful literature: he had formally met with Augusto Pinochet. "It is an undeserved honor to be received by you, Mr. President," he said in his unfortunate speech. "In Argentina, Chile, and Uruguay, liberty and order are being restored," he continued, without any encouragement. And he concluded impassively: "This is happening in a continent overrun by anarchy and undermined by communism." It's easy to assume that all these successive inanities were only meant to make fun of Pinochet. But the Swedish do not understand the Argentine sense of humor. Ever since then, Borges's name has been absent from the nominations. Now [1980], after an unfair penance, it has reappeared, and nothing would make those of us who are his insatiable readers as well as his political adversaries happier than to see him finally free of his annual anxiety."[4]

Some people will receive the prize who don't deserve it; and others, well deserving of the honor, will die without receiving it; some will win it through politics; and still others, as in García Márquez's case, will have received it for both reasons. García Márquez is a sensational writer, and no less sensational an "emergency" politician, as he puts it. His campaign for the Swedish Academy in the late seventies contrasts with some statements he had made to Juan Gossaín in 1971 for Bogota's *El Espectador*, claiming that he would like to win the Nobel Prize once he had earned so much money from his book sales that he could refuse the prize without any regret, because the prize had become "a huge international spectacle." Eleven years later, either it wasn't a spectacle any more,[5] or he didn't think that the millions of copies of his books he had sold, and the money he earned from that, was sufficient to turn down the prize; or, perhaps, he had just changed his mind. We tend to think that his decision had to do with the political consequences to be gained from the prestige associated with the prize, for since the eighties he has not hesitated to use his power for political purposes. He also declared, after soaring so high, that he would never accept another literary prize again, since the Nobel Prize was the very height of glory, and he had to leave the rest of the awards to the many writers who were deserving of them. He has kept that promise to this day, and fate has winked at him conspiratorially for this show of faith. Vargas Llosa told us that in 1997, he was a member of the jury that awarded the Cervantes Prize. That year, García Márquez was chosen as the winner, he declined to accept it, and a new winner was immediately chosen for the "Nobel" of Spanish letters: Cabrera Infante, one of the writers who has often taken García Márquez to task for his collaboration with the Castro regime, calling him "our man in Havana," borrowing the title of a Graham Greene novel, and accusing him of having a very serious case of "Castroenteritis."

What García Márquez has never turned down is power, but only his own brand of it. He was twice invited to run for president in Colombia, but he summarily rejected the offer. "President of Colombia? I'm too serious for that," he once remarked.[6] On November 13, 2002, seated around a table in the lobby of the Hotel Habana Libre, Angel Augier, a Cuban poet who had worked with Gabo at Prensa Latina, told us that on one occasion, shortly before receiving the Nobel Prize, García Márquez had been at the UNEAC offices when Augier was vice president and Nicolás Guillén was president of that prestigious Cuban institution, head-quartered in a beautiful mansion in El Vedado. As he was leaving the offices one day, García Márquez invited the two Cubans to have a drink with him at La Bodeguita del Medio, located on a busy street in Old Havana, near the cathedral. The recently appointed Cuban ambassador to Colombia was also there. García Márquez remarked: "Don't accept the appointment, because Bogotá is uninhabitable." García Márquez doesn't want power as such; he simply admires it and is obsessed by being around it. One of his best-known sayings is "I have a great fascination for power, and it's no secret."[7] His way of getting close to it is by moving in the same social orbit as those who possess and use it, and to have some influence over them, but without having to make the decisions himself.

Betancur, the conservative Colombian president from the early eighties who congratulated García Márquez as soon as he won the Nobel Prize, following a period in which Gabo had exiled himself from Colombia, recalls that he offered him various government posts and the ambassadorships in Madrid and Paris, but he was always turned down. "He likes to be close to power, but not to take it,"[8] Betancur concluded. One of Gabo's greatest pleasures is confirming that he can call Castro on the phone for any reason, at any hour of the day or night, with the assurance that his call will be taken. And that's not all: he knows that the presidents, dukes, and secretary generals who are really his friends will do arbitrary things he asks of them, to satisfy his peculiar method of exercising power. This is the case when political prisoners are freed upon his request, which we will discuss in more detail, and also with more mundane matters.

Dasso Saldívar is, no doubt, the man who knows Gabo the best, judging from his spectacular biography *García Márquez: El viaje a la semilla*, published by Alfaguara in 1997, and by the insightful information he provided us in a steady stream of e-mails. Saldívar told us that in the early eighties, right before he won the Nobel Prize, but already firmly ensconced in the highest echelons of power, García Márquez wanted to celebrate his mother's birthday on July 25. As he had left his home country and was living in Mexico, Fidel lent Gabo his private jet and had him flown to Colombia incognito, so that he could spend a wonderful evening with the daughter of the telegraph operator from Aracataca. Power and its trappings had begun to be like a toy to him. But Castro hasn't been his only political playmate. There are many powerful men, and the wheels of power don't always turn slowly.

In the late seventies, Gabo also worked with various organizations that struggled against certain abuses of power, or that fought for political and humanitarian rights. Through the magazine *Alternativa*, he helped create the FIRMES movement, which, for a while, successfully realized its goal of overcoming the differences between various Leftist groups, forming a broad, progressive front. In late 1978, he founded the Latin American Organization for Human Rights (HABEAS), which was funded in part with various grant awards and a share of his author's royalty earnings. Through that organization he appealed to Colombian president Julio César

Turbay Ayala (1978–1982), regarding the torture political prisoners were subject to in his country.[9] But his most decisive intervention was definitely with the Russell Tribunal, starting in 1975. The first tribunal was held in 1961 and had been created by the English philosopher and mathematician Bertrand Russell to judge the war activities of the United States in Vietnam. Another tribunal was held in 1973 and again in 1976, to denounce human rights violations and repression in Latin America. In an interview in 1975, García Márquez describes how he was elected vice president, and why he accepted:

The Russell Tribunal proposed that I take part in it, and I accepted. First of all, I accepted for this reason: I am not a political leader; I do not have a vocation to be a leader. I know that I could not be one, I would be a bad leader, I'm not going to attempt it; I don't play to lose, and I'm sure that I would lose. That's why I don't belong to any organization, I'm sort of a loose cannon. I run the risk of not knowing exactly what should be done; so instead I make statements, take part in protests, send telegrams every time arrests are made, every time that someplace in Latin America or anyplace else in the world there is some injustice [. . .]. The most interesting thing about the Russell Tribunal to me was, and still is, its power to throw a media spotlight on the problems of Latin America. It's like an echo chamber [. . .]. To put it even more crudely: it's a big theatrical production we're staging to publicize the situation in Latin America.[10]

AS A RESULT . . . PRESIDENT FELIPE

One of the best-known trademark phrases of former president of Spain Felipe González was "por consiguiente" (translated "as a result"). All of the political humorists and impersonators of our country made good use of his "por consiguientes," which conveniently rhymes with "presidente." Nobody remembered Adolfo Suárez's "Puedo prometer y prometo" (I can promise and I do promise) any more, and Aznar hadn't appeared on the scene yet with his "España va bien" (Spain's doing great), the catchphrase he was somehow able to shout without even moving his moustache. Gabo's friendships with Felipe and other European and Latin American socialist leaders either began or were cemented, in almost every case, in those years of the seventies up to the early eighties. He first met González in a crowded hotel room in Bogotá in 1975. It's a shame that we were not able to talk to the former president of Spain for this book. For a year we tried to firm up a date to meet, but in the end it never worked out. His secretary always told us that he didn't have time, and when we gave him the open-ended timeframe of a year and a half to squeeze in an interview, he never responded. He really must be very busy, judging from the dust that must be gathering on the seat reserved for him in Parliament, which has often been vacant when we have seen the Congress of Deputies on television. And perhaps he's simply in no rush to collect the attractive monthly salary that all of those men of good faith who represent us and govern us with such tenacity receive, religiously and punctually, even if they're in the opposition. Maybe the speaking engagements pay better, with fewer headaches. The fact is that in 1975, he went to Colombia as Spain's socialist leader, at a time when his country's political structures were in a state of flux, in anticipation of the end of Francoism. Representing the magazine *Alternativa*, Enrique Santos Calderón, Antonio Caballero, and García Márquez went to the hotel where Gonzalez was staying to interview him. This is how Gabo described what took place:

The truth is that somehow he, as well as we, all understood

that that interview was just a pretext, and we agreed to meet the next day to talk without any other witnesses or microphones. Felipe took the initiative for that meeting, in a place that was comfortable and also wouldn't draw suspicion: between the shelves of a bookstore, where the customers, completely absorbed, barely noticed we were there. It seemed to me that that way of being almost invisible, but without having to hide, was an everyday habit for Felipe, having lived through so many years of bad times in Spain.[11]

That was only their first meeting. They hit it off right away; but the friendship would come later, aided by Omar Torrijos, another one of the great socialist presidents that made up that elite class of "dukes" and "secretary generals." In the latter half of the seventies, they would meet again in some of the various houses the Panamanian president had in his country. This is how Gabo remembers it in the article that he wrote shortly after visiting with González, then president, in the presidential palace in Moncloa:

One arrived with almost no advance warning at the old military base in Farallon, where the indomitable waves of the Pacific never let up, or at the Paraíso, tucked away on Contadora Island, and you always ran into someone who had something to say about Latin America's destiny, and Central America in particular, especially three people who must have been key in the long, difficult battle over the recuperation of the Panama Canal: Carlos Andrés Pérez, Alfonso López Michelsen, and Omar Torrijos himself. Among them, the young Felipe González—who was only around thirty years old, while the others were already presidents—seemed like just a privileged disciple who was just as knowledgeable and concerned as his teachers about

when he would take a turn at the pulpit. His road to victory has been so explosive that it seems as if that all took
place a very long time ago, lending a historical distance for
analysis. Maybe that was why, when I saw Felipe González
strolling through the grounds at Moncloa, I had such a hard
time getting used to the idea that our friend from vacations
in Farallon and Contadora had become the president of his
country's government, at barely forty years old.[12]

They met not only in Panama, but also at other points on the
Latin American map, like Mexico and the San Blas islands. They
have discussed Latin American politics at such length that García
Márquez readily admits that "Felipe is the best specialist in Central
American issues that I know."[13] And he emphasizes that this is not
an exaggeration, since "I don't know anyone who is not Latin American with such a strong interest in our fate, perhaps aware that, in a
way, Spain's fate could be tied with ours."[14] So he concludes that,
after having talked with González on specifically Latin American
subjects, he has "learned a lot about who we Latin Americans and
Spaniards are and where we are headed, and the conviction that our
paths will continue to cross, and we should walk down stretches of
that road together, and that Felipe could be a decisive leader not
only for Spain, but also for our common destiny."[15]

The trio was complete with Felipe's venture into Cuban territory. Although the arguments and standoffs between Castro and
González are well known, it's reasonable to assume that Gabo would
have talked with Fidel on numerous occasions, encouraging him to
support the Spanish decisionmaker, and also discussed the situation
in Cuba with Felipe, the model of a hoped-for "common destiny."
The upshot was that in spite of the disparity of opinions, in the
mid-nineties, at a very critical juncture, in the midst of Felipe's
sharp criticisms of a long list of Fidel's positions and the depressed

conditions on the island in general, González sent Carlos Solchaga, no longer Minister of the Treasury but still the most lucid analyst on the economics of Spanish socialism, to Cuba as a special envoy. Solchaga tried to convince the Cubans, especially Castro and Lage, of the need to make a change and open up a market economy, suggesting that they had been maintaining a situation of "subsidized revolution"[16] and that he had to tell his people that he was obligated to reconsider some of the positions he had zealously defended up until that point on the means of production and so forth. But Castro responded: "Look, Solchaga, you may be right; but somebody else is going to have to do what you're talking about."[17]

TORRIJOS, THE MATCHMAKER

The Panamanian leader, who was the bridge for the friendship between Felipe and Gabo, seized power by force in his country in 1969, and made contact with the writer from Colombia very early on, before any other political leader. Torrijos was not a Marxist, but he admired Tito and Fidel, and supported the Cuban leader's interventions in Guatemala, El Salvador, and Nicaragua. García Márquez voiced very sharp criticism questioning his motives for seizing power, and the Panamanian wanted to talk to him and try to persuade him of the integrity of his intentions. That first meeting was later characterized by García Márquez as marking the beginning of their friendship, over a three-day visit.[18] After that, they got together many times, until Torrijos died in a plane crash in 1981. One of the things that struck Gabo the most about his friend was his ability to stay up all night, thanks to the stimulating effects whiskey had on him, and that he usually had six women always standing by "on high alert" in case they were needed. Shortly after Torrijos's death, Gabo wrote an emotional article about him (August 12, 1981) where he commented that in recent years he had traveled to Panama at least two or three times per year, just to visit him and their mutual friends, and that he usually stayed in a hotel. But on his last visit, on July 20 of that year, he had stayed in one of Torrijos's many houses, this one in the capital, which was rarely used. On that trip, Gabo and some others had been invited to a dinner by his friend. At the end of the evening, although the president's secretary said that they had to go to attend an official event, Torrijos gave the order to have a helicopter and also a plane prepared for takeoff, indicating that he still hadn't decided what his destination would be. Gabo remembers it like this, once he returned to the room he was staying in that night:

He said that night, as he had said on so many others: "What I like most is that I never know where I'm going to spend the night." No one knew. Only once his helicopter and plane were prepared for takeoff would he tell the pilot where they were going. That night was no exception. When I got back from the dinner, I found the house lit up, but empty and silent, and I understood that he had left just a little while earlier, since the smell of his cigar still hung in the chilly air. I never knew where he had gone, but now I know that I would never see him again after that night.[19]

García Márquez wrote several articles about Torrijos in the late seventies and early eighties, all of them very flattering and punctuated with his reflections on the various current crises in Central America, the same situations he had discussed with Felipe González and other socialist leaders. Aside from the article in 1981 paying tribute to his deceased friend, other interesting pieces include "El general Torrijos sí tiene quien le escriba" in the May 1977 issue of *Alternativa*, about the potential problem of the CIA infiltrating leftist and other radical groups of the Left in exile in Panama to destabilize the situation in the Canal Zone; and "Torrijos, cruce de mula y

FIDEL AND GABO

tigre," from *Alternativa* in August 1977, about the sovereignty of the Panama Canal and the economic consequences for Central America. With the latter article, García Márquez emphasizes the positive aspects of Torrijos's rule, focusing on his personality. Gabo underscores his natural ease, his forthrightness and courage, as Torrijos demonstrated when he remarked to a high-ranking U.S. official during negotiations with Carter: "The best thing for you to do would be to give us the Canal back gracefully. If you don't, we're going to screw you around for so many years that in the end you yourselves are going to say:'Here, take your goddamn canal and stop screwing us already."'[20]

García Márquez's intervention in this matter was not limited to giving personal advice. At the final moment when the treaty on the Canal was signed in Washington in 1977, Graham Greene and García Márquez went along with Torrijos as members of a Panamanian delegation, completely drunk, to the United States, which had denied them visas for decades because of their radical Leftist politics and their criticisms of *yanqui* imperialism. Torrijos wanted to have them there to assure the success of his negotiations, but also to show his eccentric side one more time and as a mischievous jab at his political enemies. Gabo recalls that it all started as a way of making fun of the U.S. prohibition on writers that had been in place for quite some time. The Panamanian president was planning a trip to the United States, and "When they were finalizing the list of delegates that would go to Washington, Torrijos got the idea of smuggling me and Graham Greene into the country, like contraband. It was an obsession: a little while before that, he had suggested to Greene that he dress up in a National Guard colonel's uniform and go to Washington on a special mission to see Carter, just to play another one of his usual practical jokes on him [. . .]. When General Torrijos asked if we wanted to attend the treaty ceremony as ourselves, but carrying official passports from Panama and as members of that country's delegation, we both accepted with childish delight [. . .]. Conscious of the literary weight of the moment, Graham Greene said to me, as we stepped down the plane's stairway: 'My God, such things go on here in the United States.' Carter himself could only laugh with his TV-star smile when General Torrijos told him about his little prank."[21]

Once the negotiations were finished, Gabo followed the exercise of the agreements very closely, and especially the stability of the Caribbean and Central America, where Cuba sat on the Queen's throne. In his February 21, 1981 article about Alexander Haig, Reagan's Secretary of State, who was dubbed "Reagan's Kissinger," he warns the entire region to be on high alert in the face of the hard-line political stance that Haig had initiated. He observed that "El Salvador is in flames," that "Nicaragua has yet to get a good night's sleep," and that Cuba "is on the brink of war again," ever since the night that Reagan was elected. Regarding Panama, he said that its government "is the first to directly experience General Haig's imperialistic vocation and iron-fisted style, through a puzzling message that was relayed last week [. . .], [in which he] praises the good relationship between Panama and the United States. He praises it because the Panamanian government would have held elections in 1980 and planned to hold them again in 1984. He understands that there are relations between Cuba and Panama, but he is worried that they may be too close, and he is especially concerned that the commercial trade between the two countries is undermining the blockade imposed by the United States more than twenty years earlier [. . .]. He is worried about the presence of a Cuban ship in Panamanian waters, and that Cuba uses Panama to send arms and trained personnel to El Salvador."[22] Next, the writer enumerates the objections and protests of the Panamanian government to Haig's words, and concludes with a loaded remark from Torrijos: "I'm having this message 'returned to

sender' since it was sent to the wrong address. It should have been
sent to Puerto Rico."[23]

A NEW ALLY: THE SANDINISTAS

Gabo's commitment to Central America has also meant partici-
pating in negotiations to end the civil wars in El Salvador and
Nicaragua. He has collaborated with some regularity in securing
the release of hostages on both sides of the conflicts, and has tried
to ensure international protection of the Sandinista revolution,
since he has hosted the leaders of that movement in his home in
Mexico when the struggle was still underground, and he took part
in the negotiations which culminated in the unification of three
opposition groups into the Sandinista Front.[24] Sergio Ramírez, a
Nicaraguan writer and politician aligned with the Sandinistas who
would eventually reach a high position in the government,
described his relationship with Gabo: "We met in Bogotá, in
August 1977, when I came to ask for his help in the plot to remove
Somoza, and he met with me that time in the RTI studios, where
they were working on a series based on *The Evil Hour,* in an office
filled with TV monitors and videotapes, and it was no trouble at all
to convince him that the triumph of the Sandinista revolution was
at hand, since the planned offensive against the National Guard
would be unstoppable, and what we needed him to do was to go
to Caracas and have him suggest to president Carlos Andres Pérez
that he recognize the new government that would be led by Felipe
Mántica, the owner of a supermarket chain in Managua, as soon as
we set foot on Nicaraguan soil, since all of the members of this
secret government were then living in exile in Costa Rica."[25]

García Márquez, on the one hand eager to help the Sandinistas,
and on the other to demonstrate that his natural role is as an intermediary who plays with power and manipulates it by controlling
those who have it, was excited by the idea and went on the requested

trip. Ramírez continues: "He obediently went to Caracas, he told the president that unlikely story, and he believed it, and if we didn't triumph right then in any case it wouldn't be long, since the guerrilla forces marched into Managua on July 19, 1979, less than two years later. He came to Managua shortly thereafter, and he stayed with Mercedes for quite a while in our house, that house shaded by huge tropical trees that we don't live in any more, that's now occupied by a Taiwanese businessman. Now, with so much water under the bridge, and now that I'm far removed from that revolution so twisted by greed, his only casual remark on the subject is laconic, and hits the nail on the head: 'They screwed me over.'"[26]

Teodoro Petkoff, a leader of MAS (a radical leftist Venezuelan party in opposition to the communists), ex-presidential candidate for his party and director of the weekly *Talcual*, corroborates this important diplomatic gesture, but from a different perspective. He remembers that in the latter half of the seventies, García Márquez called him on the phone to let him know that he was going to Caracas incognito, that he didn't want to see anybody, and that he would explain when he got there. Once he arrived, he told him that he had been sent by Fidel Castro, not by the Sandinista leaders, to negotiate with Carlos Andrés Pérez, then-president of Venezuela and tireless defender of the interests of the progressive presidents in Central America, but since he didn't know him he needed Petkoff to get to him. The MAS leader didn't have any problem acting as the middleman, since at the time, he says, "the opposition and the government still treated each other civilly in Venezuela."[27] He summarizes Gabo's mission in these terms: "The Sandinistas were planning the first 'final offensive'—which failed, before the second, successful one—and they wanted to form a sort of provisional government in Nicaraguan territory, and in order to do this they needed international recognition. They hoped to get it from Perez. And they discussed material aid, and I think that was the beginning of Carlos Andrés Pérez's ties with Nicaragua, which, years later, no longer siding with the Sandinistas but with their opposition, would eventually be his downfall, resulting in his arrest. That time, a few hours before his departure, Gabo pulled off another one of his tricks: since, according to his wishes, no one knew about his trip there, he arranged an interview with me, for *El Nacional*, which was a great literary scoop, but also political: Gabo had come to Caracas solely to talk to 'his party.'"[28]

But the reality was much more complicated. It wasn't just about supporting the Sandinistas because they were Leftist revolutionaries, but more than anything it was about toppling Somoza, given his cozy relationship with the United States, since Carter supported maintaining stability in Nicaragua to make sure that the Sandinista Front didn't establish another regime like their neighbor Castro's in Central America. And there was one more thing: Somoza didn't have oil, since Venezuela had stopped supplying the Central American country, and Carter took over that function himself. In a long report published in *Alternativa* in 1978, featuring Gabo in a starring role, the diplomat-at-large offered some clear-eyed responses:

ALT: Moving on to other latitudes, it's well known that you have been involved in various high-level efforts relating to the crisis in Nicaragua and, more specifically, with the Sandinista movement. How do you view the situation in Nicaragua right now, and the Sandinista perspective?

GGM: One thing that I don't think has been emphasized enough is that the Sandinistas not only remained intact after the last offensive: they grew even stronger politically and militarily. Some may be under the impression that they were wiped out, when actually the National Guard never faced the Sandinista Front. The strategy they used was to bombard and massacre the civilian population. It seems that Somoza, surely under the advisement of the United States, thought that if the support of the civilian population disappeared, the Sandinistas would not get a second chance. And just the opposite happened. The people were outraged by Somoza's brutality and the Front was strengthened.

That tactic of finishing off the Sandinistas has been Carter's position from the beginning. It would have been very hard for Somoza to have survived the last general strike without oil. But Carter sent it ever since Venezuela cut them off. That's why there was a flurry of correspondence between Carlos Andrés Pérez and Carter; Carlos Andrés Pérez with his view that the highest priority is to topple Somoza, and Carter's view that Somoza cannot fall as long as the Sandinista Front exists, because they want to establish a regime like Cuba's in Nicaragua. [. . .]

Fortunately, the anti-Somoza forces, especially the Sandinistas, have had the firm, open, and we could say even brazen support of Carlos Andrés and Torrijos.[29]

The Colombian author's intervention seems, in every respect, to have been decisive, and the connections with Cuba's interests are clear: it is Castro who sends him to Venezuela to negotiate with Pérez, the same Pérez who got together with Torrijos and Gabo in the Panamanian leader's home after his first meeting with the future Nobel Prize winner in Caracas; he was supporting a revolution that had many connections to and similarities with the Cuban Revolution, and so on. García Márquez himself recognizes the common spirit when, at another point in the article, he acknowledges that "since Cuba's July 26, no other movement has surfaced in Latin America that has not only the intelligence and maturity, but also the political and military structure as the Sandinista National Liberation Front,"[30] although he underscores that there has been no specific military aid: "The SNLF at no time would permit the true nature of their movement, which is independent, democratic, and national, to be discredited. Somoza and the United States, it should be pointed out, have desperately tried to uncover signs of direct support from Fidel Castro to the Sandinistas, and they haven't been able to find a single weapon."[31]

However, it is now common knowledge that Cuba was one of the first countries to send not only a large quantity of arms, but also a large number of well-trained, professional troops of the highest caliber for the conflict on Nicaraguan soil. By 1978, German López, a Cuban official of the Department of America, and Renán Montero, an official of the Cuban Special Troops, who acted under the code name Moleón, operated out of a Cuban business office in Costa Rica. Their venture into Nicaragua was imminent, and they would be accompanied by Fernando Comas, of the Department of America, and Tony De la Guardia, one of the most important Cuban colonels of the Revolution, who ended up in disgrace, as we will see later. By that time, they had set up an aerial link, thanks to the talents of Tony De la Guardia, between Havana, Panama, and Liberia, and arms were sent through that channel. The flights were daily, and they transported very well-trained guerrilla soldiers. Some of these combat personnel were Cuban, but there were also Chileans and Uruguayans, trained in Cuba to be sent into action when they were needed. But Cuba was not the only country to collaborate with the Sandinistas in this way: Carlos Andrés Pérez also sent arms from Venezuela, specifically FAL rifles, with the Venezuelan labels removed, leaving an unmistakable mark. Jorge Masetti, who witnessed the entire process, and participated in some of the events that took place in Nicaragua in those years, not only told us about it on our various trips to Paris, but he also dedicated a few memorable, very well-written pages to the subject in his book *El furor y el delirio*. Without furor, but with a touch of delirium, the Colombian Nobel laureate buries, as he tends to do, the information that he doesn't want anyone to hear, the things that could harm the image of the revolutionaries that have his unconditional support.

THE POET AND PROPHET IN HIS HOMELAND

From rags to riches. If Gabo came from the humblest origins in Colombia, his influence on its "royal court" would be increasingly notorious from the seventies onward. He transformed himself from an obscure university student poet to the most important writer in Colombia's history, a prophet in his own land. And also in terms of his people's politics, so battered by wars, violence, and terrorism. The list of presidents from across the spectrum who have succumbed to Gabo's power is very long. In 1971 he met with Misael Pastrana several times to discuss political prisoners in Colombia; it was the first time a Colombian president ever even acknowledged the term "political prisoner" and agreed to discuss the subject. Gabo had already had contact with Alfonso Lopez Michelsen (president 1974–1978), since they had first become acquainted when Michelsen had been one of his law professors around the time of the "bogotazo." Gabo had forcefully opposed his government in the radical magazine *Alternativa*. Michelsen had offered García Márquez the consulate post in Barcelona when he was the Foreign Minister under Carlos Lleras Restrepo (1966–1970). Gabo, however, rejected his offer in a sharply critical letter. But their relationship deteriorated further under Julio César Turbay Ayala (1978–1982). They had no contact until 1981, when Gabo had to exile himself to Mexico because of a growing military plot against him. He had just returned from one of his now-frequent trips to Cuba and Panama, and he had gotten wind of a plan to arrest him and accuse him of maintaining ties with the urban guerrilla group M-19. He and Mercedes holed up in the Mexican embassy and managed to leave the country. The episode was a disaster for Colombia in terms of international public opinion, since just a few months later García Márquez would be honored with awards in France, Mexico, and Cuba, and would eventually win the Nobel Prize.

Things began to change with President Belisario Betancur (1982–1986). He and García Márquez were old friends. He was a progressive conservative, a cultured, talented man, and he was the first to court the author to return to Colombia; he congratulated and praised him for winning the Nobel Prize; and he arranged for García Márquez to return from exile with honor. It might be said that Belisario was the president who domesticated Gabo, turning the old Leftist into an intellectual amenable to the national political establishment. After Betancur, it became a tradition that every future president of Colombia would seek out the novelist's friendship, or vice-versa. In fact, the next president, Virgilio Barco (1986–1990), without having any special relationship with García Márquez, entertained him several times and confirmed that he was Colombia's great ambassador to the world.

César Gaviria, Colombia's president from 1990 to 1994, was, in the style of Fidel or Torrijos, a close friend of Gabo's. During those years, García Márquez was not only a frequent guest at the palace in Nariño, he also assumed the role of mediator and counselor to the president on various national and international matters. For example, in his novel *News of a Kidnapping*, his admiration for Gaviria is readily apparent. It was Gaviria who, at a birthday celebration for Gabo at his house in Cartagena de Indias, brought up the idea of possibly arranging a meeting with Bill Clinton. He mentioned it to William Styron, who in turn passed along the message to his friend Clinton. Gabo had a pre-existing friendship with

Ernesto Samper (1994–1998). In fact, before he became president, Samper had visited Cuba as Gabo's guest and was able to interview Fidel Castro. A report for the magazine *Semana* came out of it, which was much-discussed throughout Colombia. Later they would grow apart, because of an issue that linked Samper to the mafia in Cali.

The son of Misael Pastrana, Andres Pastrana, who was president from 1998 until 2002, got to know Gabo during the presidential campaign. Plinio Apuleyo Mendoza introduced them. Pastrana relied on Gabo as a personal adviser on a number of issues. The two went on a trip to the United States together to meet with Clinton. And when the presidency came to Álvaro Uribe, a liberal independent, shortly before winning the election he went to Mexico to see Gabo, adhering to the established tradition that every future Colombian president must get in the writer's good graces and get close to him. With things being as they are, why would Gabo ever want—or need, for that matter—to be president, secretary, or ambassador?

CHAPTER TEN

★

FIRST CLASS

THE FIRST TIME GABO SET SAIL FOR THE OLD CONTINENT, his finances were in a shambles. Some hair-raising accounts of this period have appeared in various articles, in Plinio Apuleyo Mendoza's *El olor de la guayaba*, for example, and in many interviews. In the second volume of his memoirs, García Márquez will probably closely focus on this part of his life. On that first trip to Europe, he traveled extremely light: he didn't bring along extra clothes, books, or money. He was a young journalist embarking on an adventure, off to make a living through his reporting. By the end of the seventies, his situation had radically changed. His friends in high political places and his literary successes had granted him an enviable level of stability, and when he set sail for Europe again, a continent still teeming with "dukes" and "secretary generals," he had different interests. He had met Mitterrand before, but he had been in closest contact with him during the time of the Sandinista struggle, because of their common interests in Latin America, aside from their mutual literary interests. Pablo Neruda, who was Chile's ambassador to France during Allende's rule, had talked to the French president about the Colombian writer during those years and had given him some of Gabo's novels, translated into French. García Márquez and Mitterrand met sometime later, and their friendship took hold immediately and naturally, since the Chilean Nobel Prize winner had already spent hours talking to each one of them separately about his great friendship with the other. But Neruda wasn't just the initial link with Mitterrand; he also talked up his Colombian friend to French celebrities and a Swedish official at the dinner celebrating his own Nobel Prize. In an interview in 1973, Gabo recalls some omens from that evening in 1971:

Once he called me up in Barcelona. "You and your wife have to come to have dinner with me tomorrow in Paris." I protested: "Pablo, you know that I don't fly to Paris, I only go there by train." Then he sounded like he was about to cry and I said: "All right." "We're going," I told my wife. "Pablo threw a fit, and we have to have dinner with him tomorrow in Paris." When we got off the plane, I heard the news: he had won the Nobel Prize, and the first thing he said to the press was: "The one who really deserves this prize is Gabriel García Márquez." Then I understood why he had been so insistent that we have dinner with him.

At the dinner celebrating the award, held in his house, the only guests were David Alfaro Siqueiros and his wife, Jorge Edwards, the Chilean painter Eduardo Mata, Régis Debray, the photographer Henri Cartier-Bresson, my wife, and me. The delegate from the Swedish Academy who had come to tell him he had won the prize was also there. Pablo needled him all night, telling him they should give me a Nobel the following year. The poor guy just said: "Yes, Mr. Neruda, we'll see. . . ."[1]

Basically, Neruda lobbied both Mitterrand and the Nobel Prize committee on Gabo's behalf. Some time later, at a dinner in Mexico that García Márquez recalled in an article, his friendship with the future president of France was sealed. The dinner was held at the French embassy, in the Mexican capital, when Mitterrand was running for president. At Mitterrand's request, Gabo was the only non-French person invited. García Márquez remarks that this occasion was when he really started to get to know Mitterrand as a person, since, while all the other guests expected him to talk about the latest happenings in French politics, Mitterrand steered the conversation to literature. "The specter of disappointment fell over the room," Gabo recalled. "Most of them thought that Mitterrand, who is a very practical politician, had gathered that group together to talk about the most pressing matter at hand. But after a few minutes, we were all transfixed by our charming host's breadth of knowledge, and he was truly in his element as his conversation navigated around the great names and timeless themes of universal letters."[2]

Then he realized that Mitterrand was not a political animal, but a real man of letters; and that precisely because of this quality, if he won the election, Mitterrand would govern intelligently. That is what García Márquez said in an article dated April 14, 1981, a few days before his French friend was proclaimed president: "It seems to me that his vision of the world, more than that of a politician, is that of a man burning with the fever for literature. That's why I have always thought that he would be—will be?—a wise leader. He is a man who takes an interest in all things in life, even the simplest, and he does it passionately, with an enthusiasm and lucidity that is his greatest virtue."[3] A month later, he published another article in which he described the dinner that took place on May 21, 1981, in the Elysee Palace, where Mitterrand wanted to celebrate his victory with his Latin American friends. In attendance were Carlos Fuentes, who had arrived on the Concorde jet from the United

States, where he had given some lectures at a small university; Matilde Neruda, the widow of the poet; Miguel Otero Silva, who came from Caracas in spite of his notorious fear of flying; and Hortensia Allende, Salvador's widow, who had returned to America just a few days before because she hadn't believed that Mitterrand would win, so she had to make another trip to France for the sixth time that year. Julio Cortázar, Gabo recalls, "had the easiest time getting there. He got on the subway at the corner of his street and got out at the Concorde metro station, twenty feet away from Elysee Palace."[4] Gabo's glee is typical: he talks about "the happiest, rowdiest bash I can remember since that other historic May 1968," in the streets of Paris, and he recalls a snippet of private conversation he had with the president:

> I said: "For the first time, we Latin Americans feel like the French president is one of our own." Mitterrand smiled. "Yes," he said, "but which Latin Americans?"[5]

That friendship became so intense, and the trust between them so apparent, that within political circles in Latin America, Gabo came to be regarded as an intermediary between Nuestra America ("our America") and France, between Latin America and socialist Europe. In fact, in the *Playboy* interview published in 1983, he basically confirms this as being the case, but plays down the importance of any possible political consequences their personal friendship might have:

> *Playboy:* Another friend in a high place is France's president, François Mitterrand. Is it true that you serve as an unofficial adviser for him on Latin-American affairs?
>
> **García Márquez:** Did you use the word "adviser"? No.

President Mitterrand doesn't need advice on Latin America. Sometimes he needs information. Then we talk.

And the interview goes on to suggest a connection between Mitterrand's interest in Latin America and the friendship between Gabo and Mitterrand with the Sandinista regime, which had been in power in Nicaragua for almost three years. The interviewer understands very well the degree of Gabo's involvement in that matter; the role played by Cuba through its material and personnel support as the Soviet satellite in the Caribbean, although Gabo had denied this; the Nobel laureate's mediation efforts on various fronts; and the speed with which the newly elected President Mitterrand's administration had committed to aiding the Nicaraguans:

Playboy: Paris had a confrontation some time back with Washington when it decided to send military aid to the left-wing Sandinista regime in Nicaragua. Is that the sort of thing you talk about?

García Márquez: The decision to sell them the arms? No. Discussions on that matter, apparently, were very, very secret. But in the case of the commercial and economic help the Nicaraguans were seeking, that I knew about. The people now in power in Nicaragua, they're good friends. We worked together during the years they were fighting the Somoza regime. If you want to know what I told President Mitterrand about Nicaragua and, indeed, about the entire Central American situation, I'll be glad to repeat what I said.

Playboy: Please do.

García Márquez: It's my view that the big problem in

Latin America, in Central America in particular, is that the Reagan administration interprets everything as a result of Soviet–American dynamics. Which is ridiculous. And also unrealistic. The Reagan administration sees any nonconformity by the people of Latin America not as the end product of the miserable conditions in those countries but as some kind of Soviet operation. In believing that, the Reagan administration is creating a self-fulfilling prophecy—just as Kennedy did with Cuba in the early sixties. I happen to know the Sandinistas very well, and I know they are making great efforts to work out their own system—independent of any world power. Unfortunately, the Nicaraguans are now facing all kinds of internal conspiracies and raids from the old Somoza forces operating out of Honduras and attempts to destabilize the government by elements funded by the United States. At the same time, the Nicaraguans have a desperate need for funds for food, development, and self-defense. If the West refuses them that, they will be forced to seek it from the only government that will give it to them—the Soviet Union.[6]

And Mitterrand, socialist-to-socialist, would talk to Sweden. Olof Palme, the Swedish prime minister, who had also taken an interest in Latin American issues, wanted to meet with some distinguished Latin Americans who were in France on one of his trips to Paris. That led to a gathering in Mitterrand's house in the Bievre section of Paris, filled with high-profile people from the worlds of politics and literature. At around midnight, the Latin Americans at the party went out with the Nordic leader to La Coupole, and for more than two hours Palme asked each of them in turn to describe the situation in their country. "Finally," Gabo wrote, "when Olof Palme insisted on paying the tab, the woman at the next table asked him in Swedish if he had paid with his own personal money, or with government money. Then Palme sat down at his compatriots' table and gave them all kinds of explanations. Actually, he had paid with his own money, but he thought that in any case it would have been legitimate to have paid with money from the state, since it seemed to the Swedish prime minister that the informative meeting on Latin America had been an important official event."[7]

On the list of "dukes" and "secretary generals" who were more or less his friends, the name Pierre Schori should be added, the Swedish Vice-Minister of Foreign Affairs, and the French Régis Debray and Jack Lang, the Minister of Culture under Mitterrand, who was charged with launching an international cultural project between France and Mexico in 1981. But if it seems like a key individual is still missing from the list, Artur Lundkvist, a permanent secretary of the Swedish Academy, is also on it. In October 1980, in one of his articles about the Nobel Prize, García Márquez demonstrates the detailed knowledge he has about the institution and the prize's history: he describes the founding of the Swedish Academy in 1786, and points out that the Nobel Prize at that time was only in Literature, since the other four categories are awarded by other Swedish academies, institutions, or committees. He describes the Academy's eighteen members, its origins, characteristics, and so forth, and the little that can be gleaned about the nomination process and how the final winner is chosen. At the end of the piece, he talks about the secretary, giving us a better understanding of the political and literary journey that Gabo embarked on many years earlier, from America to Europe, with a little more baggage now, culminating in Sweden with the award for intellectual and esthetic merits, but also political, of the most coveted prize given in Europe, the Nobel Prize for Literature: "The only member," Gabo writes, "of the Swedish Academy who reads in Spanish, and very well, is the poet Artur Lundkvist. He is the one who knows the work of our writers, who nominates them for the award and who wages a secret battle for them. This has, in spite of himself, made him something of a deity, remote and enigmatic, and the universal destiny of our letters in a sense rests on him. However, in real life he is a very youthful old man, with a somewhat Latin American sense of humor, and his house is so humble-looking that it's hard to imagine the destiny of anybody depending on its owner. A few years ago, after a typical Swedish dinner in that house—with cold meats and warm beer—Lundkvist suggested we have coffee in his library. I was stunned; the collection of books he had in Spanish was just incredible, the best and the worst all mixed together, and almost all of them were personally autographed by their living authors, agonizing or dead from the excruciating wait. I asked the poet if I could read some of the inscriptions, and he assented with a knowing smile. Most of them were so affectionate, and some were so heartfelt, that when it came time for me to sign my books, it seemed that just the act of signing them was an indiscretion. The complexes some people have!"[8]

AND THE WINNER IS . . .

García Márquez. Who else? But first, let's pay another visit to Cuba before getting into the Nobel Prize story. All the international connections, especially in the Caribbean and Central America, on the mainland and on the islands, put the "emergency politician" in a privileged position; and his friendship with Castro, which had grown tremendously since that first meeting at the Hotel Nacional, became a form of currency: you give me support for the revolution, with your intellectual prestige and your ability to move inside the inner circles of some very powerful people, and I'll give you privileged information on Latin America, I'll crown you as a shining example of the revolution that faced off with the United States, and I'll grant your desires to brush up against power and play with it. The interviewer for *Playboy* said to García Márquez: "Castro once said of you, 'García Márquez is the most powerful man in Latin America.' If that is an accurate quote, how do you think he meant it?" In his answer, even though he thinks just the opposite, García Márquez implies that his political weight or influence in the highest spheres of power are not as great as they may seem, and he tries to cast doubt on Castro's alleged affirmation, even though it wasn't very forceful, and we know by now that García Márquez is not always completely sincere even when he seems to be very precise: "The phrasing doesn't sound like Fidel's; but if he did say that, I'm sure he was referring to me as a writer, not as a political man."[9]

There is a very interesting article that explains how, shortly after Gabo had made his interests in Cuba clear and had met Castro, he had gotten past all the possible hurdles in his path and had achieved a status that almost no Cuban has ever managed to attain over the past forty years. The article was written by Gerardo Molina and published in the Colombian newspaper *El Espectador* on February 13, 1980. It opens with this: "To watch the Cuban Revolution unfold from close range is inherently interesting, but to see it with García Márquez as your guide is much more eye-opening. The novelist has become so identified with the revolutionary experiment that it's easy to discover hidden aspects that otherwise would go unnoticed."[10] The author of the article, who had been in Cuba with García Márquez and had talked with Cuban writers and politicians, concludes that Gabo "could pass for a leader of the Cuban Revolution. The writer makes periodic trips to the island to see how various initiatives in progress are going. His observations are quickly heeded. We were able to see how, in García Márquez's apartment in the Hotel Riviera, ideas for projects would get tossed around that would later be set into motion. Raúl Castro put a positive spin on this fact, half-joking and half-serious, when he introduced the writer to the Soviet Minister of Defense with these words: 'I introduce to you the Cuban writer Gabriel García Márquez, born in Colombia, who luckily is not a communist, because if he were, he wouldn't be so useful.'"

And Molina continues with a reflection that masterfully explains the Colombian's method of getting close to power. He discounts some of García Márquez's statements that he neither likes nor understands politics, because "the truth is that he likes it very much and understands it all too well. It shows in his journalism. García Márquez deconstructs political happenings, sifting through them, and reconstructs them, drawing conclusions that hadn't occurred to those closely involved. It's clear that García Márquez is not and never will be any kind of government official, nor will he try to be one, or run for office. But as an adviser to policymakers and high-ranking government officials, he is irreplaceable." And in the literary arena, his novels have sold like hotcakes in Cuba. Molina writes: "When we asked the Vice-Minister of Culture, Rolando Rodríguez, about sales figures for García Márquez's works, the number he gave us seemed unbelievable. When we asked him to repeat it, and remembering where we were, we understood the implications very well: a print run of 130,000 copies of any book by García Márquez would completely sell out of the bookstores within twenty-four hours."

On occasion, García Márquez has expressed that the attraction the Cubans feel for him is mutual, since his native country, Colombia, is the most solemn place in the solar system, and the one thing that he dreads most in the whole world is solemnity. He says, "Cuba is the one place where I can be myself,"[11] since the people are completely natural there and devoid of formality. Also, there he can be completely at ease with his friends, in whom he places limitless trust. The piece on Gabo published in *El Tiempo* on December 18, 2002, recalling the time around the Nobel award and celebrating the publication of the first volume of his memoirs, states that "he is an extremely sensitive, generous, and shy person; in spite of his hard protective shell, he is profoundly intuitive, simultaneously reserved and warm, who sees the friendship of his friends as the greatest blessing."[12] And in a litany of famous statements the author has uttered, there are a few standouts, such as "The only time in my life that I feel truly myself is when I am with my friends," and "I consider myself the best friend of all of my friends, and I think that none of them loves me as much as I love the one that I love the least."[13]

This quality is particularly apparent when he accepts the honor from the Swedish Academy. The story of the Nobel Prize was "the chronicle of a prize foretold." The review we've conducted of the events of the late seventies shows that the great writer's political and diplomatic skills almost surpass his enormous talent as a novelist. He hits the right keys and waits; and knows . . . just as he knows how to interpret the waiting of previous Nobel Prize winners. In October 1980, when he's about to be passed over for that year, he remembers how others in the running in past years waited and how they reacted. Usually, a candidate who wants to win always denies this wish and expectation, if asked. Or at least dissimulates it. Octavio Paz said that the best prize is the one you don't expect. And Gabo notes: "The winners, in general, seem to be more surprised than anybody. When the playwright Samuel Beckett got the news of his award in a phone call, in 1969, dismayed, he exclaimed: 'Oh, my God, what a disaster!' In 1971, Pablo Neruda found out three days before the news was made public, through a confidential message from the Swedish Academy. But the next night, he invited a group of friends to have dinner in Paris, where he was then the Chilean ambassador, and none of us found out about the motive for the party until the newspapers printed the news the next day. 'It's just that I don't really believe anything until I see it in print,' Neruda explained later with a laugh. A few days after that, while we were eating in a noisy restaurant on Boulevard Montparnasse, he realized that he still hadn't written his speech for the award ceremony, which was to take place forty-eight hours later in Stockholm. Then he turned over one of the pages from the menu and, without pausing once, unaffected by the swirl of humanity around him, as naturally as he breathed and with the same implacable green ink he used to pen his verses, right there he wrote his beautiful acceptance speech."[14]

HAVANA WAS A PARTY, STOCKHOLM AN IMPOSSIBLE DREAM

Gabo won the Nobel Prize while he was in exile from his country, in October 1982. Although he lived in Mexico, he spent stretches of time in Havana, by that time always staying in a suite in the luxurious Hotel Riviera. The night before he won, he was in Havana and made a call to Alfredo Muñoz, a correspondent with France Presse on the island. They discussed the prize. In Cuba, and especially in Havana, there was a festive atmosphere. Everyone knew what was going to happen the following day. In fact, Alfredo Muñoz told us, when we talked with him at his home in Havana, that that same night he had written an article for the agency describing their phone conversation, portraying the Nobel laureate as a man more concerned with certain details, like the clothes he should wear when he accepts it, and what would happen if his wife has to dance with the king of Sweden, than with the prize itself.

Also on that night, to beat the Swedes to the punch and make a more formal announcement, the Council of Ministers of Cuba held a special meeting and unanimously decided to award García Márquez the Felix Varela Medal, the highest honor that the Cuban government bestowed for intellectual achievements. On October 21, 1982, the Havana newspaper *Juventud Rebelde* explained that the award was granted for "the high integrity of his work," for being a man "identified with his time, identified with the most revolutionary ideas." The next day, October 22, 1982, newspapers around the world announced the news. The official Cuban newspaper, *Granma*, made the announcement while emphasizing that, a few hours before being crowned with the Nobel Prize, García Márquez had been recognized with the highest Cuban distinction.

That same day, after the Nobel Prize victory had been announced, he was awarded the Aguila Azteca award in Mexico, the highest honor that country granted to foreigners. By that morning García Márquez was back in Mexico, and the first call that he took was from his great friend, the Swedish Vice-Minister for Foreign Affairs, Pierre Schori. The third call, paradoxically, was from the conservative president of Colombia, Belisario Betancur, who offered his effusive congratulations, in spite of his living in exile. The Spanish daily *El País*, on page 35, noted that García Márquez had had serious problems in his country in 1981, but that in March he would return to start up a new independent newspaper. The paper also described how, in parallel with the awarding of the Nobel Prize, and with no prior notice, the Cuban government had met to honor him with another award, the highest possible granted by the Cuban powers-that-be. His friend Fidel had started pulling out all the stops, and he would continue doing it two days later, and on through the end of the year.

In the Mexican paper *Unomásuno* on October 25, a story from Barranquilla and the EFE Agency explained that fifteen prisoners in Cuba, fourteen Colombian sailors, and one Dominican who had been arrested more than a year earlier for violating Cuba's territorial waters and for drug trafficking, had been suddenly released by the Castro regime, thanks to the intervention of García Márquez. On October 30, *Granma* published a letter from Gabo to Fidel dated October 20, thanking him for the Felix Varela Medal: "I am a witness of the courage, tenacity and amazing imagination with which the Cubans of today have undertaken the creation of their own world."

In light of this, the first country where García Márquez celebrated his Nobel Prize victory, and where he did so with the utmost enthusiasm, was Cuba. Only after that would he travel to Paris, and then to Stockholm. Those months leading up to the award ceremony in December were one long party. And he still found time to touch down in Cuba once again in early December, for another event: on December 3, García Márquez was honored once again by his adoptive country, to pre-celebrate the Nobel Prize presentation, and to publicize the fact that tens of thousands of copies of various of Gabo's works were to go on sale that day. And on December 6, at the Havana Book Fair, in the Palace of Segundo Cabo, he got a very warm reception at another event, which was comprehensively covered in *Granma* on December 11, where he gave a speech; also present were the Minister of Culture Armando Hart; his Vice-Minister, Antonio Núñez Jiménez, another one of Gabo's best, oldest Cuban friends; and Abel Prieto, who was then the Director of Art and Literature, and later would be Minister of Culture. Over the course of those heady days in Cuba, García Márquez still found time to write the speech that he would deliver in Sweden to an audience of kings, recording it at the Diegos' house, listening to his own words and repeating them over and over until he had memorized it. Fefe remembers that, since he was very shy and such formal proceedings made him very nervous, Gabo had to make a great effort to overcome the enormous tension that came from speaking in front of so many people under those circumstances.

On December 7, he left for Sweden, stopping first in Barcelona, where he gave a quick interview to *El País*; and then he finally arrived in the Swedish capital. On December 9, he was invited (and he alone, not the other Nobel Prize winners of that year, a group which included the renowned economist Paul Samuelson) to a dinner at the country home of the president of

Sweden, Olof Palme, in Harpsund. "Mercedes and I," Gabo recounts, "were expecting to find a medieval castle rising out of the mist, right out of an Andersen story, but we found instead a very simple, tidy house next to a frozen-over lake, in the middle of a lovely meadow where there were other identical houses for guests."[15] It was like a tribute not just to him, but to all of Latin America. In attendance were Danielle Mitterrand, the wife of the French president and Gabo's good friend, also concerned with Latin American issues; Régis Debray and Pierre Schori, also great friends of his; some Swedish writers; and Bülent Ecevit, a former prime minister of Turkey. A story Palme told about one of his many encounters with Neruda made a strong impression on Gabo: "At the dinner at his country house, he charmed us with anecdotes about our own faraway countries. He recalled a conversation he had had with Pablo Neruda at his house on Isla Negra, in 1969, a year before Salvador Allende's victory. 'We talked all night in front of the fire,' he said, 'surrounded by his somber collection of nautical figureheads that had sailed all over the world. We talked, and Neruda's reflections on dictatorship as an omnipresent phenomenon in Latin American history were unending, like the relentless waves of the Pacific Ocean that came all the way up to the house that night.' His story put the subject of Latin America squarely on the table, and it stayed there until the very late hour when we got up to go to bed."[16]

And they still had time left to fix the world, or at least Latin America—at the end of the evening, the prime minister asked Gabo to summarize the current situation in Central America, which turned into another opportunity to act politically in the region. "I hadn't slept for three days," he confessed, "overwhelmed by the endless festivities, but the prime minister's request seemed so important that I launched into a detailed analysis that went on for almost two hours, until Pierre Schori, laughing out loud, cut me off by saying: 'Don't go on, Gabriel; you've convinced us.' That was how I got the idea to call on the six presidents of Central America to urge them to make immediate efforts to establish peace in the region. The motivation for that petition, which was the same for my talk, was that never had Central America ever been so close to all-out war, nor had—and maybe for the same reason—the opportunity to reach a negotiated solution been greater."[17]

The next day, at the awards presentation, forty close friends of Gabo's accompanied him, along with a troupe of Caribbean musicians and dancers, who performed some traditional dances. During the actual presentation of the prize, music by Béla Bartók, one of García Márquez's favorite composers, was played in the background. He attended the ceremony at the Stockholm Concert Hall dressed in a white liqui-liqui, a traditional suit worn by peasants in the area where he grew up, and he carried a yellow rose, a flower that symbolizes luck and casts off evil spirits in people, objects, and situations and inspires him to write. It was the first time that a Nobel winner did not wear tails to the ceremony. The Queen of Sweden went up to accept the prize with him, since protocol dictated that the new winners be accompanied by a member of the royal family at the crowning moment. Fidel Castro, president of Gabo's adopted country, sent a very special gift: 1,500 bottles of Cuban rum, to share with his friends that day. As Swedish law did not allow alcohol to be served after ten o'clock at night, and also prohibited its consumption at establishments that did not have specific authorization, the 1,500 bottles were placed on the tables with corkscrews and empty glasses, in case "anyone interested wanted to use them." On December 15, the Swedish chancellor presented a formal complaint to the Cuban embassy, protesting the illicit distribution of such a significant quantity of alcohol.

The festivities marched on. In its edition of December 29, the Spanish paper *El País* commented that García Márquez's five-day

visit in Spain would end that day, as he headed back to Cuba to celebrate the end of the year with his friend Fidel, who, for his part,
had recently told Gabo that he really wanted to visit Galicia, the
land of his ancestors. During that particular stay in Spain, Gabo had
gotten together with his friend Felipe González several times. On
December 26, he spent five hours with the president. González
told him that he had been trying to get in touch with him for a
year and a half, to talk about the tragic accident that claimed the
life of their mutual friend General Torrijos, with whom they had
both shared some wonderful evenings. The article in *El País* also
confirmed that both men were very happy to see each other, since
it had been so long, and especially since nothing had changed
between them, in spite of the very different circumstances they
found themselves in. García Márquez congratulated his friend for
his sweeping victory in the elections, which assured him of at least
four years of an absolute majority in parliament and was a sign of
maturity for the Spanish people. González in turn congratulated
his friend for having won the Nobel Prize. The only thing that
seemed to have changed about them was that "we were both
wearing a tie," García Márquez joked. Lastly, the article explained
that García Márquez, who had spent some time exiled in Mexico,
was going to return to his country in March 1983 to found a newspaper called *El Otro*, in tribute to the Argentinian writer Jorge Luis
Borges, who never achieved the highest honor in letters in spite of
the fact that he was the best writer in the Spanish language of the
last century.

On January 5, García Márquez put his stamp of approval on
their reunion by writing an article titled "Felipe," where he
described the times he had spent with González the week before
in Moncloa Palace, emphasizing that "even though Felipe González
and I have gone to some places without wearing ties where other
people might feel a little intimidated even wearing tuxedos, I felt

obliged to put one on, not so much to pay homage to those precious places as to not seem like I was assuming the right to be informal in a place where that would have been viewed as déclassé. I arrived with Mercedes and our youngest son on a beautiful, sunny afternoon of that strange Madrid winter, and Felipe had gone out with some of his aides for a walk around the park surrounding Moncloa. When I spotted him among the trees wearing a long-sleeved blue sweater, giving him the air of a university professor more than a president, I felt overdressed for the occasion. But at least he had a tie on too."[18]

From Madrid, not quite to heaven, but almost. Gabo settled into Havana once again, his new home, and celebrated, this time more than ever, the end of the year with Fidel. He began a new stage in his life, in which the unofficial diplomat, ambassador-at-large for various presidents and countries, got ready to take a year's sabbatical. He felt so satisfied and recognized that he dedicated a whole year to fulfilling obligations and various requests relating to the prize before getting down to work and finishing *Love in the Time of Cholera*, which was published in 1985. He was probably the writer who first initiated, as Dasso Saldívar suggested to us, the tradition of Nobel Prize winners taking a year's sabbatical following the award. And there would be more Cuban surprises. . . .

CHAPTER ELEVEN

★

THE PRICE OF PARADISE

*P*ARADISO IS THE TITLE OF ONE OF THE MOST EMBLEMATIC novels in all of Cuban literature. Its author, José Lezama Lima, is without doubt the most thorough, intelligent, and erudite Cuban writer of the twentieth century. A novelist, poet, essayist, anthologist, and leader of his generation, he gave his best novel the title that many would ascribe to the tropical island. Because of Cuba's climate, its countryside, its beaches, and its crystalline ocean waters, it is an ideal place to live. And if one is lucky enough to live in the hills of Siboney, with its gardens and colonial mansions, its broad streets, crisp ocean air and singing birds, the sun-dappled trees and fresh scent of the damp earth, if one can take advantage of the privileges enjoyed by high government officials, then naturally one is not inclined to want to voluntarily abandon that ecosystem. That area of the Cuban capital, sufficiently removed from the dilapidated neighborhoods of the city center, was the refuge of the super-rich at the dawn of the twentieth century. When the Revolution began, all of the private property there was nationalized, and the best properties were set aside for the highest level of foreign visitors and heads of state; to house embassies for friendly countries, following the protocol of foreign relations; and for use as private residences of certain privileged members of Castro's inner circle, including Castro himself, and for friends in general.

As luck would have it, Gabo was rewarded with a spectacular mansion, near one of Fidel's homes, shortly after having won the Nobel Prize. The house can barely be seen from the road, and has a huge garden which was expanded shortly after Castro himself gave it to his friend. A large, luxurious Mercedes-Benz was also included in the package, which García Márquez uses only when he is on the island. This was in the eighties, when no one in Cuba had the right to private property, and there was a very long waiting list to get a Lada, a car made in Eastern Europe, on top of strict fuel rationing. All of the documents and interviews that we have had access to indicate that the house was a gift from Fidel to Gabo. Vázquez Montalbán, however, prefers to use the expression "permanent loan," as he said in an interview. Since in Cuba, absolute ownership of a property is very rare, and also because no one knows what is going to happen with property deeds from before the Revolution after Castro's death, it's possible that technically it really is an open-ended loan. Anyway, the fact is that Gabo is the only person who has "private" access to that house, and he stays there often, whenever he visits the island.

Cuba finally had its Nobel Prize, that elusive honor that had passed over Martí, who died too young in 1895, along with the twentieth century classics: Nicolás Guillén, with his *Sóngoro cosongo* and his *Sensemayá*; Lezama Lima, with his uncompromising vision of *Paradiso*; and Alejo Carpentier, in spite of his very strong ideological and political commitment as demonstrated in his *Reino de este mundo*. Cuba had its Nobel Prize, and the Nobel Prize winner

had his kingdom on the "Queen of the Caribbean." Three countries had formally nominated Gabo for the prize: Cuba, Mitterrand's France, and Colombia, as Elisabeth Burgos told us in her
lovely apartment in Paris's Latin Quarter. From the island, García
Márquez could continue exercising his own particular brand of
power. By 1980, Gerardo Molina had already described him, from
Cuba, as the diplomat-at-large for all of Latin America: "We could
see in Havana," he wrote at the time, "that there is always a Latin
American spectacle swirling around him. In that way, he carries out
a kind of diplomatic function that no one has actually assigned
him. An exiled Argentine asks him to intervene to help out
someone being persecuted. A Venezuelan solicits his analysis on the
latest schism to affect his country's Leftist movement. A Bolivian
hopes that he will collaborate on a newspaper being developed. A
Central American would like him to edit a statement on the latest
events of that tumultuous region. A Paraguayan gives him an
update on the status of their country's struggle against the dictatorship. A young person from anywhere on the map asks his advice
on how to be a writer. García Márquez has an encouraging word
for every one of them. And without taking notes on anything, he
lets this mass of first-hand information settle in his head, making
him the most complete repository on the reality of Latin
America."[1]

At that high-class mansion in Havana, García Márquez could
entertain in style. There was no need for Gabo to have a suite in
the Riviera any more or to visit his friends' homes. Fefe told us that
from then on, he visited the Diegos' home in El Vedado much less
frequently, and their relationship cooled in intensity but remained
intact. Now, Gabo would have increasing contact with another
sector of society, starting with Fidel. In the *Magazin Dominical of El
Espectador* on April 8, 1984 (number 54, p. 5), he explains: "Some
critics cannot forgive me for not only supporting the Revolution,

but also for my friendship with Fidel. I can pick up the phone and call him; and what's more, he'll answer." And vice-versa. When the Colombian writer is staying at his home in Havana, he'll frequently call up Fidel. Alfredo Bryce Echenique recounts in his *Antimemorias*: "Fidel called Gabo and me. The pretext, as usual, was to have a little cocktail to unwind, and Gabo immediately exploited the pretext to keep me from having a drink and make me out to be some kind of Carthusian monk. 'Was I okay?,' 'You don't think that I did something wrong or missed something. . .' were the routine insecurities that would surface."[2] Bryce had been a finalist for the Casa de las Americas Prize for his short stories a few years earlier, and he was invited to the island on various occasions. When Gabo had his house there, Alfredo would usually stay there when he came to Cuba, or he would at least often stop by Gabo's mansion, especially for the late-night get-togethers. He describes one of those gatherings: "That night at Gabo's house, we were no doubt waiting for Fidel, who usually showed up when you'd least expect it, every once in a while, and he would stay for hours just to rest and talk, revealing his most private side and his solitude of a thousand years, for hours that one may have rather spent getting a good night's sleep. First, a hushed silence would descend, a deafening silence, and you could hear the noise of the very air in that silence. Then Fidel would appear and we would all be happy except for Gabo, who would intermittently flash an expression that seemed to say 'We're all screwed. No one's going to get any sleep here tonight.' And no one would go to bed until Fidel, at around six in the morning, would look at his watch and make his typical observation, 'I think we all have a few things to do this morning,' and that would bring the night to a close and you could hear the silence in the air again, and the whispering breeze of the fading wind."[3]

It was far removed from the days when, as the poet and journalist Luis Suardíaz said on Habana Libre, Gabo was so young that he arrived in Cuba the first time "without a passport, and the only document he had with him was a list of clothes that he had sent to the dry cleaner's in his name, and with that he got on the plane." Those were the years of Operation Truth. Now was the time of "The Truth of the Mission," the great mission that had made the Colombian writer absolutely indispensable. Cuba is the Barranquilla of his childhood, but without all the hardships of his personal past history. The following very well-known statement he made is probably heavily autobiographical: "There is no contradiction in being rich and being a revolutionary, as long as one is sincere as a revolutionary and not sincere as a rich person."[4] His defense of the Revolution sometimes goes to incredible extremes, like when, during those years of intense political commitment, one day Anthony Quinn offered Gabo one million dollars for the dramatic rights for *One Hundred Years of Solitude*, to adapt it into a television mini-series, and he assented, but with the condition that Quinn also give one million dollars for the Revolution, in Cuba and Latin America in general. That episode was described in an article published on April 21, 1982, "Una tonteria de Anthony Quinn,"[5] in which García Márquez refutes some statements that had been made by the actor and producer from the U.S. Also, as Régis Debray told us, in the mid-eighties García Márquez is disillusioned by the level of aid to Latin America, Cuba, and the Sandinistas proposed by Mitterrand and the French government. Gabo had expected a greater commitment from his friend the President of France, but he didn't get everything he had asked for. From that point on, his relationship with the leaders of France cooled.

WHAT'S LOVE GOT TO DO WITH IT?

There are a few verses by Martí that all Cubans know by heart, and some are taken from the first poem in *Versos sencillos*, by the earnest man from the land of palm trees. It goes like this:

Si dicen que del joyero	*If they say from the jewelry chest*
Tome la joya mejor,	*to choose the most precious stone,*
Tomo a un amigo sincero	*I would choose a true friend*
Y pongo a un lado el amor.	*And leave love alone.*

When it came to Castro, the highest-ranking leader of the Cuban Revolution, in the beginning of their friendship, which was stronger than love, García Márquez didn't want to voice any personal opinions about him. In 1977, a journalist pressed him, but Gabo declined to answer, because his response "would be too impassioned and seem outrageously loyal."[6] But a few lines later in the piece, he states: "Fidel is the sweetest man I know. And he is also the harshest critic of the Revolution, and constantly self-critical."[7] In 1975 he had already stated: "Fidel Castro, aside from his political and visionary genius, is an extraordinarily well-informed man. I have a great admiration for Fidel Castro for so many reasons, but above all because he faced the daily risk of power. The waste of power is terrible. Fidel Castro took that risk and has come out on top."[8] At other times, he has laconically answered: "I am a friend of Fidel's and I'm not an enemy of the Revolution, that's it."[9] However, in the wake of the Nobel Prize, the mask would fall away.

On April 28, 1982, García Márquez reviewed the book *El pez es rojo* (The Fish Is Red) by the U.S. journalists Warren Hinckle and William Turner. The title referred to the code name of the Bay of Pigs operation. With copious documentation, the book dissects the secret war the CIA has waged against Cuba since 1959, including the various plots to assassinate Castro. García Márquez observed that the clumsiness of the *yanquis* in this regard is astonishing, since none of the attempts had hit the mark in more than twenty years. And, perplexed, he shared a few anecdotes from that dirty war: "It's hard to believe that behind all of this was none other than the creator of Secret Agent 007. But he was. In the spring of 1960, according to Hinckle and Turner, the senator John F. Kennedy, who shortly thereafter would be the new president of the United States, invited his favorite author, Ian Fleming, to lunch. The senator asked the writer what James Bond would do if he were given the assignment to assassinate Fidel Castro. Fleming answered, without a blink, that there were three things that were very important to Cubans: money, religion, and sex. First, you had to blanket Cuba with a fabulous amount of counterfeit money, courtesy of the United States. Second, you had to arrange it so that a huge, luminous cross would appear in the skies over Cuba, as a sign of Christ's imminent return to Earth to eradicate communism. The third step was to airdrop pamphlets all over Cuba, signed by the Soviet Union, warning the population that the nuclear tests carried out by the United States had contaminated the revolutionaries' beards with radioactivity, and that would make them impotent. Fleming conjectured that after that warning, all of the revolutionaries would shave their beards, including Fidel. He concluded: 'Without beards, there is no revolution.'"[10]

The CIA took the novelist's little joke completely seriously and ran with it, developing some powders that, when placed in someone's shoes, would cause the hair on the wearer's entire body to fall off. But they couldn't find anybody to sprinkle the powder into Fidel's shoes. Gabo went on to mention some actual assassination attempts that the authors cited, as well as some that weren't cited but that he knew about. He also demonstrates his expertise in matters of Cuban counterintelligence, revealing a knowledge that the ordinary citizen couldn't possibly have had. The text is a bit long, but it warrants inclusion in its entirety here:

The failures that are the most difficult to explain have been, of course, the assassination attempts on Fidel Castro. Actually, Castro does have a very unpredictable daily routine, his secret service system is extremely difficult to breach, and Cuba's counterintelligence department is considered one of the most efficient in the world. But that doesn't sufficiently explain the failures of more than fifty assassination attempts planned by the CIA, drawing on all their resources and expertise. It makes one think that there's some other element at work here that can't be detected by the CIA's computers, maybe something not unlike the magic of the Caribbean.

When President Kennedy sent James Donovan, a lawyer from New York, to Cuba in 1963 to negotiate the release of a group of North American prisoners, the CIA prepared, without Donovan's knowledge, a special present for Fidel Castro. It was scuba-diving equipment, with oxygen tanks that were also carrying the tuberculosis virus. Donovan himself, for some reason, thought the equipment didn't look worthy of a head of state, and he instead brought along other scuba gear that he had purchased in New York. "In any case," a Cuban counterintelligence agent has said, "we would have analyzed the equipment."

The most surprising failures were the three attempts the CIA made on Fidel Castro during his long visit to Chile in 1971. In the first, Castro was going to be assassinated during a press conference, with a machine gun hidden inside a television camera. "It was something similar to the Kennedy assassination," the CIA agent who was responsible for planning the attempt explained, "because the person who was going to kill Castro was provided with documents that would make him look like an agent who had deserted the Cuban office in Moscow." But at the moment of truth, one of the assassins had a sudden attack of appendicitis, and the other didn't dare to fire all by himself. The second attempt was planned for Fidel Castro's visit to the mines in Antofagasta, in the north of Chile. A car that had been abandoned on the road forced them to bring the official motorcade to a stop. Inside the abandoned car were four hundred tons of dynamite, connected to a remote detonator. But, for reasons still unknown, the dynamite did not explode. The third attempt was supposed to have been a shot fired from a plane on the ground when Fidel landed in Lima; but a change in one of the plane's positions resulted in the CIA pilot-agent deciding not to fire, determining that he would not be able to escape in time. A fourth attempt, also thwarted, was when a beautiful CIA agent gained access to Castro and was going to slip a capsule of poison into his drink. But she had smuggled the poison capsules into Cuba in a jar of cold cream, and when she was ready to use them she couldn't find them: they had dissolved.

There are three incidents which the authors of *El pez es rojo* don't mention. One was when they rigged the microphone Fidel Castro was to use to address a tribunal with a high-voltage charge. Cuban security agents discovered it in time, and their explanation was simple: "We figured it would occur to somebody to try it sooner or later." The other assassination plot that never happened was for an employee of the Hotel Habana Libre to attempt, whom the CIA had supplied with colorless, odorless capsules, which had a delayed lethal reaction, so that the assassin could escape undetected. They were to be slipped into the fruit shake that Fidel Castro usually had when he went to the cafeteria in the morning. The agent waited more than six months before making an attempt, and, by the time Fidel finally showed up, the capsules had lost their effectiveness. The CIA furnished the agent with different capsules which would not lose their potency as long as they were stored in a freezer. The agent put them in the freezer, and when Fidel Castro came back, four months later, he made the fruit shake as usual; but at the last minute he couldn't break the ice that had enveloped the capsule of poison.

With all of that, the most serious danger that Fidel Castro has ever faced, and which also goes unmentioned in this amazing book—it wasn't an assassination attempt—was after the failure of the Bay of Pigs invasion, when he came back from the front in a jeep with the top down. Two survivors of the failed plot, who had hidden behind some bushes, watched him drive by from less than ten yards away, and one of them had him in his sights for a few seconds. But he didn't dare fire.[11]

On this sharply divergent path away from the United States, the defense of his friend even involves looking at differences in cultural-political customs. In an article dated December 2, 1981, "Los dolores del poder," perhaps to throw the absolute silence on Castro's health into sharp relief, and as a demonstration of his now well-known obsession with everything related to power, Gabo makes a note of the constant updates given on the health of U.S. presidents: "In 1961, the young, athletic John F. Kennedy suffered a slipped disc [. . .] in Vienna, and returned to his country on crutches, giving him the air of a returning war veteran. A few years ago, one of the sons of his brother Edward had to have a leg amputated as a result of bone cancer, and the occurrence was celebrated in the press as one more example of that family's courage. Around the same time, the wife of President Gerald Ford and the wife of Nelson Rockefeller, the governor of New York, had disfiguring surgeries, and their misfortune warranted ample coverage on the front pages [. . .]. The health of President Ronald Reagan, who has passed his seventieth birthday, has been the subject of much conjecture, until a nine-millimeter bullet ripped into his left side and settled very close to his spinal cord. His easy manner and shiny toothpaste-commercial smile as he was shown leaving the hospital made many think that Reagan was every bit the cowboy in real life that he was in the movies. But the conjecturing didn't stop. They still say that the president of the United States lost the momentum of his perennial youth after the assassination attempt, and that his workday had been scaled back to only three hours. Still, those of us who saw him in Cancun wearing a *guayabera*, with makeup that looked more like an embalming paste, didn't get the impression that he might keel over during negotiations or while fulfilling his numerous social obligations."[12]

Again, his indirect praise of Castro has both cultural and political components. On the one hand, there's the distance and irony that he evokes when talking about the *yanqui* leaders. On the other, there is the suggestion that the North Americans have a propensity for drama and theatrics, and are prone to exaggeration and disproportionate magnification of their own nationalism and its symbolic elements. That stands in contrast with the little—virtually nonexistent—public presence given to the human, personal side of the Revolutionary leader in his political image. It's a given that Fidel is a courageous, strong man, and that his health is solid as steel, and that he is so committed to the work of government that he won't spend even one minute of his five- or six-hour speeches discussing "inconsequential" matters.

ONLY LOVE INSPIRES SYMPHONIES

The most-cited poem from Jose Martí's *Versos libres* is probably the one that ends with a sentence about love as the only thing that can give rise to music. But sometimes just the opposite happens. There are melodies, artistic expressions, sensibilities, intellectual or emotional tendencies that can give rise to love, personal affinity, or friendship. Gabo has at times tried to show that this was the case between him and Castro, with literature acting as the catalyst. One of the first times that the Nobel winner talked at length about Castro was in the interview for *Playboy* published in early 1983. In response to a question about his friendship with the Cuban leader, he says: "We are good friends. Ours is an intellectual friendship. It may not be widely known that Fidel is a very cultured man. When we're together, we talk a great deal about literature. Fidel is a fantastic reader. As a matter of fact, the friendship really began after he'd read *One Hundred Years of Solitude*, which he liked very much."[13] And when the interviewer tries to steer the conversation toward politics and power, Gabo adroitly dodges those efforts and returns to literary themes: "But we don't really talk about politics that much. Most people find it difficult to believe that my friendship with Fidel Castro is almost totally based on our mutual interest in literature. Very few of our conversations concern the fate of the world. More often, we talk about what good books we've read. Whenever I go to Cuba, I always take Fidel a stack of books. Usually, upon my arrival in the country, I leave them with one of Fidel's aides and then I go about my business. A few weeks later, when Fidel and I finally get a chance to talk, he's read everything and there are a thousand things to talk about."[14]

Gabo recalls that once he gave his friend a copy of Bram Stoker's *Dracula*, a fantastic book which is often dismissed by intellectuals. It was two o'clock in the morning when Fidel took the book with him, after he had been talking with his friend for about an hour—this was a routine occurrence for Castro, since he tended to visit his close friends at night, after a long day of work. At that time, Fidel needed to study some important government documents, so that he could present them and discuss them the next day. Ten hours later, at around noon, they got together again, and Castro said: "Gabriel, you screwed me! That book; I couldn't get a minute's sleep."[15] García Márquez offers a similar response to Plinio Apuleyo Mendoza in the long interview in *El olor de la guayaba*, when he talks about the beginnings of their friendship: "Look, my friendship with Fidel Castro, which I consider very close and sustained by a strong mutual affection, began through literature. I had run into him a few times when I was working at Prensa Latina in 1960, and I hadn't felt that we had very much in common. Later, when I was a famous writer and he was the most well-known politician in the whole world, we saw each other several times and we liked and respected each other, but I didn't get the impression that our relationship would go beyond our political affinity. But very late one night, about six years ago, he told me he had to go home because he had many documents he had to read. That unavoidable task, he told me, bored and exhausted him. I suggested that he read some books of high literary quality that were also fun, to relieve the strain from the obligatory reading; I suggested many titles, and discovered something that very few people know: Fidel Castro is a voracious reader, a lover and serious student of great literature from all historical eras, and even in his most difficult times he always has an interesting book in hand to fill up any spare time. I gave him a book to take when we said good-bye at four o'clock in the morning, after talking all night, and at noon that same day I saw him again, and he had already read the whole book."[16]

Gabo uses the "literary" nature of their friendship as a shield to avoid admitting something very obvious: that in the late seventies their conversations on politics were not only routine, but also, as we have seen, García Márquez had become a statesman; and not just any statesman, but the ambassador-of-choice for Castro to use in the service of the triumph of the Revolution, within Cuba's borders and outside of them. And although no one doubts Castro's interest for some intellectual areas, Gabo's nose grows just a bit when he goes on to say: "And that is one side of his personality that very few people see, and it's in that area where our friendship has grown. Contrary to what has been said about us, we have never conspired for political ends. Fidel thinks that the work of a writer is to write his books, and not to conspire."[17] Fidel thinks, like any good absolute ruler, that if a writer can be used to support the revolution, he will be welcomed, and if he is not completely aligned with the ruler's political interests, then that writer is a counterrevolutionary. If you doubt that, just ask anyone on the long list of those condemned simply for what they thought, compiled by Eliseo Alberto in his *Informe contra mí mismo*, or ask any of the almost eighty who have recently been sentenced to prison.

Although Gabo's house in Havana is known to be near one of Castro's main residences, not even García Márquez knows exactly where his neighbor lives. And no one in Cuba knows. They say that it's "a house hidden by a dense thicket of trees, at the end of a long road that the police prevent anyone from entering."[18] When Jon Lee Anderson is clearly puzzled by García Márquez's ignorance on this point, in 1999, Gabo explains that he never asked "so that it's not something I could inadvertently reveal to anyone."[19] And he justifies Castro's precaution in this way, also demonstrating how the two friends completely trust each other: "He knows that I'm not going to betray things that he has confided in me, and that maybe I'm the person that he can trust the most. And Fidel is so mistrustful! He's only just recently started to change a little, and he's less preoccupied with security. Sometimes he even calls and says 'I'm coming over' or something like that. He never used to do that before. He always imagined that the telephones were tapped by the *yanquis*, by the CIA. And he probably had good reason to be concerned. He keeps his private life very private. He has never introduced me to his wife, for example. What's more, he's never even mentioned her. I met her because one day I was on Fidel's private plane and she was there and introduced herself. I'm not sure if it's true, but they say that Fidel hasn't even introduced her to his brother Raúl. What's private to Fidel is absolutely private ... I think that I know Fidel a lot better than most people, and I consider him a true friend, but who is Fidel in private? What is he really like? No one knows."[20]

As a result of this, in his personal life, every day Castro finds himself alone with the solitude inherent in the exercise of power, at the head of a regime that's racked by controversy. He has never publicly acknowledged any friendship, except with Gabo. García Márquez thinks that his friendship with Castro has limits, specifically because of the leader's delicate position. "Fidel has very few friends," Gabo asserts. "Somebody asked him once—I was there—if he experienced the loneliness of power. He answered no. Still, I wonder if those in power can really perceive how alone they actually are."[21]

Another bond that ties the two colossal personalities is the trust that García Márquez places in Castro's literary critiques. If *El otoño del patriarca* falls at the very beginning of their friendship and touches on a sensitive topic, giving rise to misunderstandings (or, more accurately, very interesting coincidences), from that point on all of Gabo's works would fall into Castro's hands before the manuscripts would be sent to the publisher. That first took place with *Crónica de una muerte anunciada*, published in 1981. In the *Playboy* interview, this is brought up, and García Márquez explains why he places this trust in his friend: "The reason I showed it to him is because he is a very good reader with a really astonishing capacity for concentration—and also because he's so careful. In many of the books he reads, he quickly finds contradictions from one page to another. *Chronicle of a Death Foretold* is structured as carefully as clockwork. If there had been an error in the works, a contradiction, it would have been very serious. So, knowing about Fidel's quick

ÁNGEL ESTEBAN AND STÉPHANIE PANICHELLI

eye, I showed him the original manuscript hoping he might catch any contradictions."22

Sometimes Castro has focused on details that Gabo might not notice, but which wouldn't escape the attention of a man with experience in certain aspects of life. Gabo says his friend "is an attentive, meticulous reader, finding contradictions and errors where you would least expect it. After he read *The Story of a Shipwrecked Sailor* he came over to my hotel just to tell me that there was an error in calculating the speed of the boat, and that its arrival time couldn't have been what I had said. He was right. So before *Chronicle of a Death Foretold* was published, I gave him the original draft of the manuscript, and he pointed out a mistake about the specifications of a hunting rifle. One gets the impression that he really likes the world of literature, he feels very comfortable in it, and he enjoys writing his speeches very carefully, which are becoming more frequent. One time, not without a hint of melancholy, he said to me: 'In my next life, I want to be a writer.'"23 Years later, in 1996, Gabo declared in *El País* (September 9): "I don't publish any books any more that the Commandant hasn't read first."

Although some of our interview subjects for this book assured us that Fidel has no interest whatsoever in literature, and only reads biographies of great political figures, Vázquez Montalbán offers some very significant information in his book *Y Dios entró en La Habana*. For example: on page 220 he summarizes the books that Castro read in jail in the early fifties, when he was planning the revolution that would eventually triumph on January 1, 1959. They were Victor Hugo and Marx to start; also, *Vanity Fair* by Thackeray; *Home of the Gentry* by Tergenev; the biography of Carlos Prestes, the leader of the Brazilian Communist Party; *The Secret of Soviet Strength* by Hewlett Johnson, "the Red Dean of Canterbury"; he read *Das Kapital* again, of course; the complete works of Freud; *The State and Revolution* by Lenin; Dostoevsky's *Crime and Punishment*;

works by Kant, Roosevelt, Einstein, Shakespeare, especially *Julius Caesar*, a text that was influential to Gabo in his *Autumn of the Patriarch* and other books. A few pages later, Montalbán describes one of Gabo and Fidel's meetings. He affirms that, with the exception of García Márquez, Castro has not had any real friends since 1980, the year his personal secretary Celia Sanchez died. And he states, "Fidel talks to Gabriel García Márquez and his wife Mercedes as if they were two trusted mediums who would never deceive him about what happens outside of the labyrinth. They stay up talking into the early hours of the morning, with Mercedes as the receptive, insightful listener that only women can be. And Gabo recommends stacks of books which he obediently reads, ten days in a row, with the writer always ready to listen to his critiques, debating them, and expanding on them, approving them, as if it were an intensive course in literary analysis."[24]

In October 2002, when Gabo handed over the first volume of his highly-anticipated memoirs to the press, Castro published an article about his friend, maybe his only friend, in the Colombian magazine *Cambio*, titled "La novela de sus recuerdos," which has been read around the world since it was the first time Fidel Castro has ever written an article on a literary theme, barely touching on politics.

I've known Gabo forever, and the first time we met could have been at any point in time in any leafy, poetic place in García Márquez's geography. As he himself admitted, he has on his conscience responsibility for my "addiction to fast-reading bestsellers, as a way of balancing the reading of official documents." I would also have to add that he is responsible for having convinced me that in my next life I want to be a writer, especially a writer like Gabriel García Márquez, with his obstinate attention to detail which serves as a philosophical foundation for his wild exaggerations. Once he even claimed that I had eaten eighteen scoops of ice cream, which, of course, I vehemently denied.

I remember in the first draft of *Of Love and Other Demons*, at one point a man rode by on his eleven-month-old horse, and I suggested to the author, "Look, Gabo, add two or three years to the horse's age, because one that's only eleven months old is just a baby." Later, when I read a copy of the published version, there's a scene with Abrenuncio de Sa Pereira Cao, whom Gabo characterizes as the most well-known, controversial doctor in the city of Cartagena de Indias, at the time the story takes place. In the novel, the man is weeping, sitting on a rock in the path next to his horse, who would turn one hundred years old in October, and whose heart had given out after suffering a fall. Gabo, as you would expect, had changed the animal's age into a prodigious circumstance, into an incredible event of unquestionable veracity.[25]

Castro also supports some of his friend's unusual views on linguistics and literature. After affirming that the Nobel Prize winner's work is a clear demonstration of his sensibilities, of his unchanging faith to his origins, of his uniquely Latin American inspirations, of his commitment to truth and his progressive ideals, he adds: "I share with him a scandalous theory, probably sacrilege to academics, about the relativity of the words in the language, and I do it with the same intensity as the fascination I have for dictionaries, especially the one I got for my seventieth birthday, and it's a real jewel because the definitions of the words have famous phrases from Hispanic-American literature as examples of their use. Also, as a public figure who has to write speeches and report on events, I share with the illustrious author experiencing a kind of delight in searching for just the right word, a kind of shared, tireless obsession until we are satisfied with the sentence, faithful to the feeling or idea that we want to express, but also with the belief that it could always be better. I admire him most when, not finding just the right word, he calmly makes it up. How I envy his poetic license!"[26]

And at the end of the article he reveals something we already know happened with *Chronicle of a Death Foretold* and that we can reasonably assume has been the case with the rest of García Márquez's works since then: Castro becomes an assiduous reader of his rough manuscripts and one of his most important literary advisers, not so much for style as for the credibility of the details: "Gabo has always sent me the manuscripts of his books while they're still being worked on, in the same simple, generous gesture he has always sent the rough drafts to those whose opinions he values, as a sign of our long, highly treasured friendship."[27]

One of those friends Castro alludes to is Álvaro Mutis, perhaps Gabo's most trusted literary adviser. For that reason, García Márquez wanted to introduce Mutis to Castro. Over lunch in one of the most popular restaurants in the upscale Miraflores neighborhood in Lima, Alonso Cueto, a novelist and director of the weekly magazine *El Comercio*, told us with a certain amusement, in June 2002, about their encounter. Also around the table with us that day were Javier Reverte, the tireless Spanish novelist and world traveler; and Julio Villanueva, director of the Peruvian cultural magazine *Etiqueta Negra*. The anecdotes about literary luminaries such as Borges, Kapuscinski, Vargas Llosa, Ribeyro, Bryce, and García Márquez flowed copiously, as the wine glasses were continuously refilled over the course of the meal. Cueto described how Gabo nervously decided to carry out his plan. Mutis is one of the most conservative writers in Latin America, with a very aristocratic mentality on the divisions of society, and is a hard-line defender of the monarchist values of the Europe of five or six centuries ago; that is, an absolute monarchy which posits that each part of society is exactly where it needs to be in the overall hierarchy, having been placed there by divine authority. His decision made, Gabo had no choice but to go through with it. Not wanting their initial meeting to be awkward, before arranging for his two friends to be at the same place, he spoke with Fidel and told him:

"I want to introduce you to a writer friend of mine, Alvaro Mutis, one of the best poets and novelists in all of Colombian literature. But there's one little problem: he's very monarchist."

"Don't worry about it," Fidel answered. "There's no problem, I'm sure we'll get along fine, because we both have the same enemy: the bourgeoisie."

HAVANA NIGHTS

Having reached this high level of trust in personal, political, and literary matters, it's no surprise to find that their relationship has even more facets. Ever since Gabo won the Nobel Prize, the two have carried on a tradition that involves even more people in their inner circle: the New Year's Eve celebration held at Gabo's mansion in Havana, his own little Cuban Macondo. The custom has continued for twenty years, with perhaps only a few exceptions in recent years due to Gabo's health problems. Miguel Barnet, a Cuban poet and president of the Fernando Ortiz Foundation, told us that those parties became not-to-be-missed social events in the eighties and nineties, causing them to lose their intimate feel, after Gabo won the Swedish prize. Gabo is a man who only feels completely relaxed in private. Barnet is one of the few people who managed to forge a close relationship with the Colombian writer in those decades. He often visits the mansion in Siboney, and he feels completely at home there. Sometimes he arrives there unannounced, when Gabo is writing, so Mercedes has him wait a while until his friend has finished. Barnet told us about his friend's meticulous preparations for those special parties he hosts in his home: his white shoes and white shirts, his wristwatches with the white straps, his thoroughly Caribbean, tropical style. He recalls one time he went to Gabo's house and found the writer studying a pack of cigarettes. Barnet asked him what he was doing, so pensive, with that object, and Gabo said he was editing the text on the cigarette pack, where it warned that smoking is harmful to your health, causing cancer, raising the risk of heart disease and causing addiction. He explained that he was correcting it because the tobacco company had probably hired a very mediocre advertising copy writer to come up with that text. Finally, Gabo whittled it down to two words: the name of the tobacco company, and the word "harms." To which Barnet replied, "That's enough."

The Cuban poet and writer also remembered that at those New Year's Eve parties and other gatherings, politics were almost never discussed. In fact, the subjects the two friends most often discussed had to do with popular music: the rumba, the bolero, salsa. Barnet is an expert in this area, and on other subjects in Cuban culture such as Santeria, Afro-Cuban religions, and spirituality in the Caribbean. When Gabo was writing *Of Love and Other Demons*, which was published in 1994, he often asked Barnet for some specific information on these subjects, since the book talked about miraculous, fantastic aspects of religion and superstitions in the Caribbean. Their conversations naturally often touched on literature too. They liked to talk about the favorite authors they had in common, like Azorin, Marguerite Yourcenar, and Robert Graves.

Of all the topics of conversation that arose at these parties that would be truly memorable, perhaps the subject of food was the most "appetizing." Fidel and Gabo are true aficionados of the culinary arts, and they know how to appreciate excellent cooking and fine wine. Barnet affectionately refers to Gabo as "the great hedonist," for his love of sweets, codfish, shellfish, and food in general.

アNGEL ESTEBAN and STÉPHANIE PANICHELLI

Régis Debray, another habitual guest at the parties, especially in the eighties, emphasizes the casual atmosphere of the gatherings: there would be about thirty people, and they didn't sit around a table. The food and drinks would be laid out on the table, in an attractive but simple display; everyone would serve themselves whenever they felt like it, and sit down wherever they wanted. Different conversation groups would form. It was a really nice atmosphere, with everyone eating and drinking standing up, spread around the house. Fidel always came by himself.

The two friends' shared love of good food is so well known that it was not only apparent at the very beginning of their friendship, as we saw in their first meeting at the Hotel Nacional, but it's also been indulged by the best chefs in Cuba. The great Smith, perhaps the best of all, who began his career at the Hotel Riviera before the Revolution, and who continues to set the standard for Cuban cuisine, has cooked for an illustrious list of celebrities, including Meyer Lansky, the American gangster who owned the Riviera, Hemingway, Joan Manuel Serrat, Gabriel García Márquez, Nat King Cole, and more. In an interview with Vázquez Montalbán, this Cuban chef recalled that at the beginning of the Revolution, many famous cooks had left the island, and he often cooked for Raúl and Fidel when they were hosting a special reception for foreign ambassadors, and on more than one occasion he cooked for Gabo, "who is a great fan of my cooking, and has promised to write the introduction to my memoirs, which are almost finished."[28] In that book, each of the dishes he includes is associated with a particular person who inspired them. Gabo's dish is "Lobster à la Macondo for Gabriel García Márquez," and the one for Fidel Castro is "Turtle Consommé."[29] Both men are experts in shellfish, as they discovered in their first conversation back in the seventies, and judging by the menus of many of their shared dinners. Gabo is eventually convinced that the Cuban leader knows everything there is to know about shellfish.[30] Castro explained to the mother of Frei Betto, a Brazilian priest who authored a famous book about Fidel and religion, how to prepare lobster and shrimp:

It's best not to boil shrimp or lobsters, because the boiling water weakens the substance and flavor and makes the meat a little bit tough. I like to broil them in the oven or grill them. For shrimp, five minutes of grilling time is enough. For lobster, eleven minutes in the oven and six minutes on the grill over the coals. For condiments, just butter, garlic, and lemon. Good food is simple food.[31]

And he finishes up his culinary discourse by touching on the turtle consommé that he liked so much from a very celebrated Cuban chef, who we've already met. . . .

"UBI SUNT?"

Jorge Manrique, the best medieval Spanish poet there was, wrote some verses after his father's death; and to place him on the human, spiritual, and professional level that he deserved, he compared his father with the great personalities of the day who had also died, using the literary phrase *Ubi sunt?* (Where are they?). He asks what happened to that king, that royal prince, that aristocrat-general. Similarly, when we look at the class of people that are invited to Gabo's New Year's Eve parties, and those that are regular guests at his Macondo in Havana, we ask ourselves, like Manrique, *ubi sunt* the intellectuals and the writers. Generally, the poets, novelists, and essayists who regularly visit the house are also very cozy with the political elite, like Miguel Barnet, Abel Prieto, the Minister of Culture, and Antonio Núñez Jiménez, the Vice-Minister of Culture until his death a few years ago and one of Gabo's first friends in Cuba. But *ubi sunt* the great Cuban writers? Where are they? For example, why the distancing from his friend Eliseo Diego? Alfredo Muñoz, who was a correspondent with France Presse for many years in Havana and who attended many of Gabo's celebrated parties, observed that his own friendship with Gabo was very intense at the onset; but after Gabo won the Nobel Prize, it cooled as his relationship with the political sector grew, especially his friendship with Castro.

In April 1988, in the Colombian edition of *El País*, García Márquez stated that his "friendship with politicians is as unpolitical as it could be," and he asserts that he considers himself least friendly with intellectuals, for reasons unknown to him. Maybe it's because, he conjectures, he feels "more curious about others." He toys with the issue a little more, but doesn't give a satisfactory answer that gets to the heart of the matter, his ambition and obsession for power, stating that it would be absurd to try to be friends with a president in order to exercise influence over him, since "no political leader, no head of state, really listens to anybody. They listen, but in the end they'll do what they think they have to do. So having influence over a national leader is the hardest thing in the world, and in the end they'll end up having enormous influence over you."

Again, his "noble" nose grows just a bit. Ten years had passed since Gabo first began to exercise a decisive influence over political issues affecting the Caribbean; and since 1982, his prestige soaring after the Nobel Prize victory, he's been able to say whatever he wants to whomever he wants, and his skills in the art of diplomacy have accomplished more than one serious political objective. His friendships in Cuba were increasingly approaching the highest circles of power, closing in on the "dukes" and "secretary generals," and moving further away from the intellectuals. Some statements he has made corroborate this, such as "I hate the intellectual life, writer's conferences, the roundtable discussions on literature on television,"[32] and "the critics are very serious men, and such seriousness hasn't interested me for a long time."[33]

During our last trip to Havana, several of our interview subjects provided indirect evidence of this phenomenon. In a beautiful house in Reparto Playa, the novelist Julio Travieso was our gracious host, serving drinks and hors d'oeuvres. We looked at the first editions of the classics of Cuban literature that were displayed on the bookshelves in his study, where those jewels of letters perfectly complemented the exquisite antique furniture pieces. On top of the table, a single object interrupted the harmonious atmosphere: a computer, where the writer sat down to work every day and answered his e-mails. We also looked at the various editions of his latest novel, *El polvo y el oro*, definitely his best work to date, which had won various national and international prizes and had been published in English, French, and Italian, aside from the various editions published in Spanish in Cuba, Mexico, and Spain. We went out onto the patio at the back of the house: a veritable jungle filled with ancient fruit trees, which were probably home to many birds and provided succulent fruit to more than one family, since the higher branches of the trees extended out beyond the garden walls.

But the most "ancient" specimen of all, but by no means decrepit, was Sandor, Julio's father-in-law, who, having seen his hundredth birthday, came out to greet us effusively, with a firm handshake and a warm embrace. And to think that Sandor had been born the same year as Alberti, Dulce Maria Loynaz, and Nicolás Guillén, the same year the Republic of Cuba was founded, and in 1929 he would emigrate there, from the cold lands of Eastern Europe, and there he would remain, in the island country that so fascinated him, into the next millennium . . . Julio told us that Sandor had never given up his daily cocktails and cigar, although a few months earlier he had caught a cold, and the doctor had ordered him to stop smoking and drinking. He was able to follow his doctor's orders for one entire day, but the next day he was feeling better, and he saw no reason to continue to follow his doctor's "absurd" restrictions.

Julio remembered one occasion in the eighties when Gabo had come to Havana to launch the publication of a book, and there had been a dinner with other writers. Julio was seated near Gabo for a long while, and they had had a friendly chat. Two days later, Travieso went to the reception for Gabo's book, and he took a copy with him, so the author could sign it. He greeted Gabo confidently, because of their friendly conversation a few nights earlier, but Gabo was cold, clearly putting some distance between them. Leonardo Padura told us that around the same time, he got a call from Lichi Diego (Eliseo Alberto), because Gabo had asked him to get together three excellent young writers for a dinner at the Riviera, where they could discuss literary topics. Lichi chose Padura, Senel Paz, and Luis Manuel García. There was a strange atmosphere at the dinner, because after the initial introductions were made, the host didn't take over to lead the discussion. "It was as if he had come to regret organizing the meeting," Leonardo told us, "and none of us knew what we were doing there with him." In spite of the interest that a dinner with such a personality would inevitably spark, in the end it was a tedious and somewhat Kafka-esque evening.

Virgilio López Lemus shared a very revealing anecdote with us: in the same period of the eighties, after having published his masterful work on García Márquez, he approached Gabo at a function they both happened to be attending in Havana, to show him a copy of the book, but Gabo just looked at it skeptically, and said, "Literary criticism doesn't interest me in the least." Now, it seems, we know where the intellectuals with no political benefits or ties are, and all of those who are neither dukes nor secretary-generals: "Where oblivion lives," as Becquer would say.

PART THREE

★

FROM CUBA TO HEAVEN: AND GOD ENTERED INTO HAVANA

CHAPTER TWELVE

★

FRIENDSHIP WITH FIDEL: THE FLIP SIDE

I N SPITE OF HIS PRIVILEGED POSITION WITHIN THE CUBAN universe, Gabo knows that not all that glitters is gold, and he understands very well that his friendship with Castro has its downside too. And it's not just the resulting loss of some very valuable friends like Vargas Llosa, but also an onslaught of criticism fired at him from the right and the left, from Europe and the Americas, and even from some of his own friends. For example, his great lifelong friend Plinio Apuleyo Mendoza, who had been much more of a revolutionary and political activist in his youth than Gabo ever had, who put him in touch with contacts in Cuba in 1959 for Operation Truth and then with Prensa Latina, started to differ with his friend over the Padilla case, some details of which are still clouded in confusion. Then, when Apuleyo Mendoza wrote *El olor de la guayaba* about Gabo's life and works, Mercedes, Gabo's wife, remarked to her husband: "Apuleyo doesn't like us,"[1] a schism that became very well known upon the publication of another book about Gabo, *El caso perdido: La llama y el hielo*, which focuses at length on certain aspects of the Revolution.

In the late nineties, Plinio wrote another book that also alludes to his friend: *Manual del perfecto idiota latinoamericano*, a collaboration with Alvaro Vargas Llosa and Carlos Alberto Montaner. The book, which has been harshly criticized for its lack of objectivity, shoddy research, and an insufficient depth of understanding of Latin American cultural–political reality, says that anyone who has supported any of the Latin American revolutionary movements or has ascribed to what Plinio calls "your grandfather's socialism" is "an idiot."[2] At one point, Apuleyo Mendoza said: "I think that when Fidel dies, the same thing is going to happen as when Stalin died. We're going to hear about all the atrocities that went on under his rule. And I don't think having been such a good friend of his is going to help Gabo very much."[3] For his part, Vázquez Montalbán asserts that the price Gabo pays for the friendship he cultivates with Fidel is not adequately compensated for by the comforts and privileges he enjoys in Havana.[4]

In any case, the special treatment and the level of mutual trust their friendship has achieved still don't mean Gabo is entirely exempt from the same sort of control that all influential personalities are subject to. In Cuba, everybody minds everybody else's business, everyone is spied on, controlled, and everyone is the subject of investigation. Anyone's friend could potentially be a government agent who later reports on the activities of their "friend." For Cubans, this role could be played by anyone, even family members or extremely close friends. In Gabo's case, it's well known that there are always three or four people following him around wherever he goes in Cuba. Ricardo Vega told us that García Márquez is very aware of this, and that he views it with a sense of humor. Every once in a while he'll walk up to them and bring them a beer. If he is at a bar having a drink with friends, he'll tell the waiter to tell the men at that table in the back—the "secret" surveillance team—that the next round is on him. That is a part of the price of being friends with a dictator. On one occasion, Antonio Valle Vallejo, a professor of Marxism and a good friend of Gabo's, asked him: "Why do you put up with such contradictory treatment?" and García Márquez answered: "Because I want to write the book about Fidel."[5]

When it comes to Fidel, it's useful to note that he has very rarely been able to sustain a friendship over a long period of time. Generally, he gets bored and cuts off close relationships. That has never happened with Gabo. On the contrary, this particular friendship grows even stronger with the passage of time. In November 2002, a month after having published the heartfelt article about his friend's memoirs, Fidel appeared together with his Colombian friend in the press half the world over, at a huge stadium for the opening ceremony of an international tournament. Gray-haired and looking their age, they still wore youthful smiles, conveying the customary complicity and mutual pride they tend to put on display for the cameras when they are together, showing off the friendship they both enjoy so much. Now, Gabo no longer remembers his critical spirit of about thirty years earlier, when—in the earliest days of their friendship—he told the Leftist magazine *El Manifiesto*: "In general, my most difficult problems of conscience don't stem from the simple fact of being a writer, but from my somewhat illusory desire to maintain my position among a diaphanous group of Leftists of consequence. My political conscience boils with anger with the closing of the Soviet Union in the face of internal pressure from democratic forces, for example, from the ease with which Fidel Castro accuses a writer of being a CIA agent, a writer that Fidel Castro himself knows perfectly well is not, or with China's stupidity, that breaks off relations with Beethoven while maintaining them with Pinochet. On the other hand, my writer's spleen processes so much bile together, since literature has such a broad spectrum, inside of which these enormous contradictions become reduced to simple stumbling blocks of history."[6]

ÁNGEL ESTEBAN ᴀɴᴅ STÉPHANIE PANICHELLI

THE UNITED STATES: BOTH SIDES OF THE COIN

Gringa coins, like any other, have heads and tails. The consequences
of Gabo's close relationship with Cuba and its Revolution, in relation to the natural enemy, also have a flip side. Not everything that
comes from the North is bad. In an article from the early eighties,
when Reagan was elected president, Gabo posits that his victory
represented "a devastating cataclysm with very few precedents in
the life of that awesome country, whose immense creative power
has produced some of the greatest things of this century, and some
of the most abject."[7] And in the *Playboy* interview, he flatly concluded that "No cultured man can exist today without traveling
frequently to the U.S."[8] Finally, and as a still-positive note to a story
with more downsides than not, when Gabo was diagnosed with
lymphatic cancer in the summer of 1999, a condition complicated
by his age and his previous bout with lung cancer, which had been
operated on in 1992, the medical treatment that kept him alive
came from California. There he underwent a therapy that contained the lymphoma and that, a year later, allowed him to appear
before the cameras to announce that he was able to live a normal
life, and that he was still writing his memoirs and working on various stories and novels, and that the letter that had been widely circulated on the Internet, in which he supposedly bids farewell to the
world, was a hoax. Some skeptics may ask: Why didn't Gabo go to
a Cuban hospital, where he surely would have received a level of
care appropriate for his high-ranking position within the Revolution? In fact, around that same time, none other than Diego
Armando Maradona, the soccer superstar and friend of the Revolution, chose to go to Cuba, not the United States, to undergo
detox treatment to get off of drugs, something that he hadn't been
able to accomplish in Italy or Argentina.

In spite of having been crowned the author of the "great American Novel" by New York Times critic John Leonard,[9] and in spite

of his great acceptance as a novelist in the United States, because of his work with Prensa Latina and his politics, from 1961 until 1971 García Márquez had been denied a visa to live in that country and to work in New York. That changed somewhat in 1971 when Columbia University awarded him an honorary degree. "Since then," he explained in 1983, "I have had some sort of conditional visa that makes me feel insecure. It's a game established by the State Department."[10] And he added that "It is unpleasant. It's as if I had a mark on my forehead, and it shouldn't be that way. I am one of the great propagandists for North American literature. I have said to audiences everywhere in the world that the North American novelists have been the giants of the century. Moreover, great cultural changes are taking place in the United States because of the influence of Latin America—and my work is part of that influence. I *should* be able to participate more freely."[11]

In fact, the only Academy of Letters that he belonged to when he received the Nobel Prize is in the United States, and the critics in the U.S. are the ones who had given his works the warmest reception up to that point. Gabo wanted to make his position completely clear and coherent, underscoring the positive and negative aspects: "Sometimes I have the impression that in the United States, there is a tendency to separate my writing from my political activities—as if they were opposites. I don't think they are. What happens is that, as an anti-colonial Latin American, I take a position that many people in the United States find annoying or uncomfortable. What I'd like to correct is the problems and errors in the Americas as a whole. I would think the same way if I were a North American. Indeed, if I were North American, I would be even more of a radical, because it would be a matter of correcting the faults in my own country."[12]

His criticism of U.S. imperialism focuses on even the smallest details, such as the country's name itself. He laments that the people of the U.S. appropriate the word *America* as if they were the only

Americans, when in reality everyone from the North Pole on down to Patagonia is equally "American." What's more, they live in "a country without a name. They should find a name, because right now they have none. We have the United States of Mexico, the United States of Brazil. But the United States? The United States of what? Now, remember, that is said with affection. [...] But as a Latin American, as a partisan for Latin America, I can't help but feel resentful when North Americans appropriate the word America for themselves."[13] The imperialism is particularly noxious, he continues, when it involves small countries that are unfortunately too geographically close to them. For those cases, Gabo has a radical defense, like the one he adopts for the "Queen of the Caribbean": "Cuba is very much a part of this American ship. Sometimes I think it would be safer for the Cuban Revolution if its people could get a tugboat and tow themselves elsewhere—somewhere other than ninety miles from Florida."[14]

In recent years, in spite of the open hostility between the writer and the country still "without a name," Gabo has acted as an intermediary between political forces of "his island" and of Colombia and the United States. He introduced Pastrana, the conservative president of Colombia from 1998 to 2002, to Fidel, who could facilitate a dialogue with the guerrillas. He also helped to restore relations between Bogotá and Washington. The U.S. Secretary of Energy, Bill Richardson, affirmed that, although Gabo hadn't planned the meeting, he had at least been "a catalyst."[15]

Gabo met with President Clinton several times, to act as mediator between Cuba and the U.S. on such important subjects as lifting the embargo, the crisis of Cuban rafters, and so on, and at the same time to tell the U.S. president about results of agreements between the guerrillas and the government of Colombia, a process in which Cuba played a leading role: "The United States needs Cuba's participation in the Colombian peace process because the

Cuban government has the strongest contacts with the guerrillas. In addition, Cuba is ideally located only two hours away by plane, so Pastrana could go there any time, conduct any necessary meetings, and go back without anyone finding out. The U.S. wants that to happen."[16] Gabo's impression of Clinton was different, at least in the first years of his administration, than that of most other U.S. presidents, whom he had harshly criticized. He even sympathetically defended Clinton in one of his newspaper articles, referring to the "Lewinsky case," recalling with amusement that he was present when Fidel found out about the story, and the dictator said furiously: "Those damn *yanquis* get on you about everything!"[17] Gabo met with Clinton several times. Roberto Fernandez Retamar told us what precipitated their contact to try to resolve the rafter crisis. It was in the mid-nineties, when the Cuban economy was in a shambles. With massive numbers of Cubans leaving the island and heading for the Florida coast, it was feared that a crisis similar in scale to the Mariel boatlift was imminent, and Clinton spoke to Mexican president Salinas de Gortari to try to find a solution, knowing that Mexico had very good relations with Cuba. De Gortari got in touch with Fidel, who in turn contacted García Márquez, once more his minister, ambassador-at-large, diplomat, go-between, and negotiator-of-choice for Cuban crises.

One of those meetings also included Carlos Fuentes. Clinton seemed very open and interested, living up to a description of him as "a U.S. president who collected intellectuals."[18] Clinton was said to have listened attentively to the Latin Americans' arguments on various topics, but he didn't offer any responses to comments on subjects related to Cuba. On the trip back, Gabo said to Fidel something like: "He didn't say anything about Cuba, but what he didn't say was promising."[19] Vázquez Montalbán notes that, after that meeting, Gabo had another meeting, this time one-on-one, with the U.S. president, and he got the impression that Clinton was "very opportunistic, he's only thinking about the elections, but he doesn't have a clear philosophy completely against lifting the embargo, and if he doesn't lift it, it's so he won't cause any problems politically."[20] That's all we know about that second talk, since the first meeting has been described in detail by Carlos Fuentes to Vázquez Montalbán, and the conversation revolved around nothing more than good literature. The Catalan journalist and novelist described Clinton:

MVM: He was receptive, I think.

CF: He started by saying: "I'm going to listen to you very carefully, but I'm not going to give any opinions, just listen. . . ." And basically, we talked. Gabo talked, he talked about Bernardo Sepúlveda, the former Foreign Minister of Mexico who was there, and I talked, and it seemed like Clinton went pale, he didn't give away any emotion, he was perfectly controlled. That went on for forty or fifty minutes, an hour; then he said: "All right, I'm among writers here; why are we talking politics? Let's talk about literature. . . ." And then the fun part of the dinner began.

MVM: What writers did he talk about?

CF: Faulkner more than anything. He said he had read a lot of him, from the perspective of having come from a very dysfunctional family, very violent, the stepfather, the mother, and him, in the middle of the South, racked by racism, lynchings, intolerance. And he told us that when he was young, around fourteen or fifteen years old, he got on his bicycle and rode to Oxford (Mississippi), to see Faulkner's house, to confirm that the South was more than all those problems—that the South was Faulkner too. He talked about Cervantes like people who have actually read *Don Quixote* will talk about him. He talked about his habit of reading two hours before going to sleep, every night, of his preference for certain writers, Marco Aurelio, for example. Police procedurals and the mystery writers, Paco Ignacio Taibo II, *two*, he insisted, *Taibo two*.

MVM: Paco Ignacio is in his glory.

CF: Just imagine. When he talked about books, he showed that he was a reader. He recited a passage from Faulkner's *The Sound and the Fury*, and when the evening was winding down, Gabo and I went to the library to look up that passage: he had remembered it almost verbatim.

MVM: And what about Cuba? Had he read anything from Cuba?

CF: He didn't say anything. He got up from the table twice to take phone calls; later he said it had something to do with the crisis in Ireland, Gerry Adams and Sinn Fein. But he had already said that he wasn't going to say anything about Cuba, and he didn't. He is a very controlled man, at least politically.[21]

In that first round, in spite of his silence on Cuba, it seemed that Gabo and Clinton had made a connection. Later, negotiations would continue. But they wouldn't bring particularly positive results, and the possible agreements that might have been reached were still in a gray area: "I would love," García Márquez said later, "to see Clinton again now, but it's no longer possible. Everything's changed since Kosovo. The situation in the world has completely changed. With

Kosovo, Clinton has found the political legacy that he wants to leave behind him: the North American imperialist model."[22] At least, even though Gabo didn't win the battle on the embargo and imperialism, the battles related to his health have been waged very successfully in the United States, and his photo appeared every now and then in a newspaper, in the middle of 2003, almost four years after he was first admitted to a clinic in California. Around that time, Roberto Fernández Retamar also had to be hospitalized for cancer treatment. He told us at his home in El Vedado that in mid-1999, when they both knew about each other's diagnoses and the necessity of hospitalization, one day they were joking about the coincidence. By chance, Michael Jackson had also just been admitted to a hospital, and Gabo mentioned to Roberto, ironically: "Michael Jackson, you, and myself in the hospital: the culture is in trouble."[23]

THE SHINIEST SIDE OF THE COIN: POLITICAL PRISONERS

Cubans of the twenty-fifth century will say that when Fidel died, not that long ago, he went up to heaven, but Saint Peter, horrified, wouldn't let him in, because he wasn't on the list, and he sent him down to Hell. There, Satan welcomed him with all the honors befitting a head of state, rolling out the red carpet and serving a turtle soup worthy of the most discerning palate.

"Hello, Fidel! We've been waiting for you, come on in, make yourself at home."

"Thank you, Satan, but I have to send out a messenger right away. I was just up in heaven and I left my bags there."

"Don't worry about it, I'll send two demons from the third inferno on the left to collect your things."

So two security agents from Hell went up to heaven, but the gates were closed, since Saint Peter was out to lunch and his fill-in had the day off.

"It doesn't matter," one demon said, "we'll just climb over the gate and take the bags without anybody noticing."

They started to climb the gates when two angels passed by and saw them. One angel said to the other, "Look, Fidel hasn't even been in Hell for half an hour yet, and we have political refugees already."

This anecdote, as real as Remedio the Beauty's ascension to heaven while hanging the sheets out to dry, hoping to meet Fidel there, reveals the almost natural relationship between any dictatorial government and the large numbers of political exiles, many of whom have spent, just as "naturally," a certain period of time hiding in the shadows. Gabo, who is a political figure who supports a dictatorship, while he is also an intellectual (and knows fully well what it means to be an intellectual), is aware of the level of independence that a writer can have with respect to a political regime, and what the limits are. And he understands that, sometimes, a poem can be more powerful than a bullet. Consequently, his political commitment has led him to try to secure the release of political prisoners on many occasions, and to try to help people in the literary world who find themselves in dire straits on the island. Plinio Apuleyo Mendoza cites a figure of 3,200 prisoners freed on his behalf. Gabo has often carried out this task with the utmost discretion, out of the media spotlight, and he doesn't easily discuss the subject. This is, perhaps, the brightest side of a relationship with ample downsides. Jon Lee Anderson wrote:

When I pressed him to talk about it, García Márquez confirmed that he had helped people to leave the island, and he mentioned an effort that had resulted in the release and permitted exile of "more than two thousand people. I know how far I can go with Fidel. Sometimes he says 'No.'

Sometimes he comes to me later and says that I was right." He said that the power to help people made him happy, and he gave the impression that from Fidel's point of view, he had no problem with seeing them go. "Sometimes I go to Miami," he said, "although not that often, and I've stayed in the homes of people whom I had helped to leave. They are eminent *gusanos* [worms] who call up all their friends and throw huge parties. Their children ask me to autograph their books. Sometimes people that approach me are people who have denounced me before. But in private they show me another face." Enrique Santos Calderón says that "Gabo knows perfectly well what the Cuban government is and he has no illusions about it, but Fidel is his friend and he has chosen to live with the contradictions."[24]

As we see once again, the revolution is not perfect. Having come to know Cuba from one end to the other, it's reasonable to admit that there have been certain victories, but it's not quite so reasonable to suggest that it is the best system the world has ever seen. Between the time of that article in 1975 and the present, García Márquez has seen too many things, and simple common sense does not allow for irrational apologies. In an October 2002 article, Teodoro Petkoff describes a scene that is difficult to imagine having taken place five years earlier: "Around Christmas 1997, at his house in Havana, Gabo told me a stunning anecdote. A group of high-ranking officials had been talking with him and Fidel. Gabo made a few critical observations about the regime, and one of those present asked him what, exactly, he was trying to say. Fidel answered for him: 'What Gabo is trying to say is that neither he nor I likes the revolution that we have made.' You can imagine the shocked silence that followed that bitter confession."[25]

November 1978 marked the opening of a new chapter in the

relationship between the two friends that still exerts palpable political consequences. The radical Colombian newspaper *Alternativa*
interviewed the writer:

ALT: Let's look at Cuba. The national and international
press is filled with various stories about the release of
Cuban political prisoners, a process which you are well
acquainted with. What's behind the Cuban government's
decision on this?

GGM: The most important thing to make clear here is that
we're talking about a unilateral, spontaneous decision on the
part of the Cuban Revolution, that upon marking in January
the twentieth anniversary of its triumph, considered itself
sufficiently mature and with sufficient defensive forces to
not have to continue holding all of those people prisoner,
who at a certain time were deemed to have been a real threat
to the stability of the Revolution itself, but no longer are.
The Cuban leadership also decided that the twentieth
anniversary would be a great opportunity to work toward
the reunification of the Cuban family, in the sense of establishing contacts and closer communication channels
between the Cuban exiles in the United States, Puerto Rico,
and Venezuela, mainly, and their relatives on the island.

   This Cuban community in exile, as Fidel has called it,
has begun to clearly distinguish itself from the small organized groups of "worms" that dedicate themselves to terrorism against Cuba. The government has thought that
isolating the recalcitrant "worms" could do much for
family reunification. Remember that in a long interview
he gave in Havana, Fidel asked the exile community to
form a group that could negotiate directly with the Cuban

223

government, with no intermediaries, the release of approximately three thousand political prisoners, in the shortest time frame possible.[26]

From this commentary, Gabo seems to be a recognized, well-informed member of the Cuban government, although only three years had transpired since he first began exploring it and spending time on the island. He demonstrates an in-depth understanding of the situation; he knows how to explain and defend it. He has learned his lessons well; even the one about the collective interest coming before the interest of the individual. He never suggests here that he has been deeply involved (as the interview with Jon Lee revealed) and that perhaps it had been him, and not the mature judgment of a "unilateral, spontaneous decision on the part of the Revolution," that had persuaded the Maximum Leader to open the jail cells. However, a little later on in the *Alternativa* interview, he reveals himself as the catalyst behind a prior prisoner release. He refers to "Reynol González, the Catholic leader who was imprisoned for fifteen years, and whose release I secured from Fidel in November of last year. Once he was free, Reynol immediately joined one of the negotiating committees of the exiles and returned to Cuba to coordinate the release of the remaining political prisoners. He recently called me from Miami to tell me that he had gone back there and that he was very happy. They gave him a car to use, put him up at an official government house, and he even talked to Fidel for three hours. After Reynol's visit, forty-five prisoners were freed, among them an old friend of his, Fernando de Rojas,"[27] but not as the author of *La Celestina*. In 1980 Heberto Padilla, the author of *Fuera del juego*, was released, after many long years in prison. When he was initially being persecuted, Gabo stayed out of it, and was the only intellectual who did not protest. However, after ten years had passed, Gabo helped Padilla obtain Castro's permission to leave the island.

That year also marked the exile of Reinaldo Arenas, persecuted for being a homosexual and a counterrevolutionary, and he got out thanks to the Mariel boatlift. But Gabo thought that this wasn't a good way to leave the island, because of the potential repercussions in international public opinion. So when he found out that Arenas was planning on leaving by that route, Gabo tried to get hold of him to offer him a more dignified mode of transportation, but it was too late. Everything happened very quickly, and neither the Cuban government nor Gabo had time to react. Afredo Muñoz told us that one day, he crossed paths with Gabo in the hall of the Hotel Riviera as he was stepping off the elevator. Muñoz told him that Coco Salas, one of Arenas's friends, had just confirmed that Reinaldo was leaving on the Mariel. Alarmed, García Márquez quickly placed a call to Alfredo Guevara, the director of the ICAIC and a powerful man in the Cuban government on matters relating to the world of the intellectuals. They immediately sprang into action to try to stop Arenas, but the boat had left port. Some hours later, Arenas set foot on French soil. A few years later, on April 9, 1983, Arenas sent a letter to García Márquez, with his customary irony and betraying a deep bitterness about his past on the island. He made reference to an earlier letter that Arenas had sent to Castro, which Gabo had alluded to in some of his writings. These are Arenas's words:

Mr. Gabriel García Márquez, C.M.[28]
Presidential Palace
Bogota, Colombia

Respected fabulist:

Many writers who are close to you have told me something that, thanks to you, is already *vox populi*; that your close friend, Mr. Fidel Castro, told you that I had left Cuba for strictly personal reasons, and to illustrate this point, he extracted from his ample chest a love letter addressed to him and signed by me. . . . I do not in any way deny the existence of that letter, which you told the whole world about. Just the opposite: the letter exists, and was sent by me to officials of the Department of the Interior in Cuba, as a tactic to obtain permission to leave the country. Since, apparently, you have a very close relationship with the secret police, perhaps you could send me a photocopy of the aforementioned letter, for inclusion in a book that I am in the process of writing. Then, when the letter is published in various countries, it will save you the task as directed by your commander. If not, and because of you, I will be obliged to reconstruct the letter's text from memory, a reconstruction that will, naturally, lack the impetus and passion of the original. So, as the excellent journalist that you have been, I urge you not to deprive the reading public of that particular document.

Sincerely,

Reinaldo Arenas[29]

When Arenas published this letter to García Márquez, he left the following page almost entirely blank, with just two lines: "*Author's note*: Since García Márquez did not send the requested letter, we will leave this page blank in the hope of some day being able to publish the text."[30]

One of Cuba's most famous political prisoners, Armando Valladares, who spent almost twenty years in jail beginning in 1960 and has described being subject to tortures that almost left him crippled, was finally freed thanks to Gabo. García Márquez told the newspaper *El País* on December 8, 1982 (page 26) that he acted as an intermediary between Castro and Mitterrand to obtain Valladares's release. And he elaborated: "I like to be involved without anyone knowing about my involvement. I always thought that it was an unnecessary problem for many people and it was better to solve it." On a separate occasion, Gabo stated that Fidel had released Valladares to please him, a statement which reveals, according to Jorge Semprún, "the great writer's outsized vanity."[31] In a personal interview, Plinio Apuleyo Mendoza confirmed that Gabo helped the parents of Severo Sarduy, the great Cuban poet and novelist exiled in Paris, to secure permission to leave the island to visit their son. And Eliseo Alberto, the son of Eliseo Diego, left the island for professional reasons, thanks to Gabo. Lichi went to work on some film projects that Gabo had started in Mexico, and he never went back. Shortly thereafter, he wrote the heart-wrenching story *Informe contra mí mismo*, which his Colombian friend must not have liked very much at all.

But the most talked-about instance of assisting an exodus involves Norberto Fuentes. We have already seen how he was one of the insiders who introduced Gabo into Cuba's "high society." García Márquez, so loyal in friendship, suffered an unexpected reversal at the end of this relationship, perhaps all the sadder because of the element of surprise. At a time when he had certain connections to the shadowy world of arms traffickers, Fuentes met Colonel Tony De la Guardia. When Ochoa and De la Guardia were executed by firing squad in 1989, Fuentes, who had enjoyed a level of friendship with both of them, was never imprisoned or detained, not even for just a few hours, something that did occur with most of De la Guardia's relatives and friends, according to Jorge Masetti and his wife, Ileana De la Guardia. This was surely because of Fuentes's friendship with Raúl Castro, who protected him from those sorts of humiliations and promoted him as one of the most prominent, valuable young intellectual Revolutionaries. In any case, Norberto couldn't help experiencing an uncontrollable fear, and he felt compelled to denounce his imprisoned friend on his own. He called up the State Security and informed them that Colonel De la Guardia had left a suitcase full of dollars in his house.

After the arrest and execution of the two military men, Fuentes started to feel persecuted. He obsessed about it and grew increasingly paranoid. He decided to leave the country, but the state would not allow it, so he launched a hunger strike in his apartment in Havana. Gabo had always been Norberto Fuentes's great protector; so he intervened so that the Cuban government would allow Fuentes to leave. Finally, they both left on the president of Mexico's private plane and flew off to the land of the Aztecs. For performing that intervention, Gabo received the support of the American writer William Styron. Some time later, Fuentes went to the United States, where he fell into the hands of the U.S. Secret Service. One day, Alfredo Muñoz, the reporter for France Presse who told us this story, spoke with Fuentes on the phone and asked him: "How are you doing?" and Norberto Fuentes answered: "I'm between Miami and Virginia," that is, between the Cuban counter-revolutionary "worms" and the headquarters of *yanqui* intelligence. Barely out of Cuba, Norberto "committed the inanity of renouncing Gabo: he bit the hand that had fed him," Alfredo explained to us. Fuentes's articles and some of his books written in the nineties spew rancor at the man who had done nothing more than try to help him.

García Márquez's glowing reputation as an intercessor on behalf of lost causes, in spite of the anonymity with which he preferred to carry out much of that work, resulted in many people approaching him as if he were some kind of saint. For example, a humble family, with no connections to the worlds of literature or politics, asked the world-famous writer to help their father, who was imprisoned in Cuba, to leave the island. Gabo made the necessary overtures, and that man was able to reunite with his family in exile. This family's testimonial shall remain anonymous for posterity, and that family will be eternally grateful to the man who helped them, an act which was just a minor detail to him but meant the whole world to them.

So organizations and individuals from all walks of life began to ask Gabo for some really outlandish favors. García Márquez had a very interesting article published on August 11, 1982, titled "Even Humanitarianism Has Its Limits," in which he told a story that sounded like something out of a Hollywood movie: in December 1980, a boat carrying twelve Colombians was intercepted in Cuban waters, and those aboard the vessel were sentenced for violating Cuba's territory and for drug trafficking. In April 1981, another boat with nine Colombians aboard was intercepted for similar reasons: a large quantity of marijuana was found, and they were charged with violating territorial waters and illegal entry into the country. When Gabo arrived in Cuba in November 1981, a big pile of letters from the family members of those imprisoned awaited him, telling him that the Foreign Relations Department in Colombia refused to do anything on their behalf, since the people involved were common criminals, not politicians. Gabo pled their case to Fidel, and he presented it to the State Council, but when Gabo returned to Cuba in March to see how the process was progressing, the number of prisoners was no longer twenty-one, it had grown to thirty, since another boat had been intercepted in February, while the people aboard that vessel would be released a short time later. The problem was that later that year, when Gabo returned to Cuba in the summer to see what had transpired on the issue, he found out that in May, they had arrested sixteen more Colombians. So, at the end of the article, he had to make clear: "I am not prepared to intercede on behalf of the sixteen recently arrested prisoners or any of the others who will, no doubt, be captured in the future. The reason is very simple: at that stage, out of pure humanitarianism, I as well as the Cuban authorities would end up involuntarily, but very efficiently, serving the interests of the real drug traffickers. The families of those prisoners, in any case, now have the opportunity to make an appeal to the new government of Colombia, which perhaps has a bigger heart than the regime that has recently departed, for everyone's good."[32]

Vázquez Montalbán recognizes that Gabo's mediation has been decisive in many cases, but it would be an exaggeration to talk about some three thousand political prisoners released because of his "powers of persuasion" or, simply, thanks to his power, which has steadily grown over the years. The figures cited by Jon Lee Anderson, Plinio Apuleyo Mendoza, and others seem, when scrutinized, to be excessive. Vázquez Montalbán told us this in the interview we conducted the same day that some Spanish actors "took over" a session of Congress in Spain, in a bloodless coup without weapons, but with T-shirts that read: "NO to war in Irak."

FOR GABO, TAILS-DOWN

Once again, Fidel dies in the twenty-fifth century and goes to Hell. There, he notices that each country has its own inferno. He goes to the German one and asks,

"What do they do to you here?"

"Here, first, they put you in an electric chair for an hour, then they make you lie on a bed of nails for an hour, and for the rest of the day, the German devil comes and whips you."

Apparently, Fidel didn't like that idea, so he went around to see some infernos of other countries. He walked right by the one for the United States without even stopping. Then he went to the Russian, Spanish, and French infernos, and after asking about their various systems of punishment, he was surprised to find that they were all exactly alike. When he reached the Cuban inferno, he could see from far away that there was a huge line of people clamoring to get in. Intrigued, he asked Manolo García, the last one in line:

"Manolo, what do they do to you here?"

"Here, first they put you in an electric chair for an hour, then they make you lie on a bed of nails for an hour, and for the rest of the day the Cuban devil whips you."

"But, if it's exactly like the other infernos," Fidel replied, "why are there so many people trying to get in?"

"You'll see, Commander," Manolo said, "the electric chair doesn't work because there's no electricity, there are no nails on the bed of nails because someone stole them last week, and the devil just shows up, signs something, and leaves."

Unfortunately, for those who experienced a similar hell in real life, the scenario was different. The personal testimonies on tortures endured in Cuban prisons are numerous, and some of those giving these testimonies have a high public profile, making them difficult to dismiss. Padilla was tortured, at least psychologically, so that he would "be persuaded" to read the self-criticism. Valladares sustained life-long injuries. María Elena Cruz Varela told us one day from her office at the daily newspaper *La Razón* that she was subjected to a "hormonal treatment" that completely disfigured her. There are more. Some novelists have described the prisons' regimes, with their "methods of seduction and correction." The possibility exists, and in some cases it is more than a possibility, that certain testimonials have been exaggerated, or are completely false, but it is not likely that the hundreds of thousands of written documents on the subject all completely lack a certain objectivity and logic. Especially when we know that in all dictatorships, and also in many democracies, torture is a routine practice. Manuel Ulacia spoke plainly in a statement made in 1992: "Openly opposing him [Castro's government] has greater implications. It's common knowledge that dissidents are punished with psychiatric treatments—which include electroshock and forced ingestion of high doses of psychotropic drugs—imprisonment, torture, or death. For example, [here's what happened to] the writer María Elena Cruz Varela, winner of the National Poetry Prize in 1989, just for having written a manifesto signed by a group of Cuban intellectuals which called for 'an open dialogue between the government and the opposition to promote democracy in the country through peaceful means': after breaking into her home, beating her in public, and forcing her to 'eat' the manuscripts of her poems, in front of her children, she was then sentenced to two years in prison."[33]

For his part, Néstor Almendros made two documentaries on the subject, featuring chilling interviews with victims of some of these practices: *Conducta impropia*, about the repression of homosexuals, and *Nadie escuchaba*, about the physical and psychological tortures that Cuban political prisoners were subject to. One of the Cuban regime's most "efficient" torturers, Heriberto Mederos, was detained not too long ago in Miami after one of his victims recognized him on the street. He is charged with having tortured hundreds of political prisoners with electric shock over forty years in the Havana Psychiatric Hospital, for which he could be sentenced to life in prison. Suspicions on certain other inappropriate acts mount when coupled with the knowledge that the United Nations has formally condemned the Cuban government thirteen times for human rights violations in its prison system over the past eleven years, and the UN has requested that international monitors be allowed inside the system for annual inspections; but no one has been permitted entry. In fact, the Cuban government repeatedly refuses assistance from the International Red Cross to supervise methods of control. Humanitarian organizations like Amnesty International and Human Rights Watch denounce the state of Cuban prisons and the treatment of certain classes of prisoners every year in their annual reports.

But the most amusing commentary on these subjects comes from Fidel Castro. Some think, ironically, that it is "almost a poem,"[34] others are infuriated when they read it, and some may believe that Fidel is speaking with his heart in his hands. . . . We're referring to the interview described in Tomás Borge's book *Un grano de maíz*, published in 1992, where he affirms, in a shameless display of cynicism, that Cuba is the country "that has the most respect for human rights,"[35] because there are no child beggars, no one is without sanitation, there are no illiterates, no homelessness, no child prostitution, no discrimination because of gender or race, no differences between the rich and the poor, no exploiters or exploited, where there is not "one woman that has ever prostituted herself to make a living" (his exact words), there are no drugs, and on and on.[36] After this litany of lies and half-truths, he asserts: "Is there any country that has done more for human rights than Cuba has?"; and he answers himself, like Juan Palomo: "In over thirty years, Tomás Borge, force has never been used against the people, nor has anyone been tortured in spite of the crises, in the same way that we never beat or torture anyone in our revolutionary struggle, and that is partly why we are winning, because of the ethical dimension of our armed fight."[37]

In his analysis, Vázquez Montalbán reaches the conclusion that instances of physical torture cannot be proven (nor can they be conclusively denied), despite the thousands of accounts that have been given by the alleged victims; but psychological torture is much more clearly evident. Books like Ariel Hidalgo's *Disidencia: segunda Revolucion cubana?* and Juan Clark's *Cuba: mito y realidad* have gathered from the repressive bodies of the Revolution an inventory of"recipes" meant to physically and psychologically control the inmates.

At this junction, García Márquez finds himself in the same position as the cuckolded, defeated husband in the song from the Spanish pop group Mecano: "On Mario, three wounds: one in the forehead, that hurt the most; one in the chest, that killed him; and another, the lie in the news. . . ."[38] For those unfamiliar with the best song to come out of Spanish pop in the eighties, Mario worked at night, and his wife worked during the day. They hardly ever saw each other, and their relationship was on shaky ground. One early morning, when Mario gets off work, he sees a couple kissing in the street. As he approaches them, he realizes that it is his wife with another man, who, when he sees Mario, takes out a knife and stabs him. The betrayed husband is wounded three times: once in the head, as he realizes his wife's infidelity; once in the chest, from the actual stab wound that kills him; and the third time from the lie the newspaper prints the next day, as the story states that "two drug addicts robbed and killed Mario Postigo, while his wife witnessed the attack from a doorway."[39]

Gabo has the same three crosses to bear: one in the head, that obliges him to defend his friend and the regime that supports him; another in the chest, or the accounts of the victims that show him their scars, marking their bodies and souls; and the third, the lie: the official position that flatly denies everything that takes place within the Cuban prison system, and a strong exile community that sometimes exaggerates the brutalities committed. In an interview in 1977, Gabo was asked if he has ever visited the Cuban jails, and he replied: "Not only the penitentiaries, but also the detention centers and the interrogation rooms. Of course, when you go to those places they're not going to show you their instruments of torture, they wouldn't show you where they dismember children, even if such a place did exist. And I'm not going to be so naïve as to claim that there is no torture simply because I haven't seen it."[40] However, relying on Reynol González's account, stating that he had not been tortured, García Márquez ventures to generalize, based on this one man's word: "I'm sure that they haven't tortured anyone in Cuba [. . .]. I asked an officer responsible for determining what methods should be used to get detained suspects to confess, and he told me that the counterrevolutionaries' morale was so low that violence wasn't ever necessary as a means of coercion; and besides, the *yanqui* propaganda about torture in Cuba had made them so afraid that they came in ready to confess everything before anyone had even laid a hand on them."[41] No comment. The naïvete that he doesn't want to fall into becomes something much worse and even much less effective: putting words into someone else's mouth that he would like to say himself but doesn't entirely believe or is unsure of. And his assertions are so childish that they cause the reader to almost cringe in embarrassment for him: the low morale of the counter-revolutionaries, and the fear inspired by the enemy's propaganda machine. In the interview with Juan Luis Cebrián, his response is more grounded: "Now, in relation to Cuba, when the problem gets serious is when they start to talk about the disappeared, or political prisoners, torture and the like. . . . I'm in a position to be much better-informed about Cuba than the vast majority of the enemies of the Revolution. If I knew that they had tortured someone there, I wouldn't just not be in that position, I wouldn't have anything to do with Cuba. In Cuba, there is no torture."[42]

In his extreme defense of Castro's Revolution, he is willing to shut his eyes to some things. In 1994, the Argentine writer Ernesto Sabato recalled how he refused to sign a petition against torture in South America because García Márquez, its author, "would not include communist countries on the list."[43] When passion or ideology cloud or supersede reason altogether, a poor service is done to History. If the most basic principle of human dignity or even a person's very life hangs in the balance, we must be belligerent. Capitulating because of a friendship or a false sense of obligation is succumbing to fear and terror, it is being an accomplice to infamy. The following phrase has been attributed to Mao Tse-tung: "When the wise man raises his hand to point out the beauty of the moon, the idiot looks at his finger." Worse yet is acting the idiot without really being one.

CHAPTER THIRTEEN

★

THE DREAM FACTORY: SAN ANTONIO DE LOS BAÑOS

"**E**VERYTHING BEGAN WITH THOSE TWO HIGH-TENSION wire towers at the entrance of this house. Two awful towers, like two giraffes made of sharp metal, that some heartless bureaucrat ordered be erected there in the front yard, without any warning to the owners of the house, which, at this moment, right over our heads, carry a high-tension current of 110 million watts, enough to power a million televisions or 23,000 movie-theater projectors. Alarmed by this news, President Fidel Castro came here six months ago, trying to find out if there was some way to right this wrong, and that was how we discovered that this could be a great place to house the dreams of the Foundation of New Latin American Cinema."[1]

That was how García Márquez began his inaugural speech at the headquarters of the Foundation of New Latin American Cinema on December 4, 1986, located in the famous Quinta Santa Barbara mansion in the outskirts of Havana, close to Gabo's and Fidel's own mansions. The building is familiar to many from the film *Los sobrevivientes* by Tomás Gutiérrez Alea, which was shot there and which told the story of one upper-class family's determined struggle in the mid-twentieth century to continue to live just as they had before the Revolution. It is also the house where the poet Flor Loynaz y Muñoz, the somewhat lesser-known sister of Dulce María Loynaz, lived with her many dogs until shortly before her death in the mid-eighties.

The Quinta Santa Barbara is a lovely colonial house, painted yellow with white grilles and natural-wood window frames. With a rich variety of trees and plants, the grounds could easily pass for a botanical garden. Some of the trees look like the hundred-year-old tree in front of the Belgian ambassador's house on Fifth Avenue in Miramar. It was raining the day we visited the Foundation, unfortunately, but its charm was undiminished by the weather conditions. The many potted palms, the high ceilings, the red-carpeted staircase, and the huge spider plants that hung throughout various rooms made it an ideal headquarters location for the foundation.

The Foundation of New Latin American Cinema was established on December 4, 1985 by the Committee of Latin American Film Producers. The idea for such a place had been generated at the close of the 1985 Havana Film Festival, when Julio García Espinosa and Gabo talked to Fidel about it. Thanks in part to assistance from the Cuban government, a year later, this extremely interesting project was born.

But its origins can be traced back even further. Four dreamers, convinced, like the singer-songwriter Luis Eduardo Aute suggests, that "all of life is a movie, and dreams . . . they are movies," had their own fantasies intersect in a historic Western capital. Gabo described it in his opening speech: "Between 1952 and 1955, four of us who are now onboard were studying at the Center of Experimental Cinematography in Rome: Julio García Espinosa, Vice-Minister of Culture for Film; Fernando Birri, the great father of the New

Latin-American Cinema; Tomás Gutiérrez Alea, one of the most notable artists; and myself, who at that time wanted nothing more in this life than to be the movie director that I never was."[2] In an interview with Lídice Valenzuela at her home in Siboney shortly after the founding of the Film School, Gabo explains that this "dream" was basically a fantasy of youth: "I wanted to be a movie director, and then I realized that it was too much work. It's a job that I haven't been able to figure out, aside from [the fact] that I [realized I] can go much further, in terms of expression, in a novel. That's something that I didn't believe before. In fiction writing, you sit down and write whatever you want. And if you don't like it, you rip up the paper and start over. I don't visualize my novels; I don't think my books are visual. On the other hand, there are some stories that occur to me that I don't want to develop in literature. I know that they would make better movies than books. And those are the ones that I put on film."[3] One of these stories that "occurred" to him and was adapted for the screen was *Para Elisa*, produced by the Cubans Eliseo Alberto and Tomás Gutiérrez Alea.

Gabo has always been a passionate movie fan. His interest in film was sparked at a very young age thanks to his grandfather, Colonel Nicolas Ricardo Márquez Mejia, who took him to see the movies of Tom Mix and others.[4] "In Cartagena and Barranquilla, I was always going to the movies, developing an experienced moviegoer's eye, and together with my friends from Barranquilla, especially with Álvaro Cepeda Samudio, I came to the conclusion that film was a means of expression almost as prodigious as literature itself."[5] On February 27, 1954, García Márquez began writing a weekly movie column in the "Living" section of *El Espectador*. The column was called "Movies in Bogotá: Opening this Week." He wrote this feature on the seventh art for eighteen months. In the first volume of his memoirs, he writes about what that activity foreshadowed:

A very different kind of reality forced me to be a movie critic. It had never occurred to me that I could be one, but in Don Antonio Daconte's Olympia Theater in Aracataca, and then in the traveling school of Álvaro Cepeda, I had glimpsed the basic elements for writing a guide to films using a more helpful criterion than the one known until then in Colombia. Ernesto Volkening, a great German writer and literary critic who had lived in Bogotá since the war, broadcast a commentary on new films on Radio Nacional, but it was limited to an audience of specialists. [. . .] El Espectador was the first to face the risk, and I was assigned the task of commenting on the movie openings of the week, more as an elementary primer for fans than as pontificating criticism. One precaution taken by common consent was that I would always carry my complimentary pass intact as proof that I had bought my ticket at the box office. [. . .]

After that, in a little less than two years, I published seventy-five critical reviews, to which should be added the hours spent seeing the films.⁶

Shortly after that, he went to Europe to study at the Centro Sperimentale di Cine in Rome. He says of this period in Italy: "In those days in Rome, I had my only adventure on a film crew. I was chosen at the school to be the third assistant to the director Alessandro Blasetti on the film *Lastima que sea una canalla*, and that made me so happy, not so much for my own personal development as for the chance to meet the lead actress, Sophia Loren. But I never met her because, for over a month, my job consisted entirely of standing at a cordoned-off section of sidewalk at the corner and making sure that no curious onlookers got through. It is with that title of good service, and not with the numerous and loudly trumpeted titles from my career as a novelist, that I now have presumed to act as president of this house, as I never have in my own, and to speak on behalf of so many worthy people from the world of cinema."[7]

Between that experience in Rome and the creation of the Foundation of New Latin American Cinema and the International School of Film and Television, Gabo never completely abandoned his passion for the movies. He wrote various screenplays, which unfortunately were never as successful as he had hoped, but which, after he had secured his reputation as an internationally renowned novelist, would be published, along with the rest of his works.

The Foundation's main objective was to bring together the various national cinemas of Latin America. Cuban cinema, and Latin American cinema in general, experienced a downturn in the seventies. Then the need to create autonomous means of training and production in the film industry, independent of the United States' predominance, became apparent. According to Gabo, this could be accomplished by supporting co-productions: "When I talk about the unification of Latin American film, I'm not suggesting that there should only be one Latin American cinema and all the movies should be similar. But if you want to verify if co-production could be the answer, let's look at a specific example. Last year, Cuba and Colombia produced two films that are doing very well. Two countries that don't have relations [with one another]. That is to say, film transcends those problems. It's much easier for Latin American countries to co-produce films rather than each one trying it all on their own. That's what it's about. That is one of the basic ingredients of what I call the unification of New Latin American Cinema."[8]

The Foundation is involved with various projects such as the preservation of the Cinematic Memory of Latin America and the Caribbean, compiling and editing the History of Latin American Film, realizing studies on Audio-Visual Space in Latin America and the Caribbean, and writing screenplays under the guidance of García Márquez himself, who says that it is more like a workshop on "how to write a treatment," the phase before writing the actual script; and adds that "conducting that workshop is how I relax. Four hours spent making stuff up, making up life, making up the world, is the most relaxing thing. It's rejuvenating. No one leaves that workshop feeling tired. No one goes out feeling fatigued or in a bad mood; there hasn't been any unpleasantness. We had so much fun, that the people in the classroom next door asked what the hell we were doing in there, that we didn't do anything except laugh, that we don't work at all and we're just having a party. I think that inventing the world is the most wonderful thing there is. Now I have to call Eusebio Leal, who is the historian for the city of Havana, so that he can tell us where young couples went to have a good time in the city in the thirties. Because in the workshop, we're always bringing in expert guests to tell us about specific things that will make our movie better."9

The Foundation also has an exchange program with the Sundance Institute in Utah, run by the actor and director Robert Redford. But the most important project launched by the institution was the creation of the International School of Film and Television in San Antonio de los Baños. The School was inaugurated on December 15, 1986. Presiding over the event were García Márquez, Fidel Castro, Julio García Espinosa, and Fernando Birri. "García Márquez, in his role of president, then as now, of the Foundation of New Latin American Cinema and founder of the School; Fidel Castro, as the leader of Cuba, a nation that, in an act of graciousness and solidarity, donated the facilities and start-up equipment and managed the ample personnel team that carried out, and continues to perform, the administrative functions; García Espinosa, who first dreamed up the project, as the president of the Cuban Institute of the Cinematic Arts and Industry, ICAIC; and

Birri, who promoted the idea and is the first director of the International School of Film and Television."[10] Its main mission was to "provide artistic and technical training for professionals in film, TV, and video production, coming mostly from Latin America and the Caribbean, Asia, and Africa."[11]

In an interview with Valenzuela, Gabo explained what the project's first steps were:

Nothing has happened at the School that wasn't planned. This School was conceived of here, on paper, at this very table. A study group sat down here, and we said: "We're going to plan a School of Film and Television, international, not bureaucratic, practical, not theoretical or purely theoretical," and we tried to visualize on paper how that School would be. When we thought we had gotten it right, we made the School exactly the way we had imagined it on paper.

But in practice, we began to realize that life was richer. And that a lot of it had to be improvised. Because that started in December 1985, and it was inaugurated in December 1986. Over that year, the School was constructed and equipped. We recruited students, hired professors, did all the staff training and everything necessary to organize the school. The students and professors came, and the School opened its doors on the day we had projected. It would have been a miracle if there had not been any problems. But there weren't any; nothing happened that wasn't part of the plan.

But not all of the ideas were good ones, and the work wasn't all easy and pleasant. As with all institutions that are just getting on their feet, there were a few preliminary problems that had to be sorted out:

Currently, the School is faced with a dilemma. This dilemma has to do with trying to accommodate the various skill levels of incoming students; some students have more experience in filmmaking because they have made student films at other schools. Other students arrive who love films, but have never in their lives actually made one [. . .]. The main problems that the School has—what are they? Part of the cause for this dilemma is that we have at the School certain requirements for admission; these requirements are very broad-reaching and basic. For example, we made it a requirement, for the Basic Course, that all of the students admitted had to have graduated from high school, and had to be between twenty and thirty years old. Students who technically met these requirements applied: they were high school graduates; they were in the required age range. In some cases, however, the students had also spent up to two or three years at other film schools. These students were, in effect, overqualified; but because they did meet the minimum requirements, we simply could not turn them away.

We have to decide what we're going to do in these cases in the future. This year they have to put up with the fact that they are in a basic course; they will have to wait for the rest of the less-experienced students to catch up. One of the things that we're specifically working on now is how to improve the student recruitment and admissions so that more things like this don't happen.

[. . .]

I think the glitch came about because since the School is just starting, there is no complete Basic Course yet, just the introduction. In 1988, there will be both a Basic Course and a first-year course, which will be more advanced. As time progresses, there will be a basic, first, and second-year curriculum, and so on. In the future, if we have a student in the Basic Course who is very advanced, the solution would be to put him in a higher level, but right now we would have nowhere to put him.[12]

The School inhabits the old San Tranquilino estate and its surrounding property, about twenty-five miles outside of Havana. On one of our last trips to Cuba, we had the opportunity to visit. Thanks to the Foundation's general director, Alquimia Peña, whom we had interviewed the day before at the Quinta Santa Barbara, we received a grand reception. First, we took the bus to the School; there's a stop right behind the ICAIC, between Zapata and 10th, in front of Colon Cemetery; the bus is especially for students, professors, and actors of the School. "Are you actors?" was the first thing they asked us when we got to the School, since film people from all over the world are always visiting there to teach or take classes. After introductions were made, we were invited to have breakfast in the cafeteria, where they offered a simple meal of toast and butter, a small pastry, and coffee with steamed milk. The students, professors, actors, and guests all eat in the same place. It was an entertaining scene. There were white people, black people, Chinese, Spanish, Latin Americans, even "gringo" North Americans; but most intriguing of all was a group of Andean Indians, unmistakable in their ponchos and multicolored wool clothing, who had just arrived to take a special ethnic orientation course. Steven Spielberg had also just been in that room; he was there promoting his movie *Minority Report*, and gave a long talk to everyone at the School. We had just missed him. There were no assigned tables in the cafeteria, no special meals were prepared for anybody, and there was no cutting in line, not even for the most famous personalities. Robert Redford and García Márquez can often be spotted there when they visit the School. Our chaperone told us that the last time Gabo had been there, he had eaten a plain French omelet, and there had been a blackout that day. . . . Once we had finished breakfast, one of the School's directors gave us a guided tour, giving us a detailed description of how the School worked. In the School's brochure which we were given, one photo shows Francis Ford Coppola instructing the students on how to properly prepare one of his delicious recipes for Italian marinara sauce.

As García Márquez made clear in his inaugural speech at the Foundation, the School's creation was made possible in large part because of financial assistance provided by the Cuban government: "Next week, the Foundation of New Latin American Cinema will receive a donation from the Cuban government which we will always be grateful for, for its unprecedented generosity and the opportunity it affords, as well as for the personal dedication of the world's least-known film producer: Fidel Castro. I'm talking about the International School of Film and Television, in San Antonio de los Baños, a training ground for professionals from Latin America, Asia, and Africa, with the best resources and current technology. Construction of the facilities has been completed, just eight months after it began. Faculty from all over the world have been appointed, students have been accepted, and most of them are already here with us."[13]

With these words, the Film School, now recognized as one of the top four schools of its kind in the world, along with two in the U.S. and one in France, was off and running. The curriculum is divided into two areas: the regular two-year course, and a second training program which "consists of a series of international workshops in directing and professional growth and development."[14] The regular course provides instruction in seven different areas: screenwriting, production, directing, photography, sound, editing, and documentaries. During their first year, students get general training, which covers all of the areas; and in the second year, they specialize.

The first classes were held in 1987. At the beginning, tuition was free. García Márquez noted that at the time, this caused certain complications: "One problem of this educational center, that all schools have, is the problem of vocation. This School has a very serious danger, which is that it is developing a reputation as a privileged school. Completely free. There is no other school in the whole world like this, where everything is free. We are not unaware of the inherent danger, which is a student may have tired of studying Medicine or failed at Engineering, and says to himself: 'What do I do now?' And answers: 'Well, I'll go into film. There are pretty girls, artistic types. . . .' They meet the requirements and it turns out that yes, they are intelligent, capable people. And they come and spend a year or two here, to see what will happen. They don't like it and get the hell out of there. So how does one find their vocation? I supported the idea of giving students some time, after high school, to try and figure out if they had signs of a vocational calling. Because now, it's not that hard to make films. It was hard when we were students, learning with 35-millimeter cameras. Completely professional. Not any more. Now, the students have it easy."[15]

Despite the excellent financial and other supportive conditions the School had to offer, it still attracted primarily mid- to upper-class city kids, rather than those from more rural areas. "First, because people in cities were better informed about opportunities to apply to the school than people in rural areas. Second, because they did it mainly in an area where film activity is not common. So the social makeup of the class is not bad, but it is not fair; it is partial. That is a flaw in the student recruitment system, which is far from ideal. We are perfectly aware of this. We just had to open the School then. But each time, the recruitment will be better."[16]

Ten years after the School was founded, financial problems made it necessary to begin charging tuition. Unfortunately, since 1996, the technical equipment has needed to be updated, and because of the fall of the Soviet bloc and the change of governments in France and Spain, foreign aid has diminished considerably. At this writing, the regular two-year course costs around twelve thousand dollars. But the School does award five scholarships for the second year to the best students. The tuition may seem high to some, but the school's directors explain that it includes a great deal, such as "lodging in private rooms with private bathrooms; meals; transportation between Havana and San Antonio de los Baños; routine and emergency medical care; necessary supplies such as blank film and video cassettes, and the overall costs associated with the production of their coursework."[17] The students can use the School's Olympic-size swimming pool, and every two weeks there are student trips around the island. As Gabo's friend Ricardo Vega—who was there acting as production coordinator—told us, the School is a little world unto itself within Cuba. The students live in the same building as the School; the professors have their apartments in the building next to it. García Márquez spent a month there writing *The General In His Labyrinth*.

Selecting the students for admission is a very difficult process. Only forty students are admitted every year, and, among them, only three can be Cuban. Ricardo Vega tried to get in several times; his tenacity earned him Gabo's support, but it didn't make any difference. Later, thanks to the efforts of Fernando Birri and Lola Calviño, he got a job at the School.

Many people have told us that Gabo's relationship with the students as well as the faculty is very warm, and he treats everyone as equals. Here's just one example: on a certain occasion, Ricardo Vega and some students were preparing a rather critical report on the Minister of the Interior, José Abrantes. Since they needed a camera, they asked Gabo, who gave them one to use, without asking any questions about the content of their project. When Ricardo began having problems with the government and they classified him as a dissident because of that film project as well as other reasons, State Security tried to get him expelled from school. Gabo came to his defense and worked it out so that he could stay on until his contract ended: "Ricardo is invaluable to the School," he argued.

The San Antonio school is renowned throughout the film world, especially for the quality of its instruction. Eighty-five percent of its graduates find work immediately after graduation. This is largely due to the fact that active filmmakers are frequently invited to give lectures and workshops. Generally, about 160 instructors come through the School every year, for only forty students. This ratio allows a constant hands-on approach to the material. When Steven Spielberg was there, the most striking thing about his visit was how honest he was when it came to giving his production colleagues (actors, music supervisors, special effects artists, cinematographers, and so forth) recognition for their contributions to his films. While we were waiting for one of the School's directors, we ran into Fernando León, who was spending a few days there working on a project about Cuba, right after he had been recently nominated by the Spanish Academy to compete for an Oscar with his latest film, *Los lunes al sol*. Wearing high-heeled boots, green pants, and a black shirt, with his hair in a ponytail and a stubbly beard, we waited for him to finish talking on the phone. We congratulated him for his well-earned international recognition and for the high quality of his films in general, for Javier Bardem's spectacular performance in *Los lunes al sol*, and for the much needed wake-up call his films gave to an increasingly consumerist society, blind to its own faults.

As a result of all the hard work of so many dedicated, talented people, it's not surprising that, little by little, the School's efforts are beginning to bear fruit. In 1993, only seven years after it was founded, the School won the Roberto Rossellini award at the Cannes Film Festival. To this day, it is the only educational institution to have ever been recognized with this honor, which has in the past been presented to geniuses like Scorsese, Kusturica, and Zavattini. It's also worth mentioning that various films produced by students of the School have won awards. One feature film that has been shown all over the world is *Solas* by the Spaniard Benito Zambrano (1999), an alumnus of San Antonio, which won five Goya awards. It should also be noted that celebrated filmmakers from around the globe who give lectures and workshops at the School do not receive high salaries for their work. They go there more to enjoy the camaraderie with their colleagues, to make a contribution, or to pursue, out of genuine interest, a project they'll be working on there.

In its early years, the School was mainly focused on Latin America, the Caribbean, and Africa and Asia, for which it was dubbed the "school of three worlds." By the late nineties, it had expanded to include Spain and other European countries and North America. Now it could more accurately be called a "school of all worlds." Ricardo explained that the main reason for the change was out of financial necessity. Two years after the School had opened its doors, Gabo answered a series of questions about the institution's finances and ongoing economic support:

"And how are expenditures for the School and the Foundation going to be managed in the future? What has been the response to the call for donations that you announced in your inaugural speech at the Foundation in 1986?"

"The financial situation at the School is very clear. The School is supported by the Cuban government, which got it started and up and running, with an annual operating budget in Cuban currency. The School by necessity has a high operating cost. The materials, equipment, teacher salaries, and plane tickets are some costs, but the Foundation pays for all of that, and that's what I solicited donations for."

"And the Foundation has a budget for those expenses?"

"The Foundation, now, has funds to cover those costs, for another two years."

"But what, exactly, was the response to your public call for donations?"

"We got a response from the government of Spain. They asked something like if it should be in cash or in donated equipment. When President Felipe González came to Cuba, I told him that we weren't asking for money. Because if we asked for, say, some outrageous amount, like a million dollars, suppose they gave it to us. Then we could never ask Spain for another cent."

"So, what did you agree to . . ."

"An exchange . . ."

"What kind of exchange?"

"Spain can give us, for example, a certain number of scholarships for the School; they can send us instructors whose salaries they have paid. And they did make a donation of equipment. And every time we need something that Spain could give us, we ask Spain for it."[18]

Clearly, his friendship with Felipe González greatly facilitated this outcome, and the same thing took place with other countries which pledged to assist the School. Gabo employs his prodigious talents not only to help resolve all sorts of political conflicts at the highest levels, but he also likes to "spend his fame" promoting literature and film arts, within Cuba and Latin America. In the interview, he goes on to reiterate his personal commitment: "You can be absolutely sure that we are not out of money. When it runs out, if it runs out, I will have enough money of my own to get a plane and fly around country to country and really ask for donations. And they will give it to me. I have a reserve set aside for this. In the meantime, I have too much to do to be thinking about that. But when the day comes that I have to be a fundraiser, I will do it. I know a lot of people that will be willing to help us."[19]

As we have already noted, his willingness to help out was not enough to prevent substantial changes in the School's admission and tuition policy from taking effect in 1996. Despite the support of his friends, which dwindled in proportion to the involvement of more conservative countries in the School, the necessity of charging a rather high tuition for incoming students was unavoidable. In the face of these changes, Gabo has continued to lend his assistance however he can. He doesn't receive a single dollar for the workshops he conducts there, and this means huge help for the School. But that is not all: "Now, there's no rush, the author's royalties from my book about Miguel Litten were almost enough to cover two years of the Foundation's costs. For my part, I charge a large honorarium for my workshop. And when they give me the envelope with my payment, I automatically donate it to the Foundation."[20] And then he talks about the visiting professors and producers: "Most of the people that work there cannot donate their salary because they're not in the position I'm in. I'm set for life. But I assure you that they do it almost for the sheer pleasure of the work. They are professionals of the highest order. They have to leave their jobs for a while to come to Cuba. And that's a problem that the School will always have, since the very best film professionals cannot spend a whole year, or two or three, in Havana. And they are so accomplished that they can't be seduced by a high salary, because they surely earn much more anywhere else in the world. But they like to come here because people in the world of Latin American film have so much camaraderie and enthusiasm for this venture."[21] His personal generosity, which sets a good example for the other instructors, has sometimes been fodder for jokes between Fidel and Gabo, especially about earnings from his book sales. Vázquez Montalbán relates how, when Gorbachev went to Cuba, Gabo was invited to attend the reception for him. When introductions were being made, Castro said to the Russian leader: "Gabriel has come here to see when you're going to pay him in dollars what the USSR owes him in royalties." And Gabo teased, "First it would be nice if the Cubans paid me what they owe."[22]

Ricardo Vega and some other people involved with the Film School told us that Gabo gave generously to the School in its early years, with the condition that Fidel would donate a comparable amount of money to the School in the future. Because of the fall of the Soviet bloc and the dire economic ramifications that that had for Cuba, Fidel was not able to keep his promise. As a result, Gabo gradually distanced himself from the School's day-to-day activities. In recent years, although he still spends time at his house in Havana, he only goes to the School to give his workshop, for one week every year, which sometimes coincides with his attending the Havana Film Festival in early December. But he's always ready and willing to make a donation. When he thinks that something could be useful to the school, he doesn't pass up the chance to secure it. Ricardo Vega tells of how a group of reporters went to interview Gabo one day. After the question-and-answer session, they realized they didn't have any means to pay him, so they suggested paying him in cameras. Gabo accepted their offer, then turned around and gave the cameras to the School. In the same interview with Valenzuela, Gabo announced that from then on, he was going to charge a fee for television interviews, and use the proceeds to assist the School in San Antonio: "I get a huge amount of requests for television interviews from all over the world. I've always said no. Now, I say yes, but in exchange they have to make a donation to the School. And they are agreeing to it."[23]

By the end of the last millennium and the beginning of this one, Gabo's presence around the small town outside Havana had notably diminished. There was definitely a time between the summer of 1999 and the fall of 2000 when treatment for lymphatic cancer made it necessary for García Márquez to live in Los Angeles, and all other activities naturally slowed down or were curtailed. And, as Alquimia Peña told us in her car on the way to the Foundation, it makes sense that he was much more closely involved at the beginning, because the School had to get up and running with a minimal organizational infrastructure. So, now that the School has been functioning for a while, in spite of the financial ups and downs, Gabo's presence isn't needed as much. And García Márquez continues to be actively involved in initiatives related to the journalism world, showing great dedication to the cause. For example, he recently launched a new Foundation to revitalize Latin American journalism, headquartered in Cartagena de Indias, Colombia, a place intimately connected with the beginning of his career as a journalist. That Foundation organizes workshops for professionals run by renowned journalists from around the world, and awards prizes which have already come to have a prestigious reputation.

The Cuban economy has greatly improved since the midnineties, mostly due to the legalization of the dollar. Currently, some foreign companies have established a presence on the island and have managed to generate income in the national economy, even though they are essentially foreign investments operating in Cuba. In fact, a substantial portion of the entire country's economy revolves around the money sent every month to Cubans on the island from relatives living in exile, who help their families by sending small quantities of cash, to augment the low salaries (between two and five hundred pesos a month) they receive from the State. To gain a better understanding of this, the last time we were in Cuba, in November 2002, dollars could be exchanged at official banks at a rate of 26 pesos each. Now, if we try to imagine what it was like when Cuba was experiencing the worst of its economic crises during that "special period," neither Gabo's interviews, nor foreign assistance, nor tuition, nor reduced salaries for professors, would be able to sufficiently explain how the School managed to survive in a time when most Cubans were in desperate need. Around that time, a very peculiar Chilean man offered his economic services, his financial talents, his unique ability to quickly appear and then disappear, and his habit of working in the shadows so that his first name, Max, and his last, Marambio, would remain in the strictest anonymity.

This millionaire impresario now functions as the main nexus between Chile and Cuba. A personal friend of Fidel's, he was a key component of Cuban intelligence for a long time, and was the security chief under Salvador Allende. He was the director of CIMEX (Corporation for Importation and Exportation)[24] from 1978 until 1993, during which time he managed to amass a huge personal fortune. He is currently under investigation by the Inspector General of Spain's Treasury Department for alleged fraud, for failing to report certain commercial activities and activities of foreign holdings, such as the travel agency Sol y Son, which organizes trips to Cuba. A few summers ago, *Forbes* magazine made some very interesting revelations regarding Fidel's own Swiss bank account, which holds an amount with many zeros in it.

Marambio is also a friend of Gabo's and of Carlos Fuentes. In 1983, he formed a film production company which was an initial holding company for International Network Group, launched in 1990, which brings together companies from Chile, Ecuador, Mexico, Cuba, and Spain. Marambio was himself involved in the founding of the Foundation of New Latin American Cinema, and, from the nineties on, administration of the School has been closely tied to his financial activities. With those credentials, it's much easier to understand how this instrument for promoting the art of film in Latin America and the Third World in general can function so splendidly. Which, in a way, we can all be thankful for.

CHAPTER FOURTEEN

★

JUSTICE OR VENGEANCE?:
THE "OCHOA CASE"

O N JULY 13, 1989, THIS NEWS BRIEF RAN IN *GRANMA*: "IN THE early morning hours of today, July 13, the Special Military Tribunal's sentence was carried out in docket number 1 of 1989, the state versus Arnaldo Ochoa Sánchez, Jorge Martínez Valdés, Antonio De la Guardia Font, and Amado Padrón Trujillo." They had just executed four officials—four victims, some of them innocent, of the Revolution that for them had symbolized a new birth, as well as an explosive end.

Everything began back in June 1986 in the offices of the MC (part of Cuba's Department of the Interior, standing for "moneda convertible," or "convertible currency"), in Panama. This department was responsible for exploring possible solutions for getting around the U.S. trade embargo and importing items into Cuba through other channels. One day, in the Interconsult offices (a governmental agency that, among other things, managed to get visas approved in the most difficult immigration cases) headed by Miguel Ruiz Poo, a Cuban exile showed up to try to make the necessary arrangements to get his niece a visa. It turned out that the two Cubans were related, a fact which sped up the paperwork considerably and led to a collaboration of an entirely different sort. It started with their forming a business dealing with computers. Computers from the United States were sent to Panama, where they were in turn shipped on to Cuba. The two men encountered no problems in carrying out these transactions, and they both profited from the venture; but, gradually, an idea which could produce a much greater windfall began to take root: shipping cocaine to the United States via Cuba.

To Ruiz Poo, it seemed like a good idea, but he had to run it by his boss in the Department of the Interior (MININT), the senior Padron Trujillo. Andrés Oppenheimer[1] said that "Padron faltered. This was too much for him. In the Cuban hierarchy, there was an understanding to the effect that it was okay to allow flights transporting drugs to fly over Cuban airspace. Fidel himself had authorized flights carrying Colombian cocaine to fly in Cuban airspace in exchange for the narco-traffickers transporting arms to the guerrillas on the way back. But landing in Cuban territory was something else. Padron didn't know if that would be allowed. He would have to consult with his higher-ups."[2] One of those "higher up" individuals in the chain of command was Antonio De la Guardia, who was present at the meeting that took place a few weeks later in Havana to give the go-ahead and look the other way.

A little while after that, in a conversation between the fledgling drug traffickers and De la Guardia, one of them asked if Fidel knew about what was going on. The colonel from MININT answered, clearly and calmly, "of course."[3] Oppenheimer notes that "it's not clear if Tony De la Guardia had spoken to Castro directly about his plans for cocaine trafficking. The Commander, with his instinctive revulsion for matters of finance, rarely got personally involved in turbulent business dealings. That was Abrantes's territory, Castro's

Minister of the Interior. Abrantes had given Tony De la Guardia the green light to do whatever was necessary to get dollars—including the occasional drug deal. De la Guardia's remark to Reinaldo Ruiz could have referred to a direct conversation with Castro, or more likely it reflected the colonel's assumption that Abrantes would never sign off on something as risky as narco-trafficking without getting Fidel's blessing first."[4]

The first operation was a complete failure, but nobody got caught and there wasn't any public scandal. But they had sparked the attention of the U.S. government, which managed to plant a CIA operative inside the second operation. The CIA tape-recorded over fifty hours of conversation, which confirmed the involvement of highly ranked Cuban officials in drug trafficking. In 1982, a similar situation had arisen in the Guillot-Lara case, with high Cuban officials involved in drug trafficking, but the U.S. had no first-hand witnesses and couldn't do anything. Publicly, Castro framed it as another imperialist act against Cuba, and the case quickly faded from view. However, this time around there was first-hand testimony and very convincing proof. This time it would be impossible to hide the incident. Castro's only chance for protecting the image of his Revolution was to beat the U.S. to the punch. His brother Raúl provided the most help in this effort, while pulling off an act of pure revenge at the same time.

The Department of the Interior (MININT, by its initials in Spanish) and the Department of the Armed Revolutionary Forces (MINFAR, by its Spanish initials) had been rival agencies for a long time. MINFAR, headed by Raúl Castro, defended the country against external armed threats. The army, navy, and air force were under his command, a total force of 300,000 troops. MININT, for its part, was responsible for everything having to do with internal compliance with the law, and with counterespionage. Headed by José Abrantes, that agency oversaw 83,000 men who comprised the

National Police, the Department of State Security, the Special Forces, Border Patrol, and the Fire Department. While in theory the two departments had clearly delineated, separate responsibilities, in practice they often overlapped, and they often openly clashed. As Raúl saw it, MININT had too much power and took up too much space in the government, and, for that reason, he had long been looking for an excuse to settle the score with its leaders. The latest discovery of narco-trafficking was a tailor-made opportunity.

But there was one person in particular in the government who was a thorn in Raúl's side: Arnaldo Ochoa. General Ochoa, in charge of the Cuban armed forces in Angola and Hero of the Cuban Revolution (the highest rank possible under Castro's regime), had already expressed in public several times his dissatisfaction with some of the positions Fidel had taken. For example, he had been very frustrated and disappointed by the lack of economic assistance to the soldiers who were gradually returning from Angola. He had expressed criticism in public on various occasions, and these had reached Raúl's ears. Also, Fidel was about to appoint Ochoa the chief commander of the Western Army, a relatively important position in the Cuban government, and this was another motivation to act quickly. Raúl couldn't help but consider the general's attitude as "a serious infraction of military discipline."[5] Finally, the Castro brothers decided to combine the two issues. Ochoa, De la Guardia, and others involved would be charged with narco-trafficking and corruption, and sentenced to death. When Raúl explained this to Ochoa, the General responded: "You are trying to make a case for corruption to distract attention from the main issue, which is the fact that there are great doubts in High Command about the future of the Revolution."[6] Ochoa was a very direct, decisive man.

On June 12, 1989, Ochoa was the first to be arrested, for unethical dealings and mismanagement of funds. On June 16, the

De la Guardia twins were arrested. On that day, the term "narco-trafficker" was first introduced. This process projected an image to the outside world of Cuba as a country valiantly struggling to eradicate an evil scourge. A few days before the trial, the accused received a personal message from Castro. He requested their collaboration and cooperation. That way, things would work out okay for everyone involved. "Think of this as one more mission you have been asked to carry out. Collaborate, and you will help yourselves."[7] The testimonies of the accused were reminiscent of the poet Heberto Padilla's self-criticism. All of the Cuban public, who had just heard about these men who were trying to save their own necks, understood perfectly well that business dealings of that scope could hardly have been carried out without the Commander-in-Chief's tacit approval.

On June 25, 1989, the first session of the Ochoa–De la Guardia Military Tribunal took place. On July 13, four of the accused parties were executed by firing squad at the beach in Baracoa, on the outskirts of Havana. They first shot two lower-ranking officials, then Tony, and finally they finished off Ochoa, whose last words were "I just want you to know that I am not a traitor."[8] Up until the last second of his life, he held on to his dignity.

THE FOUR HORSEMEN OF THAT CRAZY CRISIS

Tony De la Guardia was a jovial man, a prankster with an eye for the ladies. In spite of his rank of colonel, he was rarely seen wearing his olive-green uniform; he was more likely to put on a pair of Calvin Klein jeans, a checkered shirt, and a Rolex watch. He was one of the Castro government's main secret agents, which allowed him to live a privileged life in Cuba. As Oppenheimer points out, he had a lifestyle on a par with the foreign diplomats who lived on the island. He lived in a beautiful house in Siboney, number 20600 on 17th Street, and he could travel wherever he liked. Beginning in 1986, he was the chief of the foreign exchange department in CIMEX, which was in charge of organizing "a network of commercial companies with a significant presence in outside countries, to carry out transactions without anyone in other countries being able to detect that the Cuban government was behind them."[9]

Tony was also one of Castro's "protected,"[10] and he was one of the few people who could get away with taking certain liberties in his interactions with the leader. Oppenheimer tells an anecdote, for example, which illustrates how casually Tony behaved in front of Castro: "One time when Castro was showing Benes [a banker from Miami] into his office well after midnight, as was his habit, Tony started to yawn in spite of the clear indications that the meeting had only just begun, and would probably continue until dawn. At around 1:30 A.M., Benes recalls, Tony stood up and excused himself. 'I'm beat. I have to get a little sleep,' he said, saying good-bye to everyone. Only a handful of men could take that liberty in Cuba. And Tony De la Guardia was one of them."[11]

In the Cuban government, he was always associated with his brother. They were the "jimaguas De la Guardia," as twins were called in Cuba. Patricio De la Guardia, a brigadier general, head of the MININT office in Angola, was a close friend of Arnaldo Ochoa. Although the twin brothers were identical physically, they had very distinct personalities. Antonio was more of an extrovert—he liked to be the center of attention—while Patricio was quiet and seemed to be in his brother's shadow. He was also among the accused in the Military Tribunal, and was sentenced to thirty years in prison.

Ochoa was very different from Tony. General Arnaldo Ochoa had risen up from nothing and in short order had become one of the most highly decorated military officers in Cuba. He had been born in Cuato Cristo, in the province of Holguin, to a poor family of peasants. Shortly after graduating from high school, he joined up with the Revolutionaries in the Sierra Maestra. He took part in most of the skirmishes that resulted in victory on January 1, 1959, and he played an important role in the Bay of Pigs against the Cuban exiles in 1961, as a captain of the new Revolutionary army. He fought against the counterrevolutionaries hidden away in the Sierra del Escambray in the sixties. Later, he led Cuban troops in interventions into Venezuela, Ethiopia, Angola, Yemen, and Nicaragua. In 1984 he was granted the title of Hero of the Revolution. By 1976, he was known as one of the most powerful commanders of Cuban forces in Angola. With all that, it's very strange that he was not cited even once in García Márquez's report on Operation Carlota. That piece was published in January 1977, in the early years of García Márquez's nascent friendship with Fidel. Why did the piece heap praise on Fidel and the Cuban people but not make reference to any particular official responsible for the armed forces in Angola? Possibly as a precaution: the Commander could have reacted badly to a piece in which a subordinate had more of a starring role than he did.

Oppenheimer notes that "Ochoa had been a close friend of Castro's, one of the few people who dared to address the Commander with the familiar form *tu* [instead of *Usted*, the formal term for 'you' in Spanish]."[12] They had become friends over the course of Fidel's many trips abroad. Castro called him "the black Ochoa,"[13] when he made an informal reference to his friend. But over time their relationship had cooled. The general's biggest mistake was that he began to act autonomously, a behavior completely incompatible with Castro's regime. It reached the point that Ochoa stopped following Castro's orders because, as he saw it, the supreme commander could not know, all the way from Havana, what the actual situation in Angola was, and, consequently, how to act.

When Fidel decided the time had come to put an end to Cuba's intervention in Angola and that the best solution would be a political agreement, he invited nine generals to witness the passing of the official act at the United Nations in New York. The only one missing was Arnaldo Ochoa. To him, his exclusion symbolized Fidel's negation of the role he had played in that war. Ochoa had never suffered from delusions of grandeur, in spite of his impressive titles and brilliant résumé. He had continued to live with his second wife, Maida González, in his house in Nuevo Vedado, on 24th Street, an unassuming house that had nothing in common with Tony's mansion in Miramar. Ochoa was a discreet man and didn't like to draw attention to himself. For example, like most high Cuban officials, he had a Mercedes Benz; but because of the reaction of his neighbors on the few occasions that he took it out of the driveway, he ended up giving it away to a Sandinista general. Still, the humiliation of his exclusion in New York was a deep disappointment.

Ochoa was also the only one of the accused who was completely innocent of all drug-trafficking charges, as Oppenheimer explains: "Unlike Tony De la Guardia, Ochoa had never carried out any cocaine smuggling. But the close associations of his aide-de-camp [Jorge Martinez Valdés] with the De la Guardia group—and Ochoa's consent for his trip to Medellin—would be used by Fidel Castro a few weeks later to mount a spectacular case against the Hero of the Cuban Revolution."[14] The only thing he could be accurately accused of was being an "unhappy general."[15] He died at the age of forty-nine. Tony and Ochoa hadn't been close in life, but now they are neighbors for all eternity in Colon Cemetery, the former in grave plot number 46427, the latter in number 46672 in the cemetery's row K.

The head of the Department of the Interior, José Abrantes, was stripped of his post shortly after sentences were handed down in the Ochoa–De la Guardia tribunal, and Colomé Ibarra, a protégé of Raúl Castro's, would take his place. A few weeks after the executions, Abrantes was also brought before the tribunal. He was accused of "negligence"[16] in controlling his subordinates' activities and of "corruption and tolerance of corrupt practices."[17] He was sentenced to twenty years in prison. In early 1991, he suffered a heart attack that cost him his life. He had never had any heart trouble before. Since he was the only survivor in the case who could have shed light on whether or not Fidel had been informed of the drug trafficking, some people suspect that the heart attack was not the real cause of death. According to Patricio, Tony's brother, Abrantes told him once in prison that Fidel had been aware of the drug trade.

AND WHAT ABOUT GARCÍA MÁRQUEZ?

When Gabo found out about the arrests of the high-ranking Cuban officials, he was in his house in Mexico City. The first thing he did was to place a call to Cuba to find out exactly what had happened. He was told that that very night, Raúl was going to deliver a speech on television which would explain everything. He hung up the phone and immediately called his travel agent to purchase a plane ticket to Havana. He wanted to know the truth. Oppenheimer notes that "the improvised speech that Raúl Castro delivered to the nation in the main salon of the Ministry of the Armed Forces building that night, on June 14, 1989, was the most disastrous of his life."[18] Instead of clarifying the situation, he had left his fellow countrymen even more confused.

When Ileana De la Guardia and Jorge Masetti found out that Gabo was in Havana, they immediately headed over to his house, despite the late hour. They had to talk with him, because he represented their last hope for saving Ileana's father and the others. Jorge was the son of Jorge Ricardo Masetti, the Argentine founder of Prensa Latina, where Gabo had worked during the Revolution's early years. And García Márquez had served as godfather at Jorge's step-sister's wedding. Ileana is Tony's daughter, and he was a very close friend of Gabo's. They had seen each other recently at Tony's house, when Gabo had autographed a copy of his latest book, *The General in His Labyrinth*, a title so devastatingly appropriate to the situation, with these words: "To Tony, who plants the seeds of good."

But as fate would have it, on the night of July 9, 1989, hours before the final verdict was announced, Castro paid Gabo a visit. Oppenheimer provides a good description of that visit. He explains that Fidel was a little worried about that encounter, because he knew that Gabo was opposed to capital punishment, especially in the case of the four Cuban officials: "Gabo had made it clear in conversations with members of Castro's inner circle that he wanted the lives of the four officials to be spared. And Castro knew very well that García Márquez was a close friend of Tony De la Guardia."[19] They talked for two hours, but no mention was made of the specific reason for the visit. Gabo noticed his friend's unease; and as they said good-bye in the doorway, he broached the subject and asked that the lives of the four officials be spared. He added: "I wouldn't want to be in your shoes. Because if they are executed, no one on earth will believe that you didn't give the order."[20] And Castro replied, "You think so? You think the people will see it that way?"[21]

Castro couldn't allow himself to think that his people no longer shared his faith in the Revolution. And Oppenheimer continues: "Standing in Gabo's doorway, gesturing with his hands to punctuate his words, Fidel started to explain the fairness of the legal process that had culminated in the military court's verdict. He said that the tribunal's unanimous opinion had been that Ochoa and Tony De la Guardia deserved to die. 'I've consulted with all the departments of the State, and I've found that a clear majority support execution by firing squad.' 'You don't think they say that to you because they think that's what you want to hear?' García Márquez asked. 'No, I don't think so,' Fidel answered. García Márquez was sad when Fidel said good-bye and left. He was convinced that the State Council would not save the lives of Ochoa,

Tony De la Guardia, and his aides. A few months later, pondering the executions and his conversation with Fidel in his doorway, Gabo told me: 'I know many heads of state, and there's one constant in all of them: no leader believes that people tell him what he wants to hear.'"22

Fidel had barely left when Jorge and Ileana showed up. Hanging on a wall in the foyer was one of Tony's paintings; both he and his twin brother painted. Tony's style was a good reflection of his personality. He tended to paint simple landscapes, but in bright, vibrant colors. Patricio had a different style. We were able to see this for ourselves in Jorge and Ileana's living room in Paris. They had several of Tony's multi-colored paintings, and also one of Patricio's, of a nude woman at the ocean, which he had painted in prison. The ocean represents a powerful life force for Cubans. The ocean and a woman were probably the two things he missed the most while he was in jail.

García Márquez told them that he had already been trying to save Tony and the others.23 First, because Tony was a friend; second, because he was completely opposed to the death penalty and executions. Ileana and Jorge told us later that he used phrases like "this can't happen," "Fidel would be crazy if he authorized those executions," and "neither the friends nor the enemies of the Revolution want this." Gabo told them that they had to stay calm and have faith, and not to get in touch with well-known crusaders or organizations that defended human rights. Ileana told us this with a certain sadness and a feeling of betrayal: "I believed him; I believed what he was telling me." Gabo gave them hope, but he knew that Fidel had already made up his mind. It was the only way to save the image of the Revolution and his own image. Plinio Apuleyo Mendoza told us in a conversation in Madrid that García Márquez had told him that he had done everything he could to save them, but that he had arrived in Havana too late.

Shortly after the trial of Abrantes, the chief of the Department of the Interior, Fidel went to visit Gabo. García Márquez considered taking down Tony's painting and moving it to his house in Mexico, but in the end he decided to leave it where it was, in honor of his friend who had been executed, and in spite of what Fidel might think. The conversation that we had with Jorge and Ileana in their apartment in Paris's Latin Quarter was also an homage to Tony. They had paintings by Tony and Patricio on the walls in the living room. In the library, they had Ileana's book (in French and Dutch editions), and Jorge's book, and a book that can be found in the homes of Cuba-loving French-speakers everywhere, *La Lune et le Caudillo* by Jeannine Verdès-Leroux. Tony is also the name of Jorge and Ileana's son: Tony Masetti De la Guardia. Well-known last names. His father, an Argentine–Cuban ex-guerillero who had trained in the most elite military camps on the island; his mother, a Cuban woman from a prominent family that had been influential in the first decades of the Revolution. His paternal grandfather had been a great friend of Che Guevara's and had died, as Che had, in a guerrilla struggle in the sixties, after having led the Revolution's press agency; his maternal grandfather had been one of the most highly regarded colonels of the Revolutionary army. A child with a stunning *curriculum vitae*, even before reaching the age of reason. A boy marked, without knowing it yet, by a tremendous history of heroism and betrayal. At first he eyed us warily; he didn't want his parents' attention to be diverted to a couple of strangers. Later, in the middle of the conversation, while we uncorked the first bottle of rioja, he abandoned his toys, looked away from the motorcycles careening through the air on the television screen, and started to run around the living room and the adjoining room while shouting "Verde que te quiero verde," a line from a García Lorca poem. We asked him if he had already read García Lorca in school, or if his father had taught him the verse. He gave us a defiant look and, without answering the question, said, "Verde que te quiero coca-cola."

After spending several hours with them, we found out about many details that are not generally reflected in the history books. We got the background on Gabo's friendship with the De la Guardia family, Tony in particular, dating from the late seventies. In fact, we discovered that our host Jorge Masetti had, from a very young age, felt perfectly at home in the world of international political leaders, military generals, and renowned writers in orbit around the Revolutionary elite, and he had had long conversations about his father and the Prela years with Gabo. With his father, Ricardo Masetti, deceased, the son became a real "child of the Revolution," raised in the image of the great social experiment that his father had sacrificed his life for, and the highest military leaders thought of him as a natural extension of a hero, who had to be carefully looked after out of a sense of justice. Ileana told us that, after her father had died, she found out from a trusted source that García Márquez had attended part of the trial, with Fidel and Raúl, watching from behind a large "mirror" in the main military courtroom where that drama played out on a world stage.

The couple's disillusion and disappointment went beyond García Márquez's "false comforts" on that "night of cynicism"; Jorge told us that the next day, Gabo went to meet with Mitterrand in France, where he still played the role of "official ambassador of Fidel, to explain and justify the executions—it had to do with—according to Gabo—a problem among the military leaders, and Fidel had found himself caught up in a situation that didn't allow him to react in any other way."

Later, when Ileana and Jorge were able to get out of Cuba, they went to Mexico City and stopped by Gabo's house. Mercedes greeted them and told them that Gabo would be back the next day; he wasn't there. "The wives of the great writers are the filters you need to pass through to get to them," Jorge observed. But Gabo wasn't there the next day either; an unusual occurrence, since García Márquez was meticulously organized and never missed an appointment. Mercedes attended to them again: "She interrogated us like she was part of the Secret Police," Jorge lamented. It was the last time they dropped by.

They never had any contact with Gabo again, except once, indirectly, when they arrived in Paris a few years ago. Plinio Apuleyo Medoza called the couple and told them that Gabo wanted to intervene to help get Ileana's uncle Patricio out of prison, but that "please, Ileana should write a letter to him summarizing the case and asking for his help." They didn't do it: Gabo already had all the information he would have needed to help Patricio however he saw fit. "Gabo always covers himself for history," Jorge explained, "so that in the future he can say: I intervened . . . I've helped free so many political prisoners, et cetera." It is true that he does get those kinds of favors done, but he does it, according to Masetti, in a mercenary way. "It's not humanitarian assistance. He helps because it's good for Fidel's government. He's never shown the slightest concern for people's freedom and human rights, except maybe in his book *News of a Kidnapping*. He only concerns himself with his friend's prisoners, but he has no interest in the ones held in Argentina or Chile. Freeing ones in the Cuban regime results in getting favors for his friend Fidel."

It also seems that regarding the Ochoa–De la Guardia trial, according to the reporters Jean-Francois Fogel and Bertrand Rosenthal, "To avoid testimony surfacing in Colombia, Panama, or wherever else that would focus on the past, they wiped out the possibility by discreetly releasing seventeen Latin American drug traffickers, almost all of them Colombian, who had been held in the main Cuban jail, Combinado del Este. [. . .] The Colombian writer García Márquez, a friend of Fidel Castro's, takes charge of this matter, since in the past he had overseen many humanitarian missions to help get prisoners released from Cuban prisons."[24] Another black page in Cuba's recent history. Ochoa and De la Guardia had such high profiles that their case would not go unnoticed by many Cubans, nor would it make for very high public opinion of the government's actions. Gabo was torn between two loyalties: to Tony, and to Fidel. Jorge and Ileana think he could have done more. The situation was very delicate, but García Márquez never opened his heart to show them how hurt he was. That would have been defying Fidel. When most of the intellectuals closed ranks in support of human rights and against the executions, García Márquez was silent. Not one word of protest. More Catholic than the Pope. Faithful to Fidel.

CHAPTER FIFTEEN

★

NAILED TO THE CROSS: ELIÁN IN HIS GOLGOTHA

The "Boomerang" Raft

O
N NOVEMBER 22, 1999, FOURTEEN CUBANS SCRAMBLED onto a makeshift raft and set off for the United States. Among them were Elizabeth Brotons, her son Elián, and her husband Lázaro Rafael Munero. Tragically, they ran into trouble, the raft sank, and eleven perished. Before drowning, Elizabeth, who was then twenty-eight years old, managed to lift her son onto one of the inner tubes that they had carried on board as life preservers. Two days later, a fisherman from the Fort Lauderdale area spotted Elián clinging to the inner tube, plucked him from the water, and immediately took him to the hospital. The next day, Elián was released from the hospital and went to stay with his great-uncle, Lázaro González. Juan Miguel González, Elián's father, didn't waste any time in demanding that his son be returned to him in Cuba. The rafter boy's story had begun, which would be taken up as the passionate cause of the Cuban exile community in Miami, and would become the center of a new diplomatic crisis between Cuba

and the United States, having serious repercussions in the next presidential election.

In spite of the good relationship that Elián's parents had maintained after their divorce, Juan Miguel González had not been informed by his former wife of her decision to flee to Miami, taking their son with her. Elián usually spent a few days a week with his mother and the rest of the week with his father. When Juan Miguel went to pick his son up at school, he found out that his ex-wife had taken him out of school that morning and they had never returned. A few days later, he found out about the plan to get to Miami by the dangerous route across the Caribbean Sea.

When a hospital in Miami called Juan Miguel a few days later to get some of Elián's medical history, he understood what had happened to his son, and the only thing he wanted was to get his child back. Things weren't that simple, however. On December 10, Elián's great-uncle Lázaro González petitioned the U.S. government on Elián's behalf for political asylum. After a representative from the INS (Immigration and Naturalization Service) visited Juan in Havana, they decided on January 5 that "Juan Miguel González is the only person who has the legal authority to speak for Elián González. This boy, who has suffered such a terrible tragedy, needs to be with his father."[1] The boy had to be returned to Cuba before January 14, 2000.

The relatives in Miami refused to accept the decision and tried to appeal the ruling. Lázaro González asked for temporary custody; but on January 1, Janet Reno, the U.S. Attorney General, announced that Elián's father had custody and that he had every right to have his son returned to him without delay. At the end of January, both of Elián's grandmothers traveled to Miami to speak with him. They only managed to talk to their grandson for fifteen minutes, but even in that short time, they could easily see how the boy had changed. In early April, having obtained a visa to come to the U.S., Elián's father; his wife, Nelsy Carmeta; their six-month-old son and Elián's half-brother; and a group of Elián's classmates from school, accompanied by a family member, traveled to Washington.

A week later, Attorney General Reno went to Miami and tried to persuade Elián's relatives to relinquish custody to his father; but they not only refused to do so, they managed to have Elián stay in the United States until after all of the judicial proceedings had been exhausted.

One of the many jokes that circulated about Cuba and its problems with the United States immortalized this period in Elián's life. The joke is about a little rafter boy who sent a telegram to his father in Cuba, which only contained the letters: "E.L.I.A.N." Juan Miguel, overcome with emotion, went to the Government Palace and asked Fidel to interpret the mysterious message.

He responded without a pause: "It's as clear as day. It stands for: 'Espero Luchen Intensamente Ante Norteamericanos. [I hope you will fight hard against the North Americans.]'"

The father called his son and assured him that he would keep fighting for him, that he shouldn't give up hope, that soon the whole mess would be happily resolved; perplexed, the boy asked how he had interpreted his telegram. When the father told him, the boy started to laugh, and replied, "Dad, what the telegram meant was 'Estoy Libre, Idiota. Aprenda a Nadar. [I'm free, you idiot. Learn to swim.]'"

Going back to reality, after negotiations between Elián's Miami relatives and federal authorities reached a standstill, on April 22, before dawn, police forces took custody of the boy by force, breaking into the house of Elián's great-uncle, where he had lived for the past five months. The first images of the police action released by the press included a photo of a police officer in full riot gear and armed with a huge machine gun pointed at a terrified, sobbing Elián, as he hid in a closet, held in the arms of the fisherman who had rescued him. The televised images that went around the world were no less eloquent: the police on one side, the boy's relatives and their supporters on the other, forming a kind of gauntlet of their own peculiar Golgotha, with Elián forced to walk that path carrying the cross, still smelling of wet wood; the remains of the sunken raft. Elián was immediately taken to Washington, where his father and the others who had made the journey were waiting for him. They stayed at Andrews Air Force Base for a few days, in Maryland, and then were taken to the "Wye Plantation," a government-owned estate. After a few more days of negotiations and getting reacquainted, the rafter boy returned to the island where he had been born, with his entourage, bringing his own walk with the cross to an end. After the dramatic rescue, Fidel Castro asserted that it was "the first day of cease-fire" between his country and the United States in the last forty years. Now, Elián is back at home in his neighborhood of Cárdenas, with his father and friends. No doubt, that five-month adventure, and the tug-of-war he was in the middle of, must have left something more than just a vague memory in the young protagonist's mind, rescued from the sea . . . something that will mark him for the rest of his life.

The INS has been harshly criticized for its handling of the Elián González case and its use of force; but, as Janet Reno explained, "We tried every way we could to encourage Lázaro González to voluntarily hand over the child to his father. . . . Unfortunately the Miami relatives rejected our efforts, leaving us no other option but the enforcement action." Elián spent five months in his great-uncle's house, where his twenty-one-year-old cousin, Marisleysis, also lived, taking on the role of adoptive mother.

But the story doesn't end there. This incident served to fan the flames of animosity between the two countries. The political conflict that resulted from the custody battle reignited a historic enmity, and the case was used within the context of the impending presidential election in the U.S. and the struggle for freedom in Cuba, especially by the Cuban exiles living in Miami. They argued that respecting the last wishes of Elizabeth Brotons, who wanted to offer her son a life with more "freedom," justified keeping him in Miami.

GABO'S DILIGENT PEN AND TELEPHONE

It didn't take García Márquez long to appear on the scene, in spite of his numerous health problems. On March 15, 2000, García Márquez wrote an article in *Cambio*, his Colombian magazine, titled "Naufrago en tierra firme" (Shipwreck on dry land), which also was published on the Internet and in Cuba, where the newspaper *Juventud Rebelde* devoted eight pages to it (a huge amount, taking into account the paper shortage in Cuba), accompanied by several photo illustrations. His position is clear; he defends the Cuban government's petition in favor of returning the boy to his father as the most objective, fair solution, from the viewpoint of the blood ties that bind the son with his progenitor.

Gabo provides a very detailed history of Elián's parents up until their divorce, two years before the drowning. While he presents Juan Miguel as a good father whose son was stolen from him, he describes Elián's mother as a guilty Eve who bit the apple, abandoned her husband for another man, and took too many risks to try to get to Miami, bringing her family to a most tragic end.

The image that he presents of Elián's father is dramatic, inspiring feelings of compassion in the reader. He explains how Juan Miguel got the "bad news,"[2] and quotes his exact words: "That day my life ended" (1), he said. A little later in the piece he quotes for dramatic effect, highlighting the close family ties, Elián's exact words when he told his father about his mother's drowning: "I saw when Mama sank under the water" (3), the boy had said on the phone shortly after the tragedy. Thirdly, referring to a conversation between Elián and his teacher in Cárdenas, Gabo indirectly implies that Elián wanted to return to Cuba, illustrated by his desire to return to his old school which he had attended until leaving the island: "His attachment to his school," Gabo wrote, "which is well known among his teachers and classmates, like his wish to return to his classroom, was clearly demonstrated a few days later, when he spoke to his teacher on the phone: 'Take good care of my desk'" (3). This affirmation from García Márquez contrasts with the image Elián's Miami relatives tried to project, when they released a videotape to the press in which the boy says to his father that he does not want to return to Cuba.

As if it were a story straight out of García Márquez's fabled Macondo, told in a style reminiscent of *One Hundred Years of Solitude* and *Love in the Time of Cholera*, he goes on to summarize the Cuban couple's history through a masterfully realized flashback. "She fell in love with him when she was just fourteen years old. They were married four years later, and they lived together in Cárdenas, near where Elizabeth worked as a waitress in the Hotel Paradiso in Varadero. 'We were like brother and sister,' said Juan Miguel, a thoughtful, good-natured man, who also worked in Varadero as a cashier in Josone Park. After they divorced, they continued to live together with their son in Cárdenas [. . .] until she fell in love with the man who would cost her her life: Lázaro Rafael Munero, a good-looking, womanizing guy with no fixed employment, who had learned judo not for the physical training, but as a weapon to use on the street. He had been sentenced to two years in prison for an armed robbery of the Hotel Siboney de Varadero. Juan Miguel, for his part, later married Nelsy Carmeta, and they now have a six-month-old son together who was the love of Elián's life until Elizabeth took her son away to Miami" (1–2). An adept master of narration, he uses his prodigious talents to paint a glowing, overwhelmingly positive picture of Juan

Miguel, in sharp contrast to the image he draws of Lázaro Rafael Munero: "Everybody knew that the idea to go to Miami had been Lázaro Munero's, and he had already taken two clandestine trips to the U.S. to lay the groundwork. So it would seem that he had the necessary contacts and sheer guts to take not only Elizabeth and her son, but also a younger brother, his own father, over seventy years old, and his mother, still recuperating from a heart attack" (2), Gabo reports. His reasoning is clear: no one but a complete idiot, or a disloyal Cuban, would consider abandoning his country under such dangerous conditions, with elderly and ailing family members. What García Márquez fails to consider is why hundreds of thousands of Cubans have done just that over the past forty-three years, braving the perils of the sea, sharks, the dangers of drowning, and potential reprisals from the regime aimed at family members left behind on the island. "Either you shut him up, or I will" (3): García Márquez puts these words in Munero's mouth, to describe how the stepfather roughly warned the mother to keep the young boy from crying.

But Elián's stepfather is not the only one targeted by Gabo's sharp criticism: Elizabeth Brotons is, too. First, because she apparently kept her plans to flee the island a secret from Juan Miguel, even though she planned to take their son with her. Secondly, for separating Elián from his little half-brother Hianny, who meant a lot to him, and finally for the irresponsibility of her decision: the vessel she climbed aboard with her son was not safe for such an expedition: "The final product was a ramshackle little boat no longer than a car, without a roof or seats, so the passengers had to sit on the floor, fully exposed to the sun. [. . .] Three inner tubes were taken on board to act as life preservers for fourteen people. There was no room for any more" (2).

Further on, the Miami relatives are not spared Gabo's condemnation, for not showing any concern for the child's psychological anguish after experiencing a horrendous trauma and witnessing his mother's death: "No one in Miami seems to care about the damage being done to Elián's mental health by the culture shock they are subjecting him to. At his sixth birthday party, this past December 6th, where he is being held in Miami, his self-interested hosts took pictures of him wearing a combat helmet, surrounded by toy guns and wrapped up in an American flag, a little while before a boy his age shot and killed a classmate in Michigan" (4). And he commented on the toys that were given to Elián: "They were not gifts of love, of course, but unequivocal symbols of a political conspiracy that millions of Cubans unabashedly support through the Cuban-American National Foundation, founded by Jorge Mas Canosa and sustained by his followers, which seems to be spending millions of dollars to prevent Elián from being returned to his father. That is: Elián's real shipwreck wasn't on the high seas, but when he set foot on United States soil" (4).

Later, García Márquez catalogs the challenges Juan Miguel faced in simply trying to talk with his son: "You should know that from the beginning they did everything they could to sabotage us," he told me. "Sometimes they screamed at the boy while we were talking, they turned up the volume of the cartoons on television as high as possible, or they would put a piece of candy in his mouth so that I couldn't understand what he was saying" (3–4). But he wasn't the only one to face those sorts of problems: "Elián's grandmothers also experienced those kinds of tricks first-hand, during their torturous visit to Miami, when a police officer, under orders from a frenetic nun, confiscated the cell phone they had brought with them to tell their relatives back in Cuba how the boy was doing. Their visit, which had been planned to last two days, was in the end cut down to just ninety minutes, with all kinds of interruptions and no more than fifteen minutes spent alone with Elián. His grandmothers returned to Cuba horrified by how much they had changed him" (4).

As you can see, the view that García Márquez presents of Elián's story conforms to a type of fiction that he had always scrupulously avoided—the textbook novel: there is a perfectly clear distinction between the good guys and the bad guys, cops and robbers, cowboys and Indians, an oversimplified analysis devoid of nuance in which the good are those who stay in Cuba, like Juan Miguel González, and the bad those who want to leave or have already left, like Elizabeth Brotons, Lázaro Rafael Munero, and the exiles in Miami. The entire scope and depth of this human drama, much more complex than a matter of solidarity—or slavish subservience—to a leader, is reduced here to an issue of latitude, 150 kilometers more to the north or to the south.

But the upside of this story, according to García Márquez, is that it served to unite the Cubans behind their leader in the face of the opposition exile community in Miami and the North American enemy. As if out of habit, with his characteristic fascination for this Caribbean people, he painstakingly recounts the numerous demonstrations that were staged in support of bringing Elián back to Cuba: "The popular support and the torrent of ideas that have been generated around the country to demand the boy's return have been spontaneous and spectacular" (4). It is true that rallies were held in the main cities, but it's also true that demonstrations in support of anything the state considers important are generally organized by the government itself. For example, to politically exploit the Pope, Fidel, a die-hard atheist and Marxist, ordered the people to attend the public events organized around the Pope's visit to the island, and even García Márquez, rarely accused of being a Catholic, put in an appearance.

In Elián's case, we witnessed for ourselves the huge effort the regime made to convert the little boy into a national hero, a new Martí who—from the United States—fought for Cuban sovereignty in the face of the enemy to the north. On a trip we made to Cuba shortly after his return to the island, we saw many people all over the place, from all walks of life, young and old, of any race, wearing T-shirts that had Elián's face on them and a message that was anything but subtle: "We have to save Elián!" What does this little boy have that Heberto Padilla, María Elena Cruz Varela, Gastón Baquero, and countless other men and women who were born on the island do not have, who have given all they could of themselves to express their love for the land of their birth, who pour their lives into each poem they write so that the shadow of that great green island can touch the farthest corners of the Western world; and if they haven't been able to return—some of them are now deceased—it wasn't exactly because their relatives in exile had kidnapped them?

Most likely, what this little boy had was not an outpouring of compassion and a cry for justice provoked by his horrible situation, but the "luck" of having landed in his "Golgotha" during a presidential election campaign, and in a place—Florida—where the Cuban exile community has gone off the deep end, often adopting extremist, abhorrent political positions, constituting a vocal special-interest group that clearly unsettles the powers-that-be in the White House. So the trials and tribulations that dragged on and on, holding the little boy a captive, were the result of a series of political maneuvers of the lowest order, through which each side hoped to achieve their own interests, or at least make sure that any blood spilled in the Caribbean did not dirty their hands.

But Gabo only saw one of the extremes. He rightfully accuses the United States of delaying the ultimate decision to order Elián returned to Cuba for political reasons, especially having to do with the upcoming elections. To the Democratic White House, it could have meant losing votes for the Democratic candidate Al Gore, and the outcome of the boy's case could have affected the makeup of the state judiciary, since the judges in the state of Florida are elected. Gabo observed that "It had not gone unnoticed that Judge King, the first that should have decided the outcome of this case, had to excuse himself because of his ties with the Cuban-American National Foundation. His successor, Judge Hoelever, suffered from a dubious brain hemorrhage. Michael Moore, the current judge, does not appear to be in too much of a hurry to announce his findings before the elections" (5). And García Márquez continues: "Nevertheless, the legal and historical loss could be far more costly for the United States than an electoral one, as more than 10,000 U.S. children are currently dispersed throughout various parts of the world, taken from their country by one of their parents without the authorization of the other. The gravity of the situation for them is that if the parents remaining in the United States wish to recover them, the precedent of Elián could be utilized to prevent it" (5).

And García Márquez doesn't hesitate to compare Elián's case with "Operation Peter Pan" in the sixties, where supposedly the Cuban government planned to snatch children away from their parents to send them to the Soviet Union for indoctrination. In spite of denials issued by Castro's inner circle, many people fled the island. We don't know, as García Márquez suggests, if the long-term negative consequences for the United States extend beyond the loss of the presidential election; what we do know, after the elections in November 2000, is that the absurdity, which took place at the ballot boxes in the country seen as a shining example of democracy, has no precedent anywhere in Western history. We were in the U.S. in November of that year, in Miami: not even the most patriotic could find the words to justify or explain the events around the recount of votes. The streets were filled with nervous laughter, cocktail-party conversations tried to gingerly sidestep the political minefield, while the beaches still overflowed with carefree foreign tourists, far removed from the drama dominating the headlines. The problem didn't have to do with perforations in a voting ballot punched by a machine; there, it was decided among judges, experts and observers, that one of the least charismatic men in the history of U.S. presidents would assume the highest office in the longest, most embarrassing electoral process in recent memory anywhere. Cubans decided it a paradox of history. And, through his own traumatic ordeal, Elián unwittingly had a hand in the drama.

THE DIASPORA IN ACTION: THE CUBAN QUESTION AND THE SORROW OF THOSE LOST AT SEA

A small boat goes from one end of the mile-long Malecon boardwalk in Havana to the other. It's a routine trip. Suddenly, several armed men force the boat's captain to break away from the coast and head north. Cuban coast guard officials follow the boat and fire at it with impunity. After a few minutes of sheer terror, the little boat outruns the police boats and passes into international waters, and those onboard begin to weigh the consequences of their strange little hijacking. Very soon, they would reach the shores of Florida. Many are happy and congratulate their "hijackers." Stalin Martinez, a dentist who makes the short boat trip along the Malecon every day to get to work, immediately gets in touch with his brother in Miami, who praises his "audacity" and helps him get everything in order to start a new life. Then Stalin, who never stops thinking about his family, decides to go back, not out of a sense of Revolutionary solidarity, but to see his wife and children. On his return to Havana, he gets a hero's welcome, since he opted for the hard reality on the island rather than the cushy existence of the deluded American dream. In interviews he gives to the press, he carefully emphasizes that he was always a faithful Revolutionary, and that he fought the hijackers on board, in vain, although he almost died in the attempt. But his time living in Florida has had a devastating impact on his family life: he discovers that his wife has gone off with another man, taking their children with her. Unable to endure such a humiliation, he decides to go back to Florida, this time completely voluntarily. That is how Jesús Díaz opens his fourth novel. Díaz, a Cuban writer and editor who lived in Spain from 1992 until his death in 2002, with a humorous style presents a very accurate picture of what many Cubans have experienced in recent years. He has also given his opinion on the Elián González case. And he puts Fidel Castro at the top of the list of those who exploited the human drama for political gain.[3] Other Cuban and Latin American intellectuals have made similar observations, many of whom write off García Márquez's views on the subject, vociferously defending his friend, as merely demonstrating an irrational submission to Castro.

Manuel Moreno Fraginals was perhaps the best Cuban historian of all time. With his article "Naufragio de un Nobel," he asks who was really the one lost at sea here. Gabo had written about the theme in one of his first short stories, "Story of a Shipwrecked Sailor," which was based on an actual event that took place in 1955. Eight sailors were lost at sea in a storm in the Caribbean, and only one of them, Luis Alejandro Velasco, was found four days later, washed ashore, barely alive, on a beach in Cartagena de Indias, Colombia. García Márquez turned the sailor's experience into a magnificent story, written in a journalistic style that brings the most harrowing, emotional moments of the incident to life. If, at that time, García Márquez was a young journalist in search of a sensational story, the new shipwreck story fifty years later was not innocently used by the writer as mere fodder for a well-written piece. Gabo chose which elements to focus on, and he had an agenda, according to Fraginals: "It is an article—the story about Elián—that has at least two objectives: to present Juan Miguel González, Elián's father, as a good, upright man, in contrast with the corrupted, immoral, irresponsible Elizabeth Brotons, who died trying to save her son from a life of spiritual and material destitution of Cuba today. And he presents Elián's stepfather as a dishonest, violent man."[4] Fraginals concludes that the criticism García Márquez aims at Elián's mother and stepfather is too fierce and subjective, since Lázaro Munero had successfully made the same trip several times before, and Elizabeth, though aware of the risks, could not be credibly characterized as acting completely recklessly. Also, to justify the clandestine nature of the stepfather's activities, Fraginals adds that García Márquez seems to have forgotten that if Lázaro Munero's plans had been discovered, "they would have executed him or sentenced him to up to thirty years in prison."[5] That also implies that Elián's stepfather, although surely acting in other interests, was, in effect, risking his life for others.

The historian makes another extremely interesting observation about Elián's parents. García Márquez points out that after their divorce, they continued to live together, giving the impression that they still loved each other and that, in spite of the separation, they were incapable of making a complete break . . . until she found the man "who cost her her life." So the readers of Gabo's article feel compassion for Juan Miguel González, who was left all alone, as abandoned as he could be. But Moreno Fraginals reminds us that "In Cuba today, couples can get divorced, but they don't always live apart, because since the triumph of the Revolution, housing shortages have become chronic."[6] The most important observation Fraginals makes about Gabo's article has to do with what Elián's father knew. According to García Márquez, Juan Miguel didn't know anything beforehand. Also, he further emphasizes this by describing how the boy's father had to find out about the trip, how surprised he was, and so on. In fact, it seems as if Elián's father did know of his ex-wife's plan to leave the island with their son, as has been pointed out by Fraginals and others such as Guillermo Cabrera Infante, who wisely observed that "when the boy was taken in by his relatives in Miami, his father did not seem angry or even surprised initially. And it is well known that Juan Miguel González had on two previous occasions entered the visa lottery conducted by the State Department in Washington every year, to award foreigners visas for entry into the U.S. [. . .] Also, González had spoken with his relatives in Miami, asking them to take care of his son; so, he was aware of their planned departure."[7]

García Márquez is an excellent journalist and a meticulous reporter. Since the late 1940s, he has written countless articles, he has conducted hundreds of interviews, and he has directed and established prestigious, well-regarded publications. So it is hard to believe that the omission of certain facts in his piece on Elián can be attributed to a lack of information or an oversight on the part of an inexperienced, sloppy reporter. Also, he reveals in the article that he made the extra effort to call Elián's father personally and he had a long conversation with him. Who gave him González's phone number? Why did Gabo take such an interest in a person he didn't know at all, who plays no role in the life of the writer who only calls his friends—and writes about whatever he likes—and has been known to get on a plane and fly halfway around the world just to spend some time with a friend?

To César Leante, the rafter boy's story became a political rallying cry, especially to Fidel Castro: "A case that should have been resolved by the family or in court has become a frankly political conflict. It's clear that the position of the Cuban exiles in Miami is political. But it's like a reaction, like an answer to how Fidel politicized this tragedy from the very first moment."[8] In fact, Leante criticizes Castro's reasons for supporting Juan Miguel González: "He apparently acted (acts) out of humanitarian, moral, and patriotic interests. What is this about? Unconditional support for a father (and some grandmothers) who is fighting to regain custody of a child after his mother's death? A nation's dignity, which feels that one of its citizens has been 'kidnapped,' even though that citizen is only six years old? Or is it simply protection of an innocent person, who should be supported out of the most basic instincts of brotherhood (since the State is also a paternal institution) and ethics? That would be wonderful if it were true. But I'm afraid that's not the case."[9] As proof, he cites the case of the tugboat *Trece de Marzo*. In 1994, Castro gave the order to attack this boat, which was carrying seventy-two people, including a dozen children ranging from six months to fifteen years old, trying to flee to Miami. Forty-two of the adults and children on board died when they were swept into the sea by water cannons. Leante says of the "new Herodes": "He must have been responsible for this crime, since without his consent, the boat would not have been openly attacked."[10] Apparently, the lives of some defenseless children are more valuable than others. Cabrera Infante hammers home this paradox: "Not one official statement was made on this tragedy [the *Trece de Marzo*]. Why were they making so many noisy threats to have one rafter boy, rescued from the sea, returned? The only explanation is the incoherence of a man who is wrestling with the inevitable: his impending death, and the end of his tyranny, and his life."[11] Leante doesn't try to minimize the efforts made by so many people to reestablish family harmony, but he does try to put things in their proper context. As Jesús Díaz observed, "Castro is using the tragedy to regain control of a situation that for the first time in forty years of dictatorship was starting to become adverse."[12]

The Elián Gonzalez case definitely served to reopen old wounds for many Cuban exiles, which cannot be forgotten. César Leante insists: "If Fidel Castro hadn't made Cuba into the hell that it is, no one would want to leave the country, much less risk their lives in the intent. No one leaves [a place] where they are happy, or at least they don't feel oppressed."[13] The longing of the exile is the pain of disconnection, of not knowing, this insurmountable barrier that keeps them unmoored. It's strange that García Márquez never focuses on the particular circumstances of each of the exiles, and he doesn't even talk about Elián's deceased mother. Leante's piece concludes, "as if so that the Cuban people will not think about her and perhaps will forget her. Coincidence, or a smokescreen in both cases?"[14] If

Elián has become a new symbol for Cuban patriotism, then perhaps Elizabeth Brotons has become another symbol of Cuban exile.

MARIO VARGAS LLOSA: AGAINST THE PATRIARCH

In the year 2000, Mario Vargas Llosa published one of his best works, *The Feast of the Goat*, which focuses on the dictatorship in the Dominican Republic from 1930 to 1961, personified by Trujillo. The international impact of this book eclipsed that of his earlier works, and he granted many more interviews than usual in the news media in numerous countries. In these interviews, he said over and over that "dictatorship is the supreme expression of evil,"[15] no matter how it is packaged, and if he focused on one regime in particular it is because that is his way of combating it, and because "throughout the history of literature, there has been a morbid fascination with evil," since "all of the sins are perversely fascinating to a much wider audience, maybe because we know we can all fall victim to those passions."[16] So he takes every opportunity to harshly criticize any manifestation of repression. In keeping with that strategy, inspired by Elián, Vargas Llosa made a series of statements that illustrate the shortcomings of the Cuban Revolution and reveal the real nature of Castro's role, "one of the most sanguine, repugnant dictators ever produced by authoritarian Latin America,"[17] and "the most long-lived tyrant,"[18] and so on. Vargas Llosa criticizes how the Cuban supreme leader reacted to the case. In contrast to García Márquez, Vargas Llosa takes Elián's side. He affirms, just as César Leante did, that the first to politically exploit the event was Castro: "From the earliest moment, first by Castro and then by the exile community in Miami, the boy was seen as a tool that could be used in the political struggle to score some points against the other side. The fatal error of the exiles, who naïvely fell right into the trap set by the dictator, was to accept the political challenge on a matter that should have remained strictly confined to the judiciary."[19]

So Elián became a "flag to rally around in the fight against the dictatorship,"[20] and for that reason Vargas Llosa completely disagrees with the U.S. decision to return Elián to his father, since it only served to perpetuate the methods of control practiced by Castro on the entire residential population of the island: "Just because this ruling was predictable and legal does not mean that it was just. I believe that it is unjust and immoral, because, given the very particular circumstances of the little Cuban boy's case, the United States courts will not be returning Elián to his father, but rather to Fidel Castro, who is the only person who truly exercises patriarchal authority over the Cubans on the island of Cuba."[21] Vargas Llosa also rejects the theory that Castro is defending an innocent boy's right to be with his father, since, as César Leante and Cabrera Infante have shown, he did nothing to save the children that perished aboard the *Trece de Marzo*. He concludes: "Therefore it is doubtful that the formidable mobilization unleashed by Fidel Castro several months ago in Elián González's 'defense' was motivated by his sentimental, altruistic support of parents' rights. In truth, it was a work of psychological distraction on the domestic front, and an astute provocation of the exiles in Miami to get them to adopt certain positions that would damage their own image and would seem to confirm the portrayal of them as extremist and menacing, as presented in Castrist propaganda. In both objectives, the dictator has completely triumphed."[22]

Finally, at the end of the article, Vargas Llosa twice refers to "Shipwreck on Dry Land," his erstwhile friend's piece. First, he describes García Márquez's report in support of Cuba and its actions as "slanderous propaganda." Then, he examines the fact that in Cuba, everyone was in favor of returning the boy to his father, swayed by the propaganda that Castro generated: "If even renowned poets, and a Nobel laureate, put pen to paper in service of such a farce, what else could be expected from the average disoriented Cuban, with no access to any other information sources other than what has been filtered through the regime's propaganda machine?"[23] Clearly, the positions of these two former friends—García Márquez and Vargas Llosa—with respect to Cuban issues have consistently been diametrically opposed ever since the Peruvian writer withdrew his support for the Cuban Revolution over the Padilla case. By that point, García Márquez had all his eggs in one basket. In the early nineties, Castro had seen how his power to mobilize his people—the most important weapon in his arsenal to prop up his legitimacy, gain support for far-reaching political projects, and simply control the population—had weakened considerably. But by the middle of the decade, this tool seemed to have stopped functioning altogether, since the people's morale had bottomed out, and the jokes about shortages and the government's much-hyped policies had stepped way over the line of political correctness: laughing at one's own misfortunes was the only way to survive in the face of such collective misery. With Elián, there was a dramatic reversal: one of the most cunning rulers ever to control a Latin American country played his hand brilliantly. The generation that had come of age in the eighties, completely cut off from the highest circles of power, gave way to a new generation of young people who finally connected with the patriarch in his autumn, thanks to the new symbol of anti-imperialist resistance: the little boy rescued from the sea.

CAUGHT IN THE CROSSFIRE: CARLOS FUENTES

The Mexican writer Carlos Fuentes, with his characteristic diplomacy, would rather not condemn one side over the other, preferring to take the high ground. Elián has been crucified by Cubans and gringos alike, and now, his arms nailed to the cross, the collective gaze is drawn downward to his side, where soon the last wound to draw blood will appear. After enduring his mother's death and a harrowing ordeal adrift at sea, further torture would then be administered as much from Cuba as from the United States. Elián is used by the anti-Castrists of Miami as ammunition in their own particular war, and by Fidel Castro, with the aim of "posing as a defender of Cuban sovereignty in the face of North American aggression,"[24] a process that will drag on right up to the presidential elections, where "the principal candidates for the presidency of the United States, the Democrat Al Gore and the Republican George W. Bush, adopt a position of heroic hysteria: we will save the boy from the Cuban despot's evil clutches."[25]

Fuentes strives for an impartial tone: he takes up neither the cause of the Cuban exiles in Miami, nor that of the Cubans in Cuba. For him, the victim of this saga will not be Castro, or the Cuban exiles, nor the presidential candidates, but Elián himself, his back against the crucifix where the horizontal beam crosses the vertical: "Used by Fidel Castro, and by the Miami exiles, and by the North American right, Elián González is just an affable six-year-old boy"[26] who has found himself in a situation similar to the protagonist's in the movie *The Truman Show*: "Elián González is a photogenic cherub who serves the Cuban exile community's political agenda, and the Cuban government's agenda, and the U.S. presidential candidates' agenda, and that of the press, television, and the avid TV viewers around the world. That's entertainment."[27] As the entire world watched, television cameras descended on the little house in Miami, at the exact moment when the police arrived to take the little boy by force. Most likely, that little Truman was also unaware that his life had been preprogrammed, ever since the tragedy at sea, so that the powers-that-be could have something to bluster about, and the common people would have something to watch on television on the nightly news, a reason to shed a tear, like a soap opera, or express self-righteous indignation. Bread and circus, all without having to leave the house. What a shame, some may have thought, that it was all over so soon.

CHAPTER SIXTEEN

★

AN EPILOGUE OF SORTS:
A LITTLE STORY ABOUT AN ELEVATOR

B Y THIS POINT, WE KNOW WHY GARCÍA MÁRQUEZ CONTINUES
to be a presence at the loftiest, most treacherous heights of
power: his impressive political and literary résumés have
given him wings. On the first page of *Chronicle of a Death Foretold*,
a verse by Gil Vicente appears: "La caza de amor / es de altanería."
Our Colombian Nobel Prize winner knows plenty about the thrill
of the chase and reaching the summit; that is why, in spite of his
age, when he has a very important appointment to keep, he won't
wait for the elevator: he'll take flight and home in on his target.
Angel Augier told us that in the summer of 2001, Gabo wanted to
visit one of his old Cuban friends, someone he had worked with
during those heady days of Prensa Latina. When he arrived at the
nonagenarian Augier's building, he was accompanied by Gabriel
Molina, another fellow journalist who had worked at the agency.
Since the elevator was out of order, they had to walk up eight
flights of stairs to reach Augier's apartment. In appreciation of this
effort, the Cuban poet and journalist wrote an article in *Granma*

International about the visit, titled "Gabo on friendship's eighth floor," dated August 28, 2001.

But fate doesn't have to be a bad thing. Speaking of high places and the thread of the conversation that took place that hot summer day, Gabo revealed a few episodes that would be included in the third volume of his memoirs, as yet unpublished. Since that book was going to be devoted to his friendships with presidents, it's not hard to guess that Fidel Castro will play a large role. Still, the first to appear will be Torrijos, as Gabo himself announced on that steamy afternoon. In response to a comment on the Panamanian president's tragic death in 1981, Gabriel Molina remarked that twenty years had passed since that fateful plane crash. Gabo said, pensively, "I was supposed to have been on that flight. I wasn't because Mercedes did everything she could to stop me."[1] Thanks to that uncanny sense of foreboding on the part of Mercedes Barcha, wife of the most important living writer in the Spanish language in recent decades, millions of fans of good literature got to enjoy such books as *Love in the Time of Cholera* (1985), *The General in His Labyrinth* (1989), *Strange Pilgrims: Twelve Stories* (1992), *Of Love and Other Demons* (1994), *News of a Kidnapping* (1996), and *Living to Tell the Tale* (2002), and we'll probably get to read two more volumes of memoirs and even some new stories and novels in this new millennium. The important thing isn't how high you fly; it's knowing where you're going and being in just the right position to get there, every step of the way. García Márquez is the consummate expert at this.

Another stellar event to catapult Gabo to the stratosphere in recent years involves Pope John Paul the Second's visit to Cuba. In the interview that García Márquez gave to Vázquez Montalbán on the subject, he said: "Now I am interested in the Pope. Maybe I will write something. Fidel is a little down. I am, too. When I come home, the person I like to talk with the most is Mercedes. Women hear things that we will never hear, and they make us say things that we didn't even know we were capable of saying. Maybe the meeting between Fidel and the Pope will be of two frustrated people. For one, the Revolution isn't what it should be or what he had hoped it would be; for the other, the beast is dead but its fury lives on. The end of the communist bloc hasn't translated into religious hegemony. They are two great historic figures who are coming together at a delicate moment for both of them."[2]

But the interest was mutual. Gabo wanted to be there, and Fidel wanted to have his "all-purpose" representative in a privileged spot, right next to him, instead of the number two man of the regime— his brother Raúl—or political authorities like Lage or Alarcon. Vázquez Montalbán mused: "When I saw García Márquez at Fidel Castro's side, in the first row of the powerful present at the mass in Havana, I remembered that historical sequence of events when Torrijos took Graham Greene and Gabo along to witness the signing of the treaty giving back authority over the Panama Canal. The fact that Fidel Castro wanted the Nobel Prize winner to accompany him to the last mass with the Pope could be interpreted as a meaningful ranking of the first row of the powerful; but I think the writer assumed a role, whether he wanted to or not, as representative bestowed upon him from having acted as a go-between with Clinton on two occasions, in an effort to build a bridge between Castro's Cuba and the government of the United States. García Márquez, together with Castro and in the Pope's presence, was not just the third power: he was also a signal."[3] It wasn't the first time that García Márquez had noticed Castro's doubts and melancholy. At other times, when this had happened, he always had tried to console him and tried to give him suggestions for how to overcome his low points. Once, García Márquez had asked his friend what he would rather be doing at that moment, and Fidel had answered: "Just hanging around on some corner."[4]

But in spite of Gabo's interest in immortalizing that encounter in an article, as he pointed out in the interview with Vázquez Montalbán, he never has written anything down on paper about the significance of those few hours. García Márquez had also been invited to attend other events during the Pope's visit, but he preferred to stay on the periphery of those public ceremonies, to protect his "independence."[5] He watched everything on television, and after a few days he concluded that, underneath the superficial harmony of the two leaders, there must have been some private conflict between them. He told Fidel that he would write an article about it, but not until he knew what had really happened between those two. "Fidel's answer, Gabo had said, consisted of asking me to do a favor with the North Americans. He said that if everything turned out all right there, he would tell me everything I wanted to know. I did the favor, which was essentially to relay certain messages, and everything turned out okay; but when I told him 'All right, now, what happened with the Pope?', Fidel brushed me off, saying 'Oh, that! I'll tell you some other time. Anyway, it's not as big a deal as you think.'[6]

Fidel and his secrets. Same as ever. Many areas of his private life are buried deep in an abyss where even his best friend is not allowed to enter. Maybe that is another reason why Gabo has such a high level of appreciation for the leader, "one of the few Cubans who doesn't sing or dance,"[7] in his own words. Maybe Gabo had Fidel in mind when he said "The virtue I admire the most is the ability to keep a secret to the grave."[8] And he really does love him, in spite of his quirks, because "there is no worse misfortune in human existence—Gabo says—than the incapacity to love."[9] He will be faithful to Castro to the end, because, as he asserts, "I am the sort that is buried with his friends."[10] In fact, during his visit to the "eighth floor of friendship" in the summer of 2001, he talked at length about this loyalty and how it had been tested, and his special relationship with Castro. Gabriel Molina, in his article "Un Gabo para saborear," writes about how he went with Gabo to Augier's apartment that day. On the way, they talked about various things, like the sad state of disrepair of Havana's city center and the renovation of the tunnel that connects the city with the beaches. During the year that the construction work was being done, only cars with diplomatic plates, or tourist vehicles, or buses were allowed to drive in it, almost completely isolating the areas on the other side, since the subterranean tunnel was the only direct mode of transportation between those areas; otherwise, a very circuitous, roundabout route had to be taken.

Finally, when they arrived at the poet's apartment, they had joked about a letter going around the Internet that was purported to have been written by Gabo, in which he bade farewell to the world when he had to be hospitalized in Los Angeles for lymphatic cancer. As the journalist friends agreed, the funniest part of the whole ridiculous episode was when the famous letter was "intercepted" by a radio station in Argentina and read on the air by an impressionist who imitated Gabo's voice perfectly. From then on, it was talked about in the international press, until García Márquez himself surfaced and made a statement during his recovery. Shortly after that, Fidel collapsed during one of his famously long-winded speeches. Gabo was in Los Angeles at the time, and he saw some television coverage of the incident from a station in Miami, in which the image of Fidel collapsing was repeated over and over in slow motion, and the commentator noted that for some time a "certain slowness" had been detectable in the dictator's movements. García Márquez wanted to see his friend and confirm that his collapse had been nothing serious. He got on a plane, arrived in Havana, and met with Fidel on August 4, after a session of the National Assembly had closed. They were together until four o'clock in the morning, joking about what may have caused the incident. And Gabriel Molina added in his article: "He confirmed it with his own eyes. The next day, he told me and Ana María: 'Fidel is going to be around for a long time.' And we would add: 'Gabo is going to be around for a long time.'[11]

Gabo and Fidel, this is a portrait of a friendship. Until death do you part.

AFTERWORD

★

SWAN SONG

WHILE THIS BOOK WAS BEING PREPARED FOR PUBLICATION, some events transpired that would further threaten Cuba's fragile stability. Between March 18 and 21, 2003, seventy-nine peaceful protesters were arrested on the island, almost all of them intellectuals committed to Cuba's future development—but as a democracy. Some were even accused of "possessing a Sony recorder."[1] They were sentenced to up to twenty-eight years in prison for crimes of conscience. The swan's song was becoming a shriek, taking advantage of the international chaos caused by the Iraq war. A few days after that event, some three hundred people from the worlds of literature, film, politics, and the arts in general signed an open letter demanding "the Cuban government imme-diately release all of the dissidents" and also calling for "an end of repression against the peaceful opposition."[2] Among them were such luminaries as Mario Vargas Llosa, Günter Grass (who, ever since his days as a militant communist, had always supported revo-lutionary "gestures"), Pedro Almodóvar, Ana Belén, Alfredo Bryce

Echenique, Elisabeth Burgos, Jorge Edwards, Juan Goytisolo, Enrique Krauze, Claudio Magris, Javier Marías, Antonio Muñoz Molina, Teodoro Petkoff, and Joaquín Sabina.

The initial phase of the war in Iraq was drawing to a close, and the triumphant spirit of the allies led some to suggest that there were still people living under oppressive regimes around the world, and they should not reject the possibility of intervention in some of those countries, such as North Korea. Cuba was one of the countries tossed around as possible targets in the press, but these conjectures were always couched in ambiguity. At this juncture, another uncomfortable situation arose for the Castro regime: within a few days of each other, Cubans who wanted to escape the country and emigrate to a freer one attempted to hijack a few planes and a boat. The boat was intercepted by security forces when it ran out of fuel, and those responsible for the attempted hijacking were arrested, immediately brought to trial, sentenced to death, and executed; all of this took place within the record time of less than one week. On April 11, the executions by firing squad were announced; the sentences had been carried out ipso facto. The three condemned men were black men under thirty. The youngest was only twenty years old, and the attempted hijacking of the boat had been non-violent. A few days after the executions were announced, the mother of one of the executed men gave a television interview to a Spanish station, and explained how they had called her a few days before, at ten o'clock in the morning, to inform her that her son had already been buried. She went to the cemetery, and they would not let her confirm her son's identity. "I didn't know if what they had inside that coffin was my son or a dog," she told the cameras from Television Española.

As might be expected, there was an immediate outcry. The International Foundation for Freedom, headed by Mario Vargas Llosa, and which counts Plinio Apuleyo Mendoza and Carlos

Alberto Montaner among its members, released a "Manifesto on Cuba," which asked: "Why has the Cuban dictatorship decided to act in such a brutal, challenging manner on the international stage? Essentially, because it is a totalitarian regime that does not allow the Cuban people any vestige of liberty or autonomy; and its dictator, owner, and master over the will of all of his subjects had nervously observed the growing revitalization of a civil society that was trying to escape his control. Castro simply wanted to punish them. He wanted to punish the opposition and intimidate the people. It's what he has always done."[3] It also challenged supporters of democracy around the world to not limit their responses to mere words and to take action, reducing Cuba's diplomatic presence within democratic countries, expelling Cuba from all international organizations, and pressuring the regime in the same way that the racist South African government had been pressured to reform.

Some writers of the left who had always taken Castro's side now said that solidarity has its limits, and that fundamental human rights must be respected. The most notorious example was the Portuguese writer José Saramago, who won the Nobel Prize in Literature in 1998; he published a short article in *El País* on April 14, 2003 titled "As Far as I'll Go." His words reverberated around the world: "From now on, Cuba can continue on its way; I'm staying here. The right to dissent is something that is found and will be found written in invisible ink on all declarations of human rights, past, present, and future. Dissenting is an irrepressible act of conscience." He talked about sentences that were out of proportion to the offenses, and the absence of any conspiracy on the part of the Cubans with the U.S. Interest Section in Havana; and added: "Now here come the firing squads. Hijacking a boat or a plane is a seriously punishable offense in any country on earth, but you don't sentence the offenders to death, especially when you keep in mind that there were no victims. Cuba has not won any heroic battle by executing these three men, but it has lost my confidence, it has squandered my hopes, it has betrayed my illusions. I will go no further."[4]

Another of the disillusioned was Eduardo Galeano. His article "Cuba duele" (Cuba hurts) was harshly criticized, as was Saramago's piece, by the Cuban press. In it, the author of *Las venas abiertas de America Latina* describes a model of power that is in decline, and that "has made obeying orders issued from on high a revolutionary virtue."[5] He affirms that he never believed in "single-party democracy," nor in the omnipotence of the state as "a response to the omnipotence of the market"; that the Revolution has been losing the "winds of spontaneity and freshness that propelled it from the beginning"; that there was a "disaster of communist states converted into police states," which represents a "betrayal of socialism"; and that the spread of democracy in Cuba is absolutely essential, but it has to come from the Cubans themselves, "without anyone from outside putting their fingerprints on it; they need to open up new avenues for democracy, and fight for the liberties that they lack."[6]

The pressure on those intellectuals was such that, in Galeano's case, he issued a correction a few days later. However, Saramago had already made an inalterable decision. Articles against him appeared in *Granma, La Jiribilla, Tiempo21*, etc., as well as the previously cited piece by Steffan. On April 23, 2003, we attended a Day of the Book event in Granada (Spain) with the Portuguese Nobel laureate. After the dedication ceremony of a new cultural center, he told us privately that he felt a tremendous sense of frustration about everything that was going on, since he had always been loyal to the Revolution, and had continued to be; but it was the Revolution that was betraying itself, it wasn't what it had been before, and, that being the case, he could no longer continue to support it as he had in the past.

The reactions in Cuba were not just from private individuals.

On April 20, *El País* collected statements from high-ranking political officials defending themselves from the international outcry that they were abusing their power. The Minister of Cuban Foreign Relations, Felipe Pérez Roque, pointed out that the executions and the mass imprisonments had been painful but completely unavoidable measures. He justified the death penalty "with exceptional character" for the "simple rise in the number of plane and boat hijackings—seven in as many months—that could provoke an immigration crisis with the United States,"[7] and could provide them with the perfect excuse for armed intervention. Similarly, twenty-seven Cuban intellectuals, including Miguel Barnet, Leo Brouwer, Roberto Fernández Retamar, Julio García Espinosa, Eusebio Leal, Senel Paz, Silvio Rodriguez, and Cintio Vitier, signed a letter on April 19 titled "A message from La Havana to our friends who are far away," which revealed the pain they felt from the devastating declarations that had been made against Cuba in recent days, especially because they had been made by "steadfast friends" of the Revolution who had been misinformed and who, because of their attitude, could unwittingly provoke a U.S. invasion into Cuba. The letter stated, "Our little country is more threatened today than ever before by the superpower that wants to impose a fascist dictatorship on a worldwide scale. Out of self-defense, Cuba has been forced to take rigorous measures that of course they would rather not have to take. Those measures should not be judged by taking them out of context."[8] And they shouted back at the exile community in Miami "Today Iraq, tomorrow Cuba," to try to reawaken solidarity with their disillusioned communist compatriots.

Those of us who are well aware of Castro's close relationship with García Márquez asked ourselves during the course of that long month: where is García Márquez? Why doesn't he come out in defense of his friend? And more importantly, why doesn't he publicly condemn the executions, since he has always opposed the death penalty? And why didn't he sign the letter with signatures from twenty-seven intellectuals who called on their old friends to support Cuba again? Susan Sontag helped us out, just as we had given up hope of getting any clear answers, a few days before García Márquez would finally sign the pro-Castrist Cuban letter. At the end of April, the American writer was invited to speak at the Bogotá Book Fair, and her presentation, titled "The intellectual in times of crisis," was given before an audience of thousands who responded to the provocative speech with thunderous applause. She stated that, if intellectuals could not be considered as "a cohesive group,"[9] in instances when freedom of expression is repressed, they cannot remain silent. Since she was in Gabo's country, and his silence with regard to recent events had surprised her, she added: "I know that Gabriel García Márquez is highly appreciated here, and his books are very popular; he is the great writer from this country and I admire him very much, but it's inexcusable that he has not made any statement regarding recent actions of Cuba's regime." She compares his stance with Saramago's: "I supported Cuba against the United States, but I quickly realized what Castro meant. Now I have seen that a man like José Saramago, who still calls himself a communist, condemns the barbarity that has taken place in Cuba. But I ask myself: what will Gabriel García Márquez say? I'm afraid the answer is: he's not going to say anything. I cannot excuse him for not talking."[10]

In the wake of this publicly issued challenge, Gabo could not remain silent. In fact, the next day, he made some statements to *El Tiempo* in Bogotá, in which he defends himself by cataloging some of his virtues with regard to the situation in Cuba in general, but without getting specifically into the matter at hand: "I could not even tell you myself exactly how many prisoners and dissidents I have helped, completely anonymously, to leave Cuba over the last twenty years. Many of them don't even know it, and the ones who do know are enough to keep my conscience at peace." When he addresses the recent execution of the three Cubans, he limits himself to abstract generalizations, to avoid clashing with Cuba's particular interests at that time: "In regard to the death penalty, I don't have anything to add to what I have said in public and in private for as long as I can remember: I am against it in any place, in any circumstance, for any reason. That's all, since I have a personal policy of not responding to unnecessary or provocative questions, even if they come from—as they do in this case—such a worthy, respectable person."[11]

As might have been expected, Gabo's answers were unsatisfying to many of those who had already openly expressed their opinions on the latest Cuban *affaire*. In an opinion column published in *El País* on May 9, Enrique Krauze wrote a piece called "Gabo in his Labyrinth." After a brief summary of Gabo and Fidel's friendship, he asked how this "fidelity to Fidel" could be explained. He wrote:

> At a conference for journalists held in 1996 in Colombia, García Márquez said: "Fidel is one of the people that I love most in the world." "A dictator," someone said, and the writer replied that elections were not the only way to be democratic. Then a Venezuelan journalist asked why he served as an honorary aide to Castro. "Because he is my friend," García Márquez answered, adding that one should do everything for one's friends.[12]

Later in the article, he repeated something Gabo had often said, about how a journalistic piece had to be accurate down to the last comma, and he asked again: "How does García Márquez reconcile this statement on journalistic ethics with his own concealing of the truth in Cuba, in spite of the fact that he has privileged access to

Cuban reality?" and he concludes that "it would be an act of poetic justice if, in the autumn of his life and at the zenith of his glory, he disentangled himself from Fidel Castro and put his prestige in the service of freedom, democracy, and human rights in Cuba."[13]

Mario Vargas Llosa was much harsher in his criticism of Gabo's statements and his position in relation to Fidel and the Revolution. At the same book fair in Bogotá, having read Gabo's response to Sontag, Vargas Llosa affirmed that García Márquez is "a writer who is a courtesan of Fidel Castro, whom the dictatorship holds up as an intellectual alibi, and he so far has come to accept very well all the abuses, the trampling of human rights that the Cuban dictatorship has committed, saying that secretly he helps some political prisoners get released. It is no secret to anyone that Fidel Castro hands over some political prisoners to his courtesans once in a while. That is how he keeps his conscience clean. To me it seems more like repugnant cynicism. Writers are how they are, and each assumes a responsibility with that kind of conduct. I have never read an article or essay by García Márquez that explains in moral and civic terms this systematic alignment that seems religiously devout, because intellectually he should explain it and he hasn't so far, and I doubt very much that he ever will."[14] Finally, as an exclamation point to his strong words, he has this to say about Gabo: "I don't know what going to Cuba to be seen with Fidel Castro accomplishes; maybe to show that the regime has an important writer they can claim."[15]

Bad times for the lone swan, which sings no more. Mortally wounded, it just thrashes about, like a fish. Until when?

ENDNOTES

CHAPTER 1: GODS AT PLAY

1. Fidel Castro, "La novela de sus recuerdos," *Cambio.com*, 7-X-2002, p. 1, http://66.220.28.28/calle22/portada/arículos/79/.
2. Dasso Saldívar, *García Márquez. El viaje a la semilla,* Alfaguara, Madrid, 1997, p. 98.
3. Ibid., pp. 119–120.
4. Ibid., p. 121.
5. Volker Skierka, *Fidel. La biografía definitiva del líder cubano*, Martínez Roca, Barcelona, 2002, p. 46.
6. Ibid., pp. 47–48.
7. Dasso Saldívar, *García Márquez*, p. 195.
8. Dasso Saldívar, *García Márquez*, p. 193.
9. Ibid.
10. Gabriel García Márquez, *Vivir para contarla*, Mondadori, Barcelona, 2002, p. 342.
11. Arturo Alape, *De los recuerdos de Fidel Castro: El Bogotazo y Hemingway*, Editora Política, La Habana, 1984, pp. 32–40.
12. Ibid., p. 60.
13. Fidel Castro, "La novela de sus recuerdos," pp. 1–2. Obviously, Gabo's reply is pure fantasy, a demonstration of his sense of humor. That scene doesn't appear in his memoirs, nor does it coincide with his evolution as a writer.

CHAPTER 2: IF THE RIGHT TO KNOW IS NOT A RIGHT, THEN IT MUST BE A LEFT

1. Plinio Apuleyo Mendoza, *El olor de la guayaba*, Mondadori, Barcelona, 1994, p. 123.

2. Ibid., p. 124.

3. Ibid., p. 76.

4. *Playboy*, March 1983, p. 16.

5. Interview with Plinio Apuleyo Mendoza in *Libre*, Sept.–Nov. 1971, p. 14.

6. Monologue of Gabriel García Márquez in Juan Luis Cebrián, *Retrato de Gabriel García Márquez*, Galaxia Gutenberg, Barcelona, 1997, p. 81.

7. Plinio Apuleyo Mendoza, *El olor de la guayaba*, p. 125.

8. Dasso Saldívar, *García Márquez. El viaje a la semilla*, p. 359.

9. Silvio Rodríguez, "Escaramujo," *Rodríguez*, EGREM, La Habana, 1994, first song.

10. Interview with Plinio Apuleyo Mendoza, p. 14.

11. Plinio Apuleyo Mendoza, *El caso perdido: La llama y el hielo*, Planeta/Seix Barral, Bogota, 1984, p. 59.

12. Gabriel García Márquez, "Pedro Infante se va. Batista se queda." In *Obra periodística 3: De Europa y América (1955–1960)*, Mondadori, Madrid, 1992, pp. 395–396.

13. Gabriel García Márquez, "Mi hermano Fidel." In *Obra periodística 3: De Europa y América (1955–1960)*, p. 455.

14. Ibid., p. 458.

15. Ana Belén, "Banana Republic," Con las manos llenas, CBS-Sony, Madrid, 1981, third song. Song written by Steve Goodman, Steve Birgh, and J. Rothermel.

16. Orlando Castellaños, "García Márquez en dos partes," *Prisma del Meridiano* 80(34): 15 (1976).

17. VV.AA., *Gabriel García Márquez*, Taurus, Madrid, 1981, p. 239.

18. Speech reprinted in *La Jornada*, 8-IV-1997.

19. Angel Augier, "Gabo en la octava planta de la amistad," *Granma Internacional*, 28-VIII-2001, p. 1, in *http://www.granma.co.cu/frances/agosto4/35gabo-f.html*.

20. From Gabriel García Márquez, *Notas de Prensa: 1980–1984*, Mondadori, Madrid, 1991, pp. 195–198.

21. Orlando Castellaños, art. cit., p. 15.

22. Raúl Cremades and Angel Esteban, *Cuando llegan las musas. Cómo trabajan los grandes maestros de la literatura*, Espasa Calpe, Madrid, 2002, p. 262.

23. Lourdes Casal, *El caso Padilla. Literatura y revolución en Cuba. Documentos*, Nueva Atlántida, New York, 1971.

24. Plinio Apuleyo Mendoza, *El caso perdido. La llama y el hielo*, p. 112.

25. Ibid., p. 127.

CHAPTER 3: FADE TO BLACK: THE PADILLA CASE

1. Raúl Cremades and Ángel Esteban, op. cit., p. 262.

2. Juan Goytisolo, "El gato negro que atravesó nuestras oficinas de la Rue de, Bièvre," *Quimera* 29: 15 (1983).

3. Juan Goytisolo, art. cit., p. 15.

4. Manuel Díaz Martínez, "El caso Padilla: Crimen y castigo (Recuerdos de un condenado)," *Encuentro de la Cultura Cubana* 4–5: 90 (1997).

5. Manuel Vázquez Montalbán, *Y Dios entró en La Habana*, El País/Aguilar, Madrid, 1998, p. 338.

6. Lourdes Casal, op. cit., p. 62.

7. Ibid., p. 58.

8. Ibid., p. 63.

9. Manuel Vázquez Montalbán, op. cit., p. 344.

10. Ottmar Ette, *José Martí: Apóstol, poeta revolucionario: una historia de su recepción*, UNAM, Mexico, 1995, p. 233.

11. Juan Goytisolo, art. cit., p. 17.

12. Ibid.

13. Manuel Díaz Martínez, art. cit., p. 95.

14. Juan Goytisolo, art. cit., p. 18.

15. VV.AA., "El caso Padilla: Documentos," Libre 95 (IX/XI-1971).

16. Excerpt from an interview conducted in October 2001. The subject of the interview wishes to remain anonymous.

17. Plinio Apuleyo Mendoza, *El caso perdido: La llama y el hielo*, op. cit., p. 136.

18. Ibid.

19. Juan Goytisolo, art. cit., p. 18.

20. Manuel Díaz Martínez, art. cit., p. 95.

21. Carlos Verdecia y Heberto Padilla, *La mala memoria: Conversación con Heberto Padilla*, Kosmos, Costa Rica, 1992, p. 78.

22. Manuel Díaz Martínez, art. cit., p. 96.

23. Felix Grande, "Imaginaciones," *Cuadernos Hispanoamericanos* 504: 139–142 (1992).

24. Nadia Lie, "Las malas memorias de Heberto Padilla," in P. Collard [with the collaboration of I. Jongbloet, M. E. Ocampo and Vilas (eds.)], *La memoria histórica en las letras hispánicas contemporáneas. Simposio internacional. Amberes, November 14–19 1994*, Col. Románica Gandensia, Librairie Droz, S.A., Geneva, 1996, pp. 187–206.

25. Raúl Rivero, Eliseo Alberto, and Marilyn Bobes also helped edit this text.

26. VV.AA., "El Caso Padilla: Documentos," art. cit., pp. 97–98.

27. Ibid., p. 102.

28. Ibid., p. 98.

29. César Leante, *Gabriel García Márquez, el hechicero*, Pliegos, Madrid, 1996, p. 9.

30. VV.AA., "El caso Padilla. Documentos," art. cit., p. 123.

31. Ibid.

32. Ibid.

33. Plinio Apuleyo Mendoza, *El caso perdido. La llama y el hielo*, op. cit., p. 139.

34. Ibid., pp. 139–140.

35. Julio Cortazar, "Carta a Haydée Santamaría," *Obra crítica/3*, Alfaguara, Madrid, 1994, p. 51.

36. Julio Cortázar, op. cit., pp. 49–50.

37. Juan Goytisolo, art. cit., pp. 21–22.

38. Plinio Apuleyo Mendoza, *El caso perdido. La llama y el hielo*, op. cit., p. 141.

39. Plinio Apuleyo Mendoza, *El caso perdido. La llama y el hielo*, op. cit., p. 8.

40. J. P. Clerc, *Les quatre saisons de Fidel Castro. Biographie*, Seuil, Paris, 1996, p. 257.

41. K. Van den Berghe, *La nueva novela latinoamericana: boom y boomerang. Un estudio polisistémico*, Leuven, 1987, p. 121.

42. Jon Lee Anderson, "El poder de Gabo," *Semana*, 4-X-1999, p. 60.

43. Ibid.

44. José Donoso, *Historia personal del boom*, Alfaguara, Madrid, 1999, pp. 59–60.

45. Juan Goytisolo, art. cit., p. 15.

46. José Donoso, op. cit., p. 143.

47. Dasso Saldívar, op. cit., p. 464.

48. Carlos Verdecia y Heberto Padilla, *La mala memoria. Conversaciones con Heberto Padilla*, Kosmos, Costa Rica, 1992, pp. 219–220.

49. Dasso Saldívar, op. cit., p. 462.

50. Jon Lee Anderson, art. cit., p. 61.

51. Plinio Apuleyo Mendoza, *El olor de la guayaba*, op. cit., p. 128.

52. Plinio Apuleyo Mendoza, *El caso perdido. La llama y el hielo*, op. cit., p. 144.

53. Ibid., pp. 142–143.

54. Plinio Apuleyo Mendoza, *El caso perdido. La llama y el hielo*, op. cit., p. 144.

55. Interview given to the journalist Julio Roca of the *Diario del Caribe*, in Barranquilla, Colombia, in VV.AA., "El caso Padilla. Documentos," art. cit., p. 135.

56. Ibid.

57. Ibid.

58. César Leante, *Gabriel García Márquez, el hechicero*, op. cit., p. 9.

59. Plinio Apuleyo Mendoza, *El caso perdido. La llama y el hielo*, op. cit., p. 137.

60. Interview with J. Roca, art. cit., p. 135.

61. Ibid.

62. Interview with J. Roca, art. cit., p. 135.

63. VV.AA., "El caso Padilla. Documentos," art. cit., p. 95.

64. Ibid.

65. Manuel Díaz Martínez, art. cit., p. 92.

66. Ibid., p. 94.

67. Speech by Fidel Castro, in VV.AA., "El caso Padilla. Documentos," art. cit., p. 119.

68. From Gabriel García Márquez, *Obra periodística 4: Por la libre (1974–1995)*, Mondadori, Madrid, 1999, pp. 61–90.

69. Gabriel García Márquez, "Cuba de cabo a rabo," op. cit., p. 86.

70. Ibid., p. 87.

71. Ibid., p. 86.

72. Ibid.

73. Ibid.

74. Ibid.

75. Ibid., pp. 87–88.

76. Interview with J. Roca, art. cit., p. 136.

77. Ibid.

78. Ibid.

79. Ibid.

80. Ibid.

81. Ibid.

82. Ibid.

CHAPTER 4: THE LURE OF POWER

1. Manuel Vázquez Montalbán, *Y Dios entró en La Habana*, op. cit., p. 328.

2. Interview with Joaquin Navarro-Valls, August 5, 2001.

3. Jon Lee Anderson, art. cit., p. 52.

4. Ibid.

5. Interview given to Plinio Apuleyo Mendoza for the magazine *Libre*, in 1972, titled "El encuentro de dos camaradas." Published later in *Triunfo* (1974).

6. Gabriel García Márquez, "Mi hermano Fidel," op. cit., p. 457.

7. Ibid., p. 455.

8. Cited by Pedro Sorela, *El otro García Márquez: Los años difíciles*, Oveja Negra, Bogotá, 1988, p. 244.

9. Plinio Apuleyo Mendoza, *El caso perdido. La llama y el hielo*, pp. 81–82.

10. Ibid., p. 82.

11. Cesar Leante, *Gabriel García Márquez, el hechicero*, pp. 16–17.

12. Juan Luis Cebrián, op. cit., p. 80.

13. Ibid.

14. Jon Lee Anderson, art. cit., p. 65.

15. Cesar Leante, *Gabriel García Márquez, el hechicero*, p. 34.

16. Juan Luis Cebrián, op. cit., p. 49.

17. Cf. Alfonso Renteria, *García Márquez habla de García Márquez*, Renteria Editores, Bogotá, 1979, p. 157.

18. Cesar Leante, *Gabriel García Márquez, el hechicero*, p. 33.

19. Cesar Leante, *Fidel Castro: el fin de un mito*, Pliegos, Madrid, 1991, p. 46.

20. Ibid., p. 45.

21. Orlando Castellaños, "García Márquez en dos partes," *Prisma del Meridiano* 80(35):31 (1976).

22. Juan Luis Cebrián, op. cit., p. 81.

23. Gabriel García Márquez, introduction to *Habla Fidel* by Gianni Minà, Edivision Compañía, Mexico, 1988, p. 14.

24. Ibid., p. 23.

25. Ibid., p. 17.

26. Ibid., p. 12.

27. Ibid., p. 16.

28. Ibid., p. 18.

28. Ibid., p. 26.

30. Ibid., p. 23.
31. Ibid., pp. 26–27.
32. Gabriel García Márquez, "Cuba de cabo a rabo," in *Obra periodística 4: Por la libre (1974–1995)*, op. cit., p. 85.
33. Manuel Vázquez Montalbán, op. cit., pp. 560–561.
34. Ibid., p. 299.
35. Alfonso Renteria, *García Márquez habla de García Márquez*, op. cit., p. 63.

CHAPTER 5: THE PATRIARCH IN HIS AUTUMN

1. Data from the excellent study by Leonel-Antonio de la Cuesta, *Constituciones cubanas. Desde 1912 hasta nuestros días*, Ediciones Exilio, New York, 1974.
2. Some of this data was taken from the article by Pío E. Serrano, "De la revolución al modelo totalitario (1959-1998)" in VV.AA., *Cien años de historia de Cuba (1898–1998)*, Verbum, Madrid, 2000, pp. 239–240.
3. Pedro Sorela, op. cit., p. 233.
4. Dasso Saldívar found a reference in his archives to another trip, in 1973, but it was very short and without repercussion for García Márquez.
5. Pedro Sorela, op. cit., p. 240.
6. Gabriel García Márquez, *Chile, el golpe y los gringos*, Editorial Latina, Bogota, 1974, pp. 20, 21.
7. Pedro Sorela, op. cit., pp. 245–246.
8. In *Playboy*, March 1983, p. 26.
9. Pedro Sorela, op. cit., p. 251.
10. Gabriel García Márquez, "Los idus de marzo," in *Notas de Prensa (1980–1984)*, Mondadori, Madrid, 1991, pp. 162–163.
11. Jon Lee Anderson, art. cit., p. 58.
12. Alfonso Renteria, op. cit., p. 172.
13. Teodoro Petkoff, "Los tiempos de la izquierda," *Cambio.com*, 7-X-2002, p. 1, in http://66.220.28.29/calle22/portada/articulos/81/.
14. Gabriel García Márquez, "Los idus de marzo," in *Notas de prensa (1980–1984)*, op. cit., p. 162.
15. Ibid., p. 163.
16. José Manuel Camacho Delgado, *Césares, tiranos y santos en "El otoño del patriarca." La falsa biografía del guerrero*, Diputación Provincial, Sevilla, 1997, p. 142. Some of the previous ideas have been extracted from the same text.

17. Gabriel García Márquez, "Algo más sobre literatura y realidad," in *Notas de Prensa (1980–1984)*, op. cit., p. 121.
18. In Alfonso Renteria, op. cit., p. 170.
19. Interview with Eva Norvind for the magazine *Hombre de Mundo* of 1977. Cited in Alfonso Renteria, op. cit., p. 152.
20. In Alfonso Renteria, op. cit., p. 172.
21. Ibid., p. 152.
22. José Manuel Camacho Delgado, op. cit., pp. 172–173.

CHAPTER 6: WHO'S NOT IN THE FAMILY PHOTO?

1. Gabriel García Márquez, English translation by Gregory Rabassa, *The Autumn of the Patriarch*, HarperPerennial Classics, New York, 1999 (first edition 1976), p. 6. From here forward, all references to this work will be made within the text, with the page number in parentheses.
2. Plinio Apuleyo Mendoza, *El caso perdido. La llama y el hielo*, p. 82.
3. César Leante, *Gabriel García Márquez, el hechicero*, p. 29.
4. Ibid., pp. 21–22.
5. Ibid., p. 22.
6. Ibid.
7. Ibid., p. 23.
8. Ibid.
9. Ibid., p. 28.
10. Ibid., pp. 28–29.
11. Ibid., p. 29.
12. Ibid.
13. Jon Lee Anderson, art. cit., p. 64.
14. This is the argument masterfully put forth in the opening poem of Heberto Padilla's book *Fuera del juego*, the work that sparked the previously described controversial events. Cf. Ángel Esteban and Álvaro Salvador, *Antología de la poesía cubana*, Verbum, Madrid, 2002, pp. 206–207.
15. Jon Lee Anderson, art. cit., p. 64.
16. Cited by Manuel Vázquez Montalbán, *Y Dios entró en La Habana*, p. 303.
17. Alfredo Bryce Echenique, *Permiso para vivir. Antimemorias*, Peisa, Lima, 1994, p. 408.
18. Manuel Vázquez Montalbán, *Y Dios entró en La Habana*, p. 303.
19. Gabriel García Márquez, translated by Edith Grossman, *The General in His*

Labyrinth, Vintage, New York, 2003 (first edition 1990), p. 48. From here forward, all references to this work will be made within the text, with the page number in parentheses.

20. Fidel Castro, *My Early Years*, Melbourne and New York, 1998, prologue by García Márquez, p. 18.

21. Cited by Manuel Vázquez Montalbán, *Y Dios entró en La Habana*, p. 14.

22. Ibid.

CHAPTER 7: THE "QUEEN OF THE CARIBBEAN": ALL ASHORE

1. Gabriel García Márquez, "Cuba de cabo a rabo," *Obra periodística 4: Por la libre (1974–1995)*, op. cit., p. 61. From here forward, references to this work will be cited in the text, with the page number in parentheses.

2. Alfonso Renteria, op. cit., p. 99.

3. Bernardo Marqués, "García Márquez: pasado y presente de una obra," *Alternativa* 93:6 (9/16-VIII-1976).

4. Ibid.

5. Ibid.

6. Roberto Fernández Retamar, "Sobre una primera lectura de Cien años de soledad—y otra lectura," *Casa de las Americas* 209: 89–90 (1997).

7. Cited by Pedro Sorela, op. cit., pp. 242–243.

8. Ibid., p. 243.

9. Ibid., pp. 242–243.

10. Josep Sarret, "Los días que, uno tras otro, son la vida," *El Espectador. Magazin Dominical*, 12-VIII-1979, p. 1.

11. Cited by Pedro Sorela, p. 243.

12. *Playboy*, March 1983, p. 20.

13. Ibid., pp. 18–20.

CHAPTER 8: CUBANS IN ANGOLA: "OPERATION CARLOTA"

1. Gabriel García Márquez, "Operation Carlota," in *Obra periodística 4: Por la libre (1974–1995)*, op. cit., pp. 127–156.

2. Ibid., p. 142.

3. Ibid., p. 148.

4. Ibid., pp. 128, 133.

5. Ibid., pp. 136, 137.

6. Ibid., p. 142.

7. Ibid., p. 132.

8. Ibid., p. 130.

9. Ibid., p. 137.

10. Ibid., p. 133.

11. Ibid., p. 140.

12. Ibid.

13. Ibid., p. 142.

14. Domingo del Pino, "*Cubanos en Etiopía: Operación García Márquez*," *El Viejo Topo 20: 28–32 (1978)*.

15. Gabriel García Márquez, "Operación Carlota," in *Obra periodística 4: Por la libre (1974–1995)*, op. cit., pp. 155–156.

16. Ibid., pp. 150–151.

17. Andrés Oppenheimer, *La hora final de Castro*, Javier Vergara, Buenos Aires, 1992.

18. Ibid., p. 137.

19. Fidel Castro, *Angola. Girón Africano*. Ed. De Ciencias Sociales, Havana, 1976, pp. 21–22.

20. Ibid., p. 22.

21. Plinio Apuleyo Mendoza, *El olor de la guayaba*, pp. 126–127.

22. Domingo del Pino, art. cit., p. 28.

23. Ibid., pp. 30–31.

24. Gabriel García Márquez, "Operación Carlota," in *Obra periodística 4: Por la libre (1974–1995)*, op. cit., p. 156.

25. Ibid.

26. César Leante, *Fidel Castro: el fin de un mito*, p. 145.

27. Gabriel García Márquez, "Operación Carlota," in *Obra periodística 4: Por la libre (1974–1995)*, p. 129.

28. César Leante, *Fidel Castro: el fin de un mito*, p. 145.

29. Domingo del Pino, art. cit., p. 29.

30. Ibid., p. 29.

31. Gabriel García Márquez, "Operación Carlota," in *Obra Periodística 4: Por la libre (1974–1995)*, p. 134.

32. Ibid., p. 135.

33. Domingo del Pino, art. cit., p. 28.

34. Ibid., p. 29.

35. Ibid.

36. Pierre Kalfon, *Che. Ernesto Guevara, una leyenda de nuestro siglo*, Plaza y Janes, Barcelona, 1997, p. 490.
37. Ibid.
38. Ibid.

CHAPTER 9: FLYING HIGH

1. Manuel Vázquez Montalbán, op. cit., p. 559.
2. Gabriel García Márquez, "El fantasma del Premio Nobel," *Notas de Prensa (1980–1984)*, op. cit., p. 9.
3. Ibid., p. 7.
4. Ibid., p. 8.
5. Alfonso Renteria, *García Márquez habla de García Márquez*, op. cit., p. 70.
6. Pedro Sorela, op. cit., p. 249.
7. "García Márquez: la soledad de la fama," in ElTiempo.com, December 18, 2002, p. 2.
8. Jon Lee Anderson, art. cit., p. 64.
9. Pedro Sorela, op. cit., p. 250.
10. "GGM al banquillo," Revista Seuil, Brussels, 1975, in Alfonso Renteria, op. cit., pp. 99–100.
11. Gabriel García Márquez, "Felipe," *Notas de Prensa (1980–1984)*, op. cit., p. 357.
12. Ibid., p. 357.
13. Ibid.
14. Ibid.
15. Ibid., pp. 357–358.
16. Manuel Vázquez Montalbán, op. cit., p. 181.
17. Ibid.
18. Jon Lee Anderson, art cit., p. 64.
19. Gabriel García Márquez, "Torrijos," *Notas de Prensa (1980–1984)*, op. cit., p. 140.
20. Gabriel García Márquez, "Torrijos, cruce de mula y tigre," *Obra periodística 4: Por la libre (1974–1995)*, op. cit., p. 184.
21. Gabriel García Márquez, "Las veinte horas de Graham Greene en La Habana," *Notas de Prensa (1980–1984)*, op. cit., p. 360.
22. Gabriel García Márquez, "El Kissinger del Reagan," *Notas de Prensa (1980–1984)*, op. cit., pp. 61–62.
23. Ibid., p. 63.

24. Pedro Sorela, op. cit., p. 249.
25. Sergio Ramírez, "Nada llega a perderse," Cambio.com, 16-X-2002, p. 2, on http://66.220.28.29/calle22/portada/articulos/75/
26. Ibid.
27. Teodoro Petkoff, "Los tiempos de la izquierda," Cambio.com, 7-X-2002, p. 3, on http://66.220.28.29/calle22/portada/articulos/81/
28. Ibid., pp. 3–4.
29. "La realidad se ha vuelto populista," *Alternativa* 188:4 XI-1978.
30. Ibid., p. 5.
31. Ibid.

CHAPTER 10: FIRST CLASS

1. "Gabriel García Márquez evoca a Pablo Neruda," *Revista Cromos,* Bogota, 1973, in Alfonso Renteria, op. cit., p. 95.
2. Gabriel García Márquez, "Mitterrand, el otro: el escritor," *Notas de Prensa (1980–1984),* op. cit., p. 88.
3. Ibid., p. 89.
4. Gabriel García Márquez, "Mitterrand, el otro: el presidente," *Notas de Prensa (1980–1984),* op. cit., p. 108.
5. Ibid.
6. *Playboy,* art. cit., p. 20.
7. Gabriel García Márquez, "Cena de paz en Harpsund," *Notas de Prensa (1980–1984),* op. cit., p. 351.
8. Gabriel García Márquez, "El fantasma del Premio Nobel (1)," *Notas de Prensa (1980–1984),* op. cit., p. 10.
9. *Playboy,* art. cit., p. 18.
10. Gerardo Molina, "Con Gabriel García Márquez en Cuba," *El Espectador,* 13-II-1980. All of the following citations taken from Molina's article have the same bibliographical reference.
11. Bernardo Marqués, art. cit., p. 7.
12. "García Márquez: la soledad de la fama (1982)," *El Tiempo.com,* Dec. 18, 2002, p. 1.
13. Ibid., p. 2.
14. Gabriel García Márquez, "El fantasma del Premio Nobel," art. cit., p. 7.
15. Gabriel García Márquez, "Cena de paz en Harpsund," art. cit., p. 350.
16. Ibid., pp. 351–352.

17. Ibid., p. 352.
18. Gabriel García Márquez, "Felipe," art. cit., p. 356.

CHAPTER 11: THE PRICE OF PARADISE

1. Gerardo Molina, art. cit.
2. Alfredo Bryce Echenique, *Permiso para vivir. Antimemorias*, Peisa, Lima, 1994, p. 410.
3. Ibid., pp. 407–408.
4. "García Márquez: la soledad de la fama," p. 1.
5. Gabriel García Márquez, *Obra periodística 5: Notas de Prensa (1961–1984)*, Mondadori, Madrid, 1999, pp. 302–305.
6. Vicente Romero, "Gabriel García Márquez habla sobre Cuba," *Pueblo*, Madrid, 1977, in Alfonso Renteria, op. cit., p. 149.
7. Ibid.
8. "GGM al banquillo," Revista Seuil, Brussels, 1975, in Alfonso Renteria, op. cit., p. 99.
9. Manuel Vázquez Montalbán, op. cit., p. 560.
10. Gabriel García Márquez, "El pez es rojo," *Notas de Prensa (1980–1984)*, op. cit., p. 253.
11. Ibid., pp. 254–255.
12. Gabriel García Márquez, "Los dolores del poder," *Notas de Prensa (1980–1984)*, op. cit., pp. 186–187.
13. *Playboy*, art. cit., p. 18.
14. Ibid.
15. Ibid.
16. Plinio Apuleyo Mendoza, *El olor de la guayaba*, op. cit., pp. 156–157.
17. Ibid., p. 18.
18. Jon Lee Anderson, art. cit., p. 62.
19. Ibid.
20. Ibid.
21. *Playboy*, art. cit., p. 20.
22. Ibid.
23. Plinio Apuleyo Mendoza, *El olor de la guayaba*, op. cit., pp. 156–157.
24. Manuel Vázquez Montalbán, op. cit., p. 301.
25. Fidel Castro, "La novela de sus recuerdos," *Cambio.com*, 7-X-2002, p. 2, from *http://66.220.28.29/calle22/portada/articulos/79/*

26. Ibid.

27. Ibid., p. 3.

28. Manuel Vázquez Montalbán, op. cit., p. 251.

29. Ibid., p. 254.

30. *Playboy*, art. cit., p. 20.

31. Manuel Vázquez Montalbán, op. cit., pp. 216–217.

32. "García Márquez: la soledad de la fama," op. cit., p. 1.

33. Ibid.

CHAPTER 12: FRIENDSHIP WITH FIDEL: THE FLIP SIDE

1. Interview with Plinio Apuleyo Mendoza, 15-VII-2002.

2. Manuel Vázquez Montalbán, art. cit., p. 303.

3. Jon Lee Anderson, art. cit., p. 62.

4. Manuel Vázquez Montalbán, op. cit., pp. 301–302.

5. Interview with Ricardo Vega, 9-X-2002.

6. Pedro Sorela, op. cit., p. 238.

7. Gabriel García Márquez, "Del malo conocido al peor por conocer," *Notas de Prensa (1980–1984)*, op. cit., p. 21.

8. *Playboy*, art. cit., p. 16.

9. Ibid.

10. Ibid.

11. Ibid.

12. Ibid.

13. Ibid.

14. Ibid.

15. Jon Lee Anderson, art. cit., p. 51.

16. Ibid.

17. Ibid., p. 64.

18. Manuel Vázquez Montalbán, op. cit., p. 506.

19. Ibid.

20. Ibid., pp. 511–512.

21. Ibid., pp. 526–527.

22. Jon Lee Anderson, art. cit., p. 51.

23. Interview with Roberto Fernández Retamar, 13-XI-2002.

24. Jon Lee Anderson, art. cit., p. 62.

25. Teodoro Petkoff, art. cit., p. 3.

26. "La realidad se ha vuelto populista," op. cit., pp. 5–6.

27. Ibid., p. 6.

28. C.M. stands for "Countess of Macondo," a term Arenas used to describe Márquez from then on, especially in his work published posthumously, *El color del verano*.

29. Reinaldo Arenas, *Necesidad de libertad*, Universal, Miami, 2001, p. 294.

30. Ibid., p. 295.

31. Pedro Sorela, op. cit., pp. 244–245.

32. Gabriel García Márquez, "También el humanitarismo tiene su límite," *Notas de Prensa (1980–1984)*, op. cit., p. 301.

33. Manuel Ulacia, "El castrismo en México," *Cuadernos Hispanoamericanos* 501:129 (1992).

34. Manuel Vázquez Montalbán, op. cit., p. 266.

35. Ibid.

36. Ibid.

37. Ibid., p. 267.

38. Mecano, "Cruz de navajas," *Entre el cielo y el suelo*, Ariola, Barcelona, 1986.

39. Ibid.

40. Vicente Romero, "Gabriel García Márquez habla sobre Cuba," Pueblo, Madrid, 1977, cited in Alfonso Renteria, op. cit., p. 149.

41. Ibid.

42. Juan Luis Cebrián, op. cit., p. 81.

43. Statement from *ABC*, October 25, 1994, p. 57.

CHAPTER 13: THE DREAM FACTORY: SAN ANTONIO DE LOS BAÑOS

1. *Fundación del Nuevo Cine Latinoamericano*, Havana, 2002, p. 1.

2. Ibid., p. 2.

3. Lídice Valenzuela, *Realidad y nostalgia de García Márquez*, Colección Pablo, Havana, 1989, pp. 105–106.

4. Dasso Saldívar, op. cit., p. 307.

5. Ibid.

6. Gabriel García Márquez, *Living to Tell the Tale*, pp. 436–437.

7. *Fundación del Nuevo Cine Latinoamericano*, op. cit., p. 2.

8. Lídice Valenzuela, op. cit., pp. 91–92.

9. Ibid., p. 102.

10. *EICTV, Fundación del Nuevo Cine Latinoamericano*, Havana, 2002, p. 7.

11. *Fundación del Nuevo Cine Latinoamericano*, op. cit., p. 7.
12. Lídice Valenzuela, op. cit., pp. 95–96.
13. *Fundación del Nuevo Cine Latinoamericano*, op. cit., p. 1.
14. *EICTV*, op. cit., p. 8.
15. Lídice Valenzuela, op. cit., p. 96.
16. Ibid., p. 97.
17. *EICTV*, op. cit., p. 21.
18. Lídice Valenzuela, op. cit., p. 98.
19. Ibid., p. 99.
20. Ibid.
21. Ibid.
22. Manuel Vázquez Montalbán, op. cit., p. 305.
23. Lídice Valenzuela, op. cit., p. 98.
24. This corporation was formed by J. L. Padron (assistant to Jose Abrantes, head of the Department of the Interior), Orlando Pérez (former president of the Banco Nacional), Regino Boti (former chief of Juceplan), and Emilio Aragonés (ambassador to Argentina and one of Castro's closest financial advisers). CIMEX was a conglomerate of import and export companies and owned a chain of department stores in Cuba that only accepted dollars. Within CIMEX was the Department of Convertible Currency (MC, in its Spanish initials), which secretly tried to circumvent the U.S. trade embargo and minimize its effects. We would again find Tony De la Guardia in this department.

CHAPTER 14: JUSTICE OR VENGEANCE?: THE "OCHOA CASE"

1. Andrés Oppenheimer is an Argentine journalist. In 1992, he published *La hora final de Castro*, which won a Pulitzer Prize. The entire first part of the book is devoted to the Ochoa–De la Guardia case; it was one of our main sources of information for facts involved in the case.
2. Andrés Oppenheimer, *La hora final de Castro: La historia secreta detrás de la inminente caída del comunismo en Cuba*, Javier Vergara, Buenos Aires, 1992, p. 29.
3. Ibid., p. 31.
4. Ibid., p. 29.
5. Ibid., p. 67.
6. Ibid., p. 91.

7. Ibid., p. 107.
8. Ibid., p. 21.
9. Ibid., p. 42.
10. Ibid., p. 35.
11. Ibid., p. 41.
12. Ibid., p. 77.
13. Ibid.
14. Ibid., p. 83.
15. Ibid., p. 71.
16. Ibid., p. 121.
17. Ibid.
18. Ibid., p. 102.
19. Ibid., p. 116.
20. Ibid., p. 117.
21. Ibid.
22. Ibid., p. 117.
23. Ibid., p. 118.
24. Jean-Francois Fogel and Bertrand Rosenthal, *Fin de siècle à La Havane*, Seuil, Paris, 1993, p. 90.

CHAPTER 15: NAILED TO THE CROSS: ELIÁN IN HIS GOLGOTHA

1. S. Kauffmann, "Les Etas-Unis se prononcent pour le rapatriement du petit naufragé cubain vers La Havane," *Le Monde*, 7-I-2000, p. 3.
2. Gabriel García Márquez, "Naufrago en tierra firme," *Cambio.com*, 15-III-2000, p. 1. From here forward, citations from this article will appear in the text, with the page number in parentheses. The article was also published in *El País*, 19-III-2000, available electronically at http://64.21.33.164/CNews/y00/mar00/2002.htm.
3. In his article "Cuba rota," *El País*, 31-I-2000, on http://www.analitica.com/va/hispanica/fuentes/9715146.asp.
4. Manuel Moreno Fraginals, "Naufragio de un Nobel," *El País*, 29-III-2000, on http://64.21.33.164/Cnews/y00/mar00/2908.htm.
5. Ibid.
6. Ibid.
7. Guillermo Cabrera Infante, "El niño prodigio," *El País*, 22-II-2000, on http://www.analitica.com/va/hispanica/fuentes/6530484.asp.

8. César Leante, "Fidel Castro y los niños," *El País*, 25-III-2000, on http://www.chez.com/jpquin/fidenino.html.

9. Ibid.

10. Ibid.

11. Guillermo Cabrera Infante, "El niño prodigio," art. cit.

12. Jesús Díaz, "Cuba rota," art. cit.

13. César Leante, "Fidel Castro y los niños," art. cit.

14. Ibid.

15. Raúl Cremades and Ángel Esteban, *Cuando llegan las musas*, op. cit., p. 381.

16. Ibid.

17. Mario Vargas Llosa, "Vida y miserias de Elián," *El País*, 30-IV-2000, on http://www.caretas.com.pe/2000/1617/columnas/mvll.phtml.

18. Ibid.

19. Ibid.

20. Ibid.

21. Ibid.

22. Ibid.

23. Ibid.

24. Carlos Fuentes, "The Elián Show," *El País*, 26-IV-2000, on http://www.analitica.com/va/hispanica/fuentes/8588773.asp.

25. Ibid.

26. Ibid.

27. Ibid.

CHAPTER 16: AN EPILOGUE OF SORTS: A LITTLE STORY ABOUT AN ELEVATOR

1. Gabriel Molina, "Un Gabo para saborear," *Granma Internacional*, 9-VIII-2001, on http://www.granma.cu/frances/agosto1/32gabo-f.html, p.2.

2. Manuel Vázquez Montalbán, op. cit., p. 561.

3. Ibid., p. 567.

4. Fidel Castro, *My Early Years*, op. cit., p. 25.

5. Jon Lee Anderson, art. cit., p. 64.

6. Ibid.

7. Gabriel García Márquez, prologue to *My Early Years* by Fidel Castro, op. cit., p. 15.

8. "García Márquez: la soldedad de la fama," op. cit., p. 1.

9. Ibid., p. 2.

10. Statements made by García Márquez on Fidel Castro to *El País*, international edition (2-X-1995), in an interview given in September 29 of that year in Biarritz, where he was attending the International Latin American Film Festival.
11. Gabriel Molina, "Un Gabo para saborear," art. cit., p. 2.

AFTERWORD: SWAN SONG
1. Enrique Krauze, "Gabo en su laberinto," *El País*, 9-V-2003, p. 14.
2. "Represión en Cuba," in *Cubaencuentro.com*, 2-V-2003, p. 1.
3. Taken from http://www.fundacionfil.org/declaracion/cuba.html, 2_v-2003.
4. Taken from http://www.lainsignia.org/2003/abril/ibe_036.htm.
5. Cited by Heinz Dieterich Steffan in *Tiempo21*, a Cuban newspaper, 2-V-2003, p. 1 of the Opinion section.
6. Ibid.
7. Taken from http://www.cubaliberal.org/04_04_21-a.htm, p. 1.
8. Ibid.
9. *El País*, 30-IV-2003, p. 36.
10. Ibid.
11. Ibid.
12. Enrique Krauze, art. cit., p. 14.
13. Ibid.
14. "Vargas Llosa crítica a Gabo," in *El Tiempo.com*, 2-V-2003, Culture section, p. 1.
15. Ibid.

INDEX